WORLD FACTS

GEDDES & GROSSET

WORLD FACTS

Published by Geddes & Grosset,
David Dale House, New Lanark ML11 9DJ, Scotland

First published 1998
Reprinted 2001 (twice), 2002 (three times)

ISBN 1 85534 331 2

Printed and bound in Poland

Countries of the World

Afghanistan is a landlocked country in southern Asia. The greater part of the country is mountainous with several peaks over 6000 m (19,686 ft) in the central region with one navigable river, the Amu Darya. The climate is generally arid with great extremes of temperature. There is considerable snowfall in winter which may remain on the mountain summits the year round. The main economic activity is agriculture and although predominantly pastoral, successful cultivation takes place in the fertile plains and valleys, although only 15% of Afghanistan's land is suitable for farming. Natural gas is produced in northern Afghanistan and over 90% of this is piped across the border to the former USSR. Large oil reserves have been discovered in the north of the country but these have not been exploited, due mainly to the war. Other mineral resources are scattered and so far underdeveloped. The main exports are Karakuls (Persian lambskins), raw cotton and foodstuffs such as dried fruit. Since the Russian withdrawal from Afghanistan in 1989, the country has still been troubled by, mainly ethnic, conflict. The general population comprises many ethnic groups, some of which are Pushtuns, Tajiks, Hazaras and Uzbeks.

Quick facts:
Area : 652,225 sq km (251,773 sq miles)
Population : 18,052,000
Capital : Kabul
Other major cities : Herat, Kandahar, Mazar-I-Sharif
Form of government : Republic
Religions : Sunni Islam, Shia Islam
Currency : Afghani

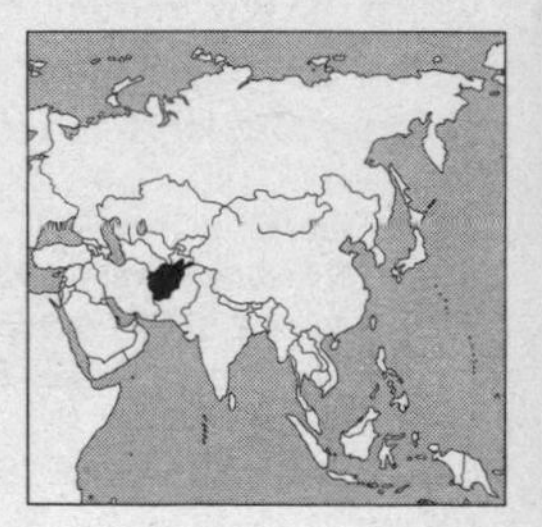

Albania is a small mountainous country in the eastern Mediterranean with one small navigable river, the Buenï. Its immediate neighbours are Greece, Serbia and The Former Yugoslav Republic of Macedonia, and it is bounded to the west by the Adriatic Sea. The climate is typically Mediterranean and although most rain falls in winter, severe thunderstorms frequently occur on the plains in summer. Winters are severe in the highland areas and heavy snowfalls are common. All land is state owned, with the main agricultural areas lying along the Adriatic coast and in the Korce Basin with about a fifth of the land being arable. Industry is also nationalized and output is small. The principal industries are agricultural product processing, textiles, oil products, cement, iron and steel. There is also potential for producing hydroelectricity, with the country's many mountain streams. Most trade is with neighbouring Serbia and The Former Yugoslav Republic of Macedonia and major imports are consumables, grains and machinery.

Albania has been afflicted by severe economic problems and in late 1996 public dissatisfaction with the government erupted into civil unrest, leading to a major revolt by citizen militias during which the government forces lost control, particularly in the south of the country. By March 1997 the country was on the brink of collapse and large numbers of refugees were leaving.

Quick facts:
Area : 28,748 sq km (11,100 sq miles)
Population : 3,420,000 (estimate prior to 1997, since when many refugees have fled)
Capital : Tirana (Tiranè)
Other major cities : Durrès, Shkodèr, Elbasan, Vlorë
Form of government : Socialist Republic
Religion : Constitutionally atheist but mainly Sunni Islam
Currency : Lek

Algeria is a huge country in northern Africa, which fringes the Mediterranean Sea in the north. Over four-fifths of Algeria is covered by the Sahara Desert to the south. Near the north coastal area the Atlas Mountains run east-west in parallel ranges. The Chelif, at 450 miles long, is the country's main river, rising in the Tell Atlas and flowing to the Mediterranean. The climate in the coastal areas is warm and temperate with most of the rain falling in winter. The summers are dry and hot with temperatures rising to over 32°C. Inland beyond the Atlas Mountains conditions become more arid and temperatures range from 49°C during the day to 10°C at night. Most of Algeria is unproductive agriculturally, but it does possess one of the largest reserves of natural gas and oil in the world. Algeria's main exports are oil-based products, fruit, vegetables, tobacco, phosphates and cork while imports include textiles, foodstuffs, machinery, iron and steel. In recent years, the country has been wracked by civil strife and terrorist attacks with the various opposing forces unable to agree peace proposals.

Quick facts:
Area : 2,381,741 sq km (919,590 sq miles)
Population : 28,321,000
Capital : Algiers (Alger)
Other major cities : Oran, Constantine, Annaba
Form of government : Republic
Religion : Sunni Islam
Currency : Algerian dinar

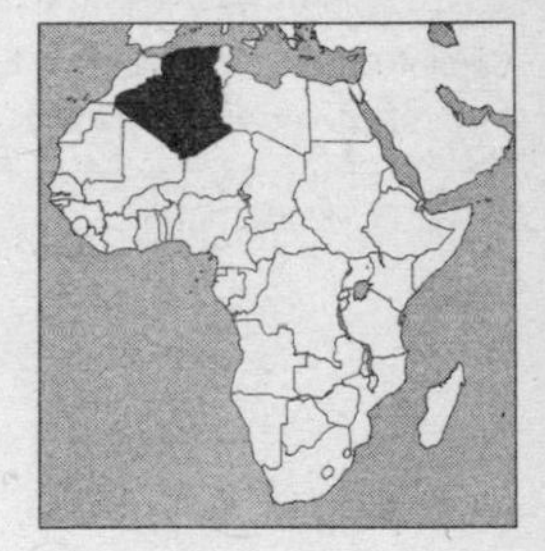

Andorra is a tiny state, situated high in the eastern Pyrénées, between FRANCE and SPAIN. The state consists of deep valleys and high mountain peaks which reach heights of 3000 m/9843 ft. Although only 20 km/12 miles wide and 30 km/19 miles long, the spectacular scenery and climate attract many tourists. About 10 million visitors arrive each year, during the cold weather when heavy snowfalls makes for ideal skiing, or in summer when the weather is mild and sunny and the mountains are used for walking. Tourism and the duty-free trade are now Andorra's chief sources of income. Natives who are not involved in the tourist industry may raise sheep and cattle on the high pastures. Although Andorra has no airport or railroad, there is a good road system. The average life expectancy from birth is 95 for women, 86 for men and 91 years overall. In 1993 an Andorran government was elected and has its own Parliament after 715 years of being ruled by France's leader and the Spanish Bishop of Urgel.

Quick facts:
Area : 457 sq km (170 sq miles)
Population : 72,766
Capital : Andorra-la-Vella
Form of government : Republic
Religion : RC
Currency : Franc, Peseta

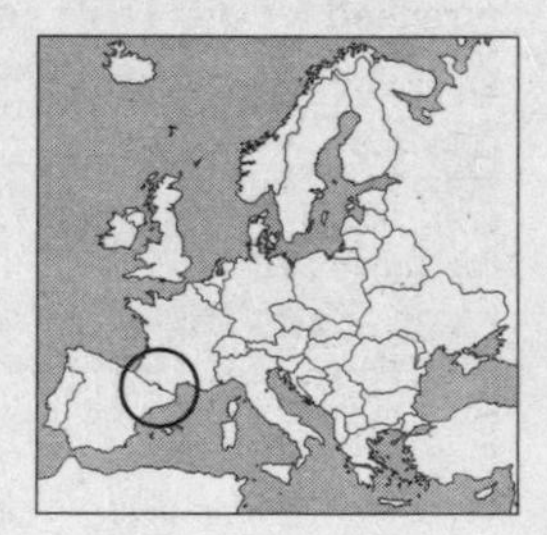

Angola is situated on the Atlantic coast of west central Africa, Angola lies about 10°S of the equator. It shares borders with CONGO, DEMOCRATIC REPUBLIC OF CONGO, ZAMBIA and NAMIBIA. Its climate is tropical with temperatures constantly between 20°C and 25°C. The rainfall is heaviest in inland areas where there are vast equatorial forests. The country is also rich in minerals, however deposits of manganese, copper and phosphate are as yet unexploited. Diamonds are mined in the north-east and oil is produced near Luanda. Oil production is the most important aspect of the economy, making up about 90% of exports which have traditionally included diamonds, fish, coffee and palm oil. Around 70% of the workforce are engaged in agriculture. Since independence from Portugal in 1975, the USA is the main recipient of the country's exports. However, the Angolan economy has been severely damaged by the civil war of the 1980s and early 1990s.

Quick facts:
Area: 1,246,700 sq km (481,351 sq miles)
Population : 11,030,000
Capital : Luanda
Other major cities : Huambo, Lobito, Benguela, Lubango
Form of government : People's Republic
Religions : RC, Animism
Currency : Kwanza

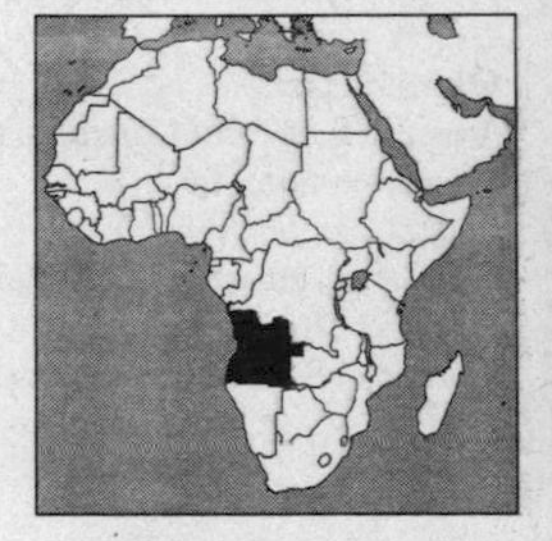

Antigua and Barbuda are located on the eastern side of the Leeward Islands, a tiny state comprising three islands–Antigua, Barbuda and the uninhabited rocky islet Redonda. Antigua's strategic position was recognized by the British in the 18th century when it was an important naval base, and later by the USA who built the island's airport during World War II to defend the Caribbean and the Panama Canal. Although mainly low-lying, the country's highest point is Boggy Peak at 405 m (1329 ft). The climate is tropical although its average rainfall of 100 mm (4 inches) makes it drier than most of the other islands of the West Indies. Tourism is the main industry as its numerous sandy beaches make it an ideal destination. Barbuda is surrounded by coral reefs and the island is home to a wide range of wildlife. Cotton, sugar cane and fruits are cultivated and fishing is an important industry in Barbuda. Great damage was inflicted on Antigua and Barbuda in 1995 by Hurricane Luis when over 75% of property was destroyed or damaged.

Quick facts:
Area : 442 sq km (170 sq miles)
Population : 66,100
Capital : St John's
Form of government : Constitutional Monarchy
Religion : Christianity (mainly Anglicanism)
Currency : East Caribbean dollar

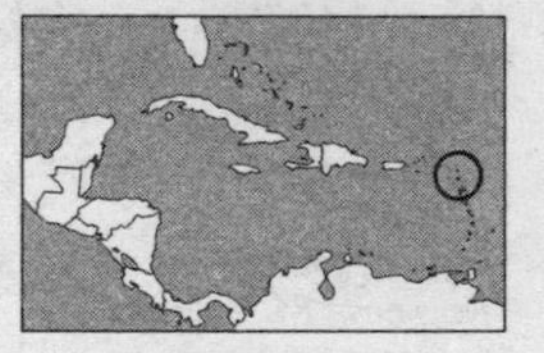

Argentina, the world's eighth largest country, stretches from the Tropic of Capricorn to Cape Horn on the southern tip of the South American continent. To the west, a massive mountain chain, the Andes, forms the border with CHILE. The climate ranges from warm temperate over the Pampas in the central region, to a more arid climate in the north and west, while in the extreme south conditions although also dry are much cooler. The vast fertile plains of the Pampas are the main agricultural area and produce cereals and wheat, while in other irrigated areas sugar cane, fruit and grapes for wine are raised. Meat processing, animal products and livestock production are major industries and also feature prominently in export trade. A series of military regimes has resulted in an unstable economy which fails to provide reasonable living standards for the population, although more recently a trade agreement has aided economic recovery.

Quick facts:
Area : 2,766,889 sq km (1,302,296 sq miles)
Population : 34,463,000
Capital : Buenos Aires
Other major cities : Cordoba, Mar del Plata, Mendoza, La Plata, Rosario, Salta
Form of government : Federal Republic
Religion : RC
Currency : Peso

Armenia, the former independent kingdom that straddled the borders of modern TURKEY, IRAN, GEORGIA, and AZERBAIJAN. Armenia is the smallest republic of the former USSR and part of the former kingdom of Armenia which was divided between Turkey, Iran and the former USSR. It declared independence from the USSR in 1991. It is a landlocked Transcaucasian republic, and its neighbours are Turkey, Iran, Georgia and Azerbaijan. The country is very mountainous with many peaks over 3000 m (9900 ft), the highest being Arragats Lerr at 4095 m. Agriculture is mixed in the lowland areas. The main crops grown are grain, sugar beet and potatoes, and livestock reared include cattle, pigs and sheep. Mining of copper, zinc and lead is important, and to a lesser extent gold, aluminium and molybdenum, and industrial development is increasing. Hydro-electricity is produced from stations on the river Razdan as it falls 1000 m (3281 ft) from Lake Sevan to its confluence with the River Araks. Territorial conflict with Azerbaijan over Nagorny Karabakh under a cease-fire since 1994, put a brake on economic development for many years.

Quick facts:
Area : 29,800 sq km (11,500 sq miles)
Population : 3,463,500
Capital : Yerevan
Other major city : Kumayri (Leninakan)
Form of government : Republic
Religion : Armenian Orthodox
Currency : Dram (= 100 luma)

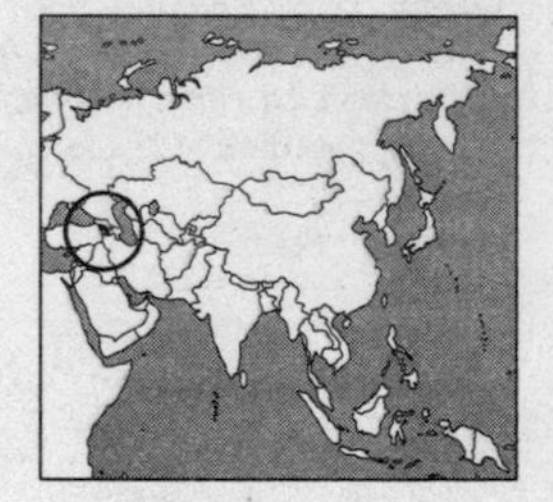

Australia, the world's smallest continental landmass, is a vast and sparsely populated island state in the southern hemisphere and is comprised of six states. The most mountainous region is the Great Dividing Range which runs down the entire east coast. Because of its great size, Australia's climates range from tropical monsoon to cool temperate and also large areas of desert. The majority of the country's natural inland lakes are salt water and are the remnants of a huge inland sea. The Great Barrier Reef is approximately 2010 km (1250 miles) long and is the largest coral formation known in the world. Central and south Queensland are subtropical while north and central New South Wales are warm temperate. Much of Australia's wealth comes from agriculture, with huge sheep and cattle stations extending over large parts of the interior known as the Outback. Australia is the world's leading producer of wool, particularly the fine Merino wool. Cereal growing is dominated by wheat. Mining continues to be an important industry and produces coal, natural gas, oil, gold and iron ore. Australia is the largest producer of diamonds.

Quick facts:
Area : 7,300,848 sq km (2,966,150 sq miles)
Population : 18,242,000
Capital : Canberra
Other major cities : Adelaide, Brisbane, Melbourne, Perth, Sydney
Form of government : Federal Parliamentary State
Religion : Christianity
Currency : Australian dollar

Austria is a landlocked country in central Europe and is surrounded by seven nations. The wall of mountains which runs across the centre of the country dominates the scenery. In the warm summers tourists come to walk in the forests and mountains and in the cold winters skiers come to the mountains which now boast over 50 ski resorts. The main river is the Danube and there are numerous lakes, principally Lake Constance (Bodensee) and Neusiedler Lake. Agriculture in Austria is based on small farms, many of which are run by single families. Dairy products, beef and lamb from the hill farms contribute to exports. More than 37% of Austria is covered in forest, resulting in the paper-making industry near Graz. There are mineral resources of lignite, magnesium, petroleum, iron ore and natural gas and high-grade graphite is exported. Unemployment is very low in Austria and its low strike record has attracted multinational companies in recent years. Attachment to local customs is still strong and in rural areas men still wear lederhosen and women the traditional dirndl skirt on feast days and holidays.

Quick facts:
Area : 83,855 sq km (32,367 sq miles)
Population : 8,015,000
Capital : Vienna (Wien)
Other major cities : Graz, Innsbruck, Linz, Salzburg
Form of government : Federal Republic
Religion : RC
Currency : Schilling

Azerbaijan, a republic of the former USSR, declared itself independent in 1991. It is situated on the south-west coast of the Caspian Sea and shares borders with IRAN, ARMENIA, GEORGIA and the RUSSIAN FEDERATION. The Araks river separates Azerbaijan from the region known as AZERBAIJAN in northern Iran. The country is semi-arid, and 70% of the land is irrigated for the production of cotton, wheat, maize, potatoes, tobacco, tea and citrus fruits. It has rich mineral deposits of oil, natural gas, iron and aluminium. The most important mineral is oil, which is found in the Baku area from where it is piped to Batumi on the Black Sea. There are steel, synthetic rubber and aluminium works at Sumgait just north of the capital Baku. However, Azerbaijan is only minimally developed, industrially, but it is hindered by its dispute with Armenia over the Nagorny Karabakh region.

Quick facts:
Area : 86,600 sq km (33,400 sq miles)
Population : 7,677,000
Capital : Baku
Other major cities : Kirovabad, Sumgait
Form of government : Republic
Religions : Shia Islam, Sunni Islam, Russian Orthodox
Currency : Manat (= 100 gopik)

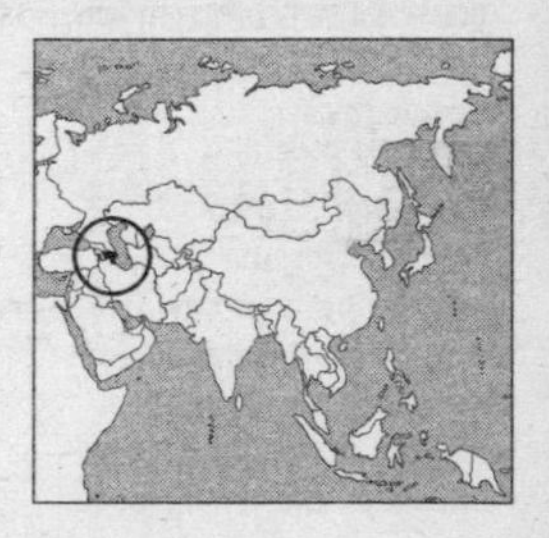

Bahamas, The consist of an archipelago of 700 islands located in the Atlantic Ocean off the south-east coast of Florida. The largest island is Andros (4144 sq km/1600 sq miles), and the two most populated are Grand Bahama and New Providence where the capital Nassau lies. Winters in the Bahamas are mild and summers warm. Most rain falls in May, June, September and October, and thunderstorms are frequent in summer. The islands are also subject to hurricanes and other tropical storms. The islands have few natural resources, and for many years fishing and small-scale farming (citrus fruits and vegetables) was the only way to make a living. Now, however, tourism, which employs almost half of the workforce, is the most important industry and has been developed on a vast scale. Offshore banking is also a growing source of income. About three million tourists, mainly from North America, visit the Bahamas each year.

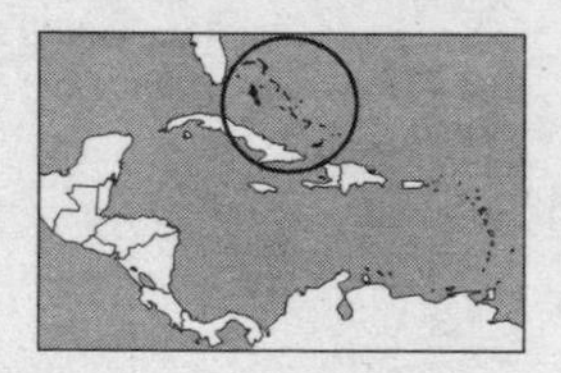

Quick facts:
Area : 13,940 sq km (5382 sq miles)
Population : 269,350
Capital : Nassau
Other important city : Freeport
Form of government : Constitutional Monarchy
Religion : Christianity
Currency : Bahamian dollar

Bahrain is a Gulf State comprising 33 low-lying islands situated between the QATAR peninsula and the mainland of SAUDI ARABIA. Bahrain Island is the largest, and a causeway, called the King Fahd Causeway, linking it to Saudi Arabia was opened in 1986. The highest point in the state is only 122.4 m (402 ft) above sea level. The climate is pleasantly warm between December and March, but very hot from June to November. Most of Bahrain is sandy and too saline to support crops but drainage schemes are now used to reduce salinity and fertile soil is imported from other islands. Oil was discovered in 1931 and revenues from oil now account for about 75% of the country's total revenue. Bahrain is being developed as a major manufacturing state, the main enterprises being aluminum smelting and the manufacture of clothing, paper products and consumer goods. Traditional industries include pearl fishing, boat building, weaving and pottery. Agricultural products include vegetables, dates and fruits with artesian wells providing irrigation mainly on the north coast.

Quick facts:
Area : 691 sq km (267 sq miles)
Population : 523,060
Capital : Manama
Other major city: Al Muharraq
Form of government : Monarchy (Emirate)
Religions : Shia Islam, Sunni Islam
Currency : Bahrain dinar

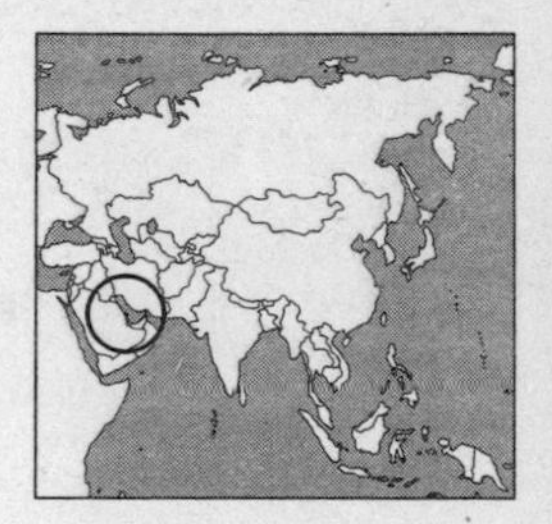

Bangladesh was formerly the Eastern Province of PAKISTAN and is the world's eighth highest populated country. It is bounded almost entirely by INDIA and to the south by the Bay of Bengal. There is a wide variety of animal life with the Sundarbans area being one of the last strongholds of the Bengal tiger. The country is extremely flat and is virtually a huge delta formed by the Ganges, Brahmaputra and Meghna rivers. The country is subject to devastating floods and cyclones which sweep in from the Bay of Bengal. Most villages are built on mud platforms to keep them above water. The climate is tropical monsoon with heat, extreme humidity and heavy rainfall in the monsoon season along with accompanying tornadoes. The short winter season is mild and dry. The combination of rainfall, sun and silt from the rivers makes the land productive, and it is often possible to grow three crops a year. Bangladesh produces about 70% of the world's jute and the production of jute-related products is a principal industry with tea being an important cash crop. There are few mineral resources although natural gas, coal and peat are found.

Quick facts:
Area : 143,998 sq km (55,598 sq miles)
Population : 116,310,000
Capital : Dacca (Dhaka)
Other major cities : Chittagong, Khulna, Narayanganj, Rajshahi
Form of government : Republic
Religion : Sunni Islam
Currency : Taka

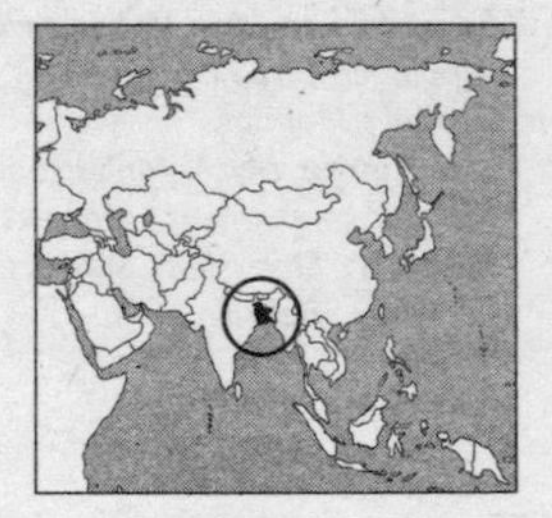

Barbados is the most easterly island of the West Indies and lies well outside the group of islands which makes up the Lesser Antilles. Mainly surrounded by coral reefs, most of the island is low-lying and only in the north does it rise to 336 m/1104 ft at Mount Hillaby. The climate is tropical, but the cooling effect of the north-east trade winds prevents the temperatures rising above 30°C (86°F). There are only two seasons, the dry and the wet, when rainfall is very heavy. At one time the economy depended almost exclusively on the production of sugar and its by-products molasses and rum, and although the industry is now declining, sugar is still the principal export. Tourism has now taken over as the main industry and it employs approximately 40% of the island's labour force, although there are industries manufacturing furniture, clothing, electrical and electronic equipment. More recently, deposits of natural gas and petroleum have been discovered and fishing is an important activity. The island is surrounded by pink and white sandy beaches and coral reefs which are visited by around 400,000 tourists each year.

Quick facts:
Area : 430 sq km (166 sq miles)
Population : 261,580
Capital : Bridgetown
Form of government : Constitutional Monarchy
Religions : Anglicanism, Methodism
Currency : Barbados dollar

Belarus (Belorussia, Byelorussia), a republic of the former USSR, declared itself independent in 1991. It borders POLAND to the west, UKRAINE to the south, LATVIA and LITHUANIA to the north, and the RUSSIAN FEDERATION to the east. The country consists mainly of a low-lying plain, and forests cover approximately one third of the country. The climate is continental with long severe winters and short warm summers. Although the economy is overwhelmingly based on industry, including oil refining, food processing, woodworking, chemicals, textiles and machinery, output has gradually declined since 1991 and problems persist in the supply of raw materials from other republics that previously formed parts of the USSR. Agriculture, although seriously affected by contamination from the Chernobyl nuclear accident of 1986, accounts for approximately 20% of employment, the main crops being flax, potatoes and hemp. The main livestock raised are cattle and pigs. Extensive forest areas also contribute in the supply of raw materials for woodwork and paper-making. Peat is the fuel used to provide power for industry and the country's power plants. Belarus has a good transport system of road, rail, navigable rivers and canals.

Quick facts:
Area : 207,600 sq km (80,150 sq miles)
Population : 10,355,000
Capital : Minsk
Other major cities : Gomel, Hrodna, Vicevsk
Form of government : Republic
Religions : Russian Orthodox, RC
Currency : Rouble

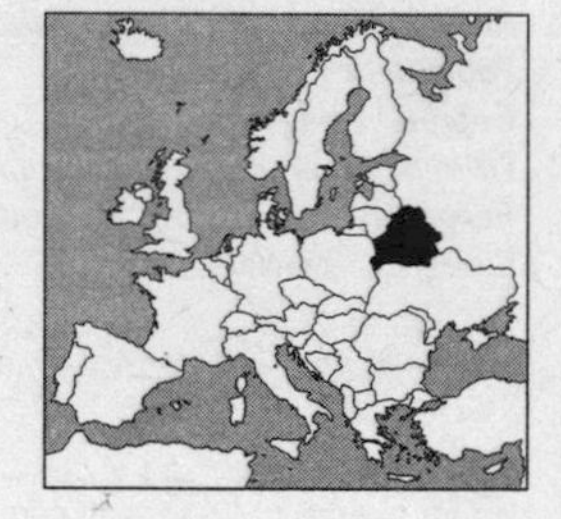

Belgium is a highly industrialized, relatively small country in north-west Europe with a short coastline on the North Sea. The Meuse river divides Belgium into two distinct geographical regions. To the north of the river the land slopes continuously for 150 km/93 miles until it reaches the North Sea where the coastlands are flat and grassy. To the south of the river is the forested plateau area of the Ardennes. Between these two regions lies the Meuse valley. Belgium is a densely populated country with few natural resources. Agriculture, which uses about 45% of the land for cultivation or rearing of livestock, employs only 3% of the workforce. About one fifth of the country is covered with forests with the wooded areas mainly used for recreation. The metal-working industry, originally based on the small mineral deposits in the Ardennes, is the most important industry, and in the northern cities new textile industries are producing carpets and clothing. Nearly all raw materials are now imported through the main port of Antwerp. There are three officially-recognized languages in Belgium — Dutch, French and German.

Quick facts:
Area : 30,519 sq km (11,783 sq miles)
Population : 10,100,630
Capital : Brussels
Other major cities : Antwerp, Bruges, Charleroi, Ghent, Liège
Form of government : Constitutional Monarchy
Religion : RC
Currency : Belgian franc

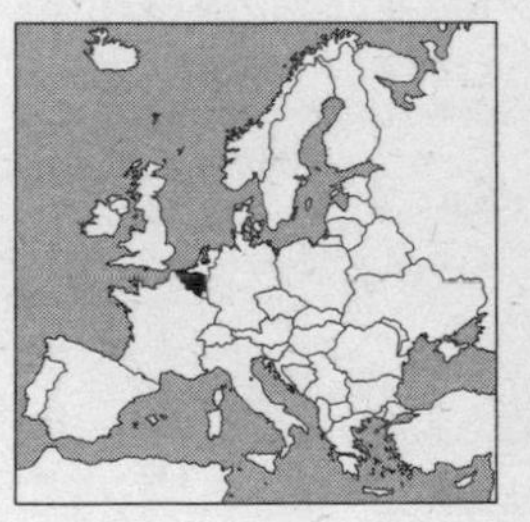

Belize is a small Central American country on the south-east of the Yucatan Peninsula in the Caribbean Sea. Its coastline on the Gulf of Honduras is approached through some 550 km/342 miles of coral reefs and keys (cayo). The coastal area and north of the country are low-lying and swampy with dense forests inland. In the south the Maya Mountains rise to 1100 m/3609 ft. The subtropical climate is warm and humid and the trade winds bring cooling sea breezes. Rainfall is heavy, particularly in the south, and hurricanes may occur in summer. The dense forests which cover most of the country provide valuable hardwoods such as mahogany. Most of the population make a living from forestry, fishing or agriculture although only 5% of the land is cultivated. The main crops grown for export are sugar cane, citrus fruits (mainly grapefruit), bananas and coconuts. Industry is very underdeveloped, causing many people to emigrate to find work. The official language is English although many others are spoken including Mayan, Carib and Spanish.

Quick facts:
Area : 22,965 sq km (8867 sq miles)
Population : 204,450
Capital : Belmopan
Other major city : Belize City
Form of government : Constitutional Monarchy
Religion : RC, Protestant
Currency : Belize dollar

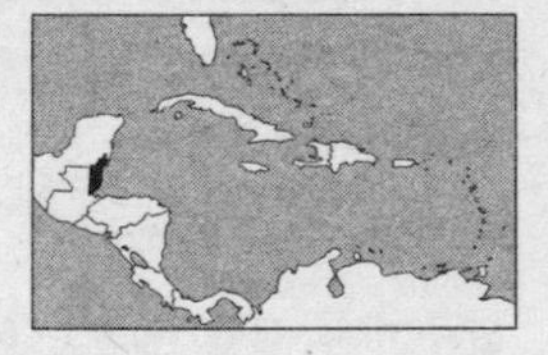

Benin on the southern coast of West Africa is an ice cream cone-shaped country with a very short coastline on the Bight of Benin. The coastal area has white sandy beaches backed by lagoons and low-lying fertile lands known as barre country. In the north-west the Atakora Mountains are grassy plateaux which are deeply cut into steep forested valleys and on the grasslands sheep, cattle and goats are reared. The main rivers of Benin are the Donga, Couffo and Niger with its tributaries. The climate in the north is tropical and in the south equatorial. There are nine rainy months each year so crops rarely fail. Farming is predominantly subsistence and accounts for around 60% of employment, with yams, cassava, maize, rice, groundnuts and vegetables forming most of the produce. The country is very poor, although since the late 1980s economic reforms have been towards a market economy and Western financial aid has been sought. The main exports are palm oil, palm kernels, and cotton. Tourism is now being developed but as yet facilities for this are few except in some coastal towns.

Quick facts:
Area : 112,622 sq km (43,483 sq miles)
Population : 5,270,000
Capital : Porto-Novo
Other major city : Cotonou
Form of government : Republic
Religions : Animism, RC, Sunni Islam, Christian
Currency : CFA Franc

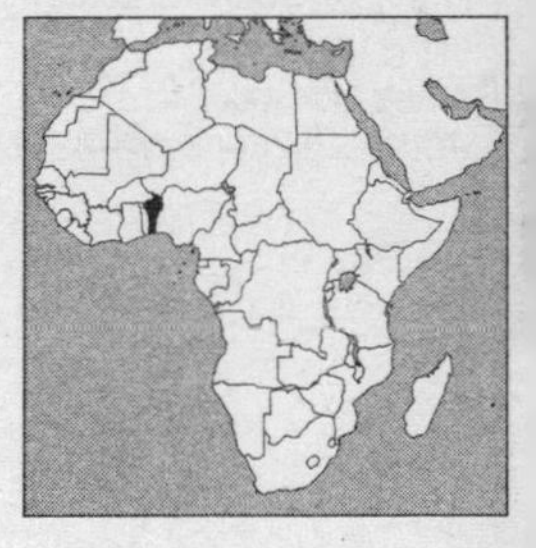

Bermuda consists of a group of 150 small islands in the western Atlantic Ocean. It lies about 920 km/572 miles east of Cape Hatteras on the coast of the USA. The hilly limestone islands are the caps of ancient volcanoes rising from the sea-bed. The main island, Great Bermuda, is linked to the other islands by bridges and causeways. The climate is warm and humid with rain spread evenly throughout the year, but with the risk of hurricanes from June to November. Bermuda's chief agricultural products are fresh vegetables, bananas and citrus fruit but 80% of food requirements are imported. Many foreign banks and financial institutions operate from the island, taking advantage of the lenient tax laws. Other industries include ship repair and pharmaceuticals. Its proximity to the USA and the pleasant climate have led to a flourishing tourist industry.

Quick facts:
Area : 54 sq km (21 sq miles)
Population : 62,100
Capital : Hamilton
Form of government : Colony under British administration
Religion : Protest, RC
Currency : Bermuda dollar

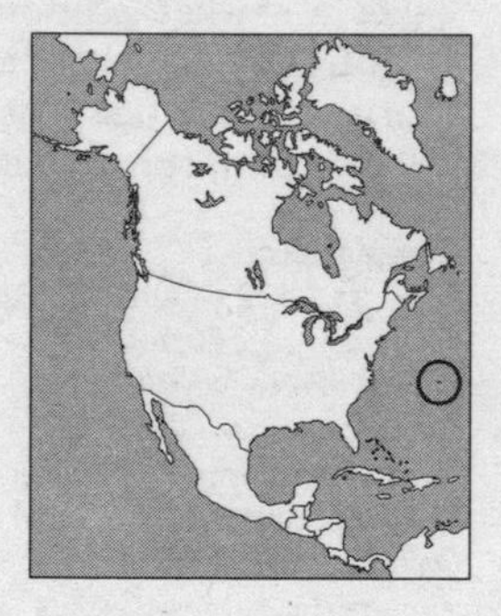

Bhutan is surrounded by INDIA to the south and CHINA to the north. It rises from foothills overlooking the Brahmaputra river to the southern slopes of the Himalayas. The Himalayas, which rise to over 7500 m/24,608 ft in Bhutan, make up most of the country. The climate is hot and wet on the plains but temperatures drop progressively with altitude, resulting in glaciers and permanent snow cover in the north. The valleys in the centre of the country are wide and fertile and about 95% of the workforce are farmers growing wheat, rice, potatoes and corn. Fruit such as plums, pears, apples and also cardamom are grown for export. There are many monasteries with about 6000 monks. Yaks reared on the high pasture land provide milk, cheese and meat. Vast areas of the country still remain forested as there is little demand for new farmland. Bhutan is one of the world's poorest and least developed countries; it has little contact with the rest of the world although tourism has been encouraged in recent years. There are no railways but roads join many parts of the country.

Quick facts:
Area : 46,500 sq km (17,954 sq miles)
Population : 1,095,000
Capital : Thimpu
Form of government : Constitutional Monarchy
Religion : Buddhism, Hinduism
Currency : Ngultrum

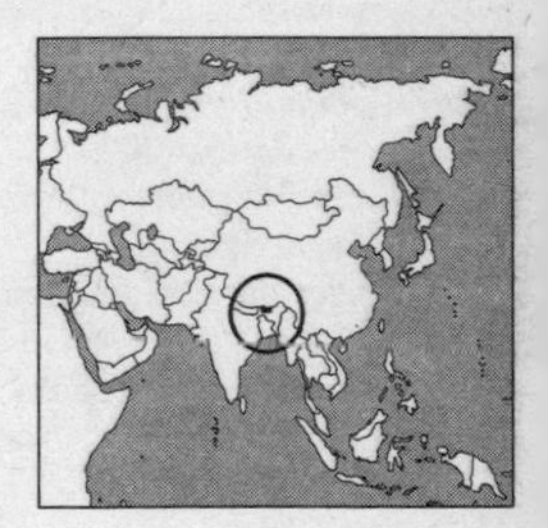

Bolivia is a landlocked republic of Central South America through which the great mountain range of the Andes runs. It is in the Andes that the highest navigable lake in the world, Lake Titicaca, is found. On the undulating depression south of the lake, the Altiplano, is the highest capital city in the world, La Paz. To the east and north-east of the mountains is a huge area of lowland containing tropical rainforests (the Llanos) and wooded savanna (the Chaco). The north-east has a heavy rainfall while in the south-west it is negligible. Temperatures vary with altitude from extremely cold on the summits to cool on the Altiplano, where at least half of the population lives. Although rich in natural resources such as lead, silver, copper, zinc, oil and tin, Bolivia remains a poor country because of lack of funds for their extraction, lack of investment and political instability. Bolivia is self-sufficient in petroleum and exports natural gas. Agriculture produces soya beans, sugar cane and cotton for export, and increased production of coca, from which cocaine is derived, has resulted in an illicit economy.

Quick facts:
Area : 1,098,581 sq km (424,164 sq miles)
Population : 8,017,000
Capital : La Paz (administrative capital), Sucre (legal capital)
Other major cities : Cochabamba, Oruro, Potosi, Santa Cruz
Form of government : Republic
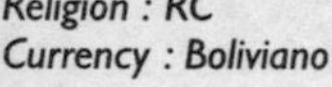
Religion : RC
Currency : Boliviano

Bosnia & Herzegovina, a republic of former YUGOSLAVIA, was formally recognized as an independent state in March 1992. It is a very mountainous country and includes part of the Dinaric Alps, which are densely forested and deeply cut by rivers flowing northwards to join the Sava river. Half the country is forested, and timber is an important product of the northern areas. One quarter of the land is cultivated, and corn, wheat and flax are the principal products of the north. In the south, tobacco, cotton, fruits and grapes are the main products. Bosnia & Herzegovina has large deposits of lignite, iron ore and bauxite, and its metallurgical plants create air pollution. Water is also polluted around these with a shortage of drinking water, the Sava river being severely affected. Despite the natural resources the economy has been devastated by civil war which began in 1991 following the secession of CROATIA and SLOVENIA from the former Yugoslavia. Dispute over control of Bosnia and Herzegovina continued, leading to UN intervention in an attempt to devise a territorial plan acceptable to all factions. A peace agreement signed in late 1995 has resulted in the division of the country into two self-governing provinces. The population of the state was significantly diminished when refugees from the civil war fled between 1992 and 1993. The economy is at a standstill and most inhabitants are dependent on UN aid.

Quick facts:
Area : 51,129 sq km (19,741 sq miles)
Population : 3,400,000
Capital : Sarajevo
Other major cities : Banja Luka, Mostar, Tuzla
Form of government : Republic
Religions : Eastern Orthodox, Sunni Islam, RC
Currency : Dinar

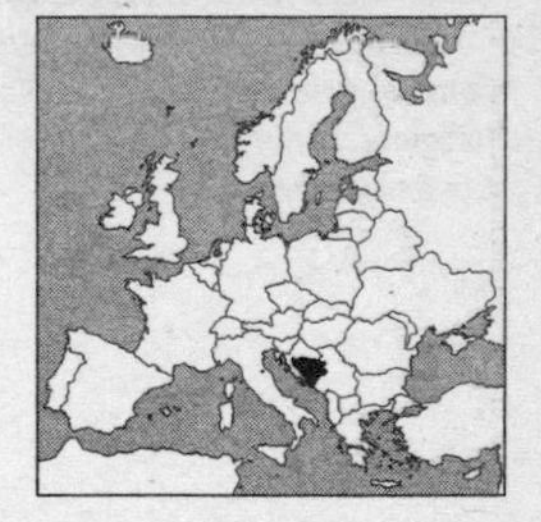

Botswana is a landlocked republic in southern Africa which straddles the Tropic of Capricorn. Much of the west and southwest of the country forms part of the Kalahari Desert. In the north there is a huge area of marshland around the Okavango Delta, which is home for a wide variety of wildlife. With the exception of the desert area, most of the country has a subtropical climate but is subject to drought. In winter, days are warm and nights cold while summer is hot with sporadic rainfall. The people are mainly farmers and cattle rearing is the main activity. After independence in 1966 the exploitation of minerals started. In 1972 the first diamond mine was at Orapa and they quickly became the country's most important export and copper from the nickel/copper complex at Selebi-Pikwe was also exported. Exploitation of these mineral resources has facilitated a high rate of economic growth within the country. Coal is also mined but the majority is for domestic use. About 17% of the land is set aside for wildlife preservation in National Parks, Game Reserves, Game Sanctuaries and controlled hunting areas.

Quick facts:
Area : 581,730 sq km (224,606 sq miles)
Population : 1,383,000
Capital : Gaborone
Other major cities : Francistown, Kanye, Molepolole, Selibi-Pikwe, Serowe
Form of government : Republic
Religions : Animism, Christian
Currency : Pula

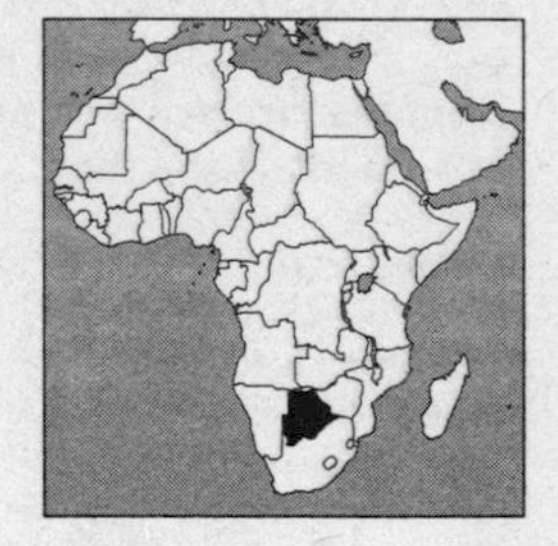

Brazil is a huge South American country bounded to the north, south and east by the Atlantic Ocean. It is the fifth largest country in the world and covers nearly half of South America. The climate is mainly tropical, but altitude, distance from the sea and prevailing winds cause many variations. The Amazon river basin occupies a huge area of land, over one third of the country's area, and much of this is covered with tropical rain forests. In the tropical areas winters are dry and summers wet and droughts may occur in the north-east, where it is hot and arid. About 14% of the population is employed in agriculture, which occupies only about 7% of the land area, and the main products exported are coffee, soya beans, orange juice and cocoa. Brazil is rich in minerals and is the only source of high grade quartz crystal in commercial quantities. It is also a major producer of chrome ore and it is now developing what is thought to be the richest iron ore deposits in the world. Since improvement of facilities, fishing is now an important industry mainly of lobsters, shrimp and sardines.

Quick facts:
Area : 8,511,965 sq km (3,285,488 sq miles)
Population : 160,015,000
Capital : Brasília
Other major cities : Balem, Belo Horizonte, Curitiba, Porto Alegre, Recife, Rio de Janeiro, Salvador, São Paulo
Form of government : Federal Republic
Religion : RC
Currency : Cruzeiro

Brunei is a sultanate located on the north-west coast of BORNEO in South-East Asia. It is bounded on all sides by the Sarawak territory of MALAYSIA, which splits the sultanate into two separate parts. Broad tidal swamplands cover the coastal plains and inland Brunei is hilly and covered with tropical rain forests which occupy almost half of the country's land area. The climate is tropical marine, hot and moist, with cool nights. Rainfall is heavy (2500 mm/98 inches) at the coast but even heavier (5000 mm/197 inches) inland. The main crops grown are rice, vegetables and fruit, but economically the country depends on its oil industry, which employs 7% of the working population. Cloth weaving and metalwork are also small local industries. Oil production began in the 1920s and now oil and natural gas account for almost all exports. Other minor products are rubber, pepper, gravel and animal hides.

Quick facts:
Area : 5,765 sq km (2,226 sq miles)
Population : 284,000
Capital : Bandar Seri Begawan
Other major cities : Kuala Belait, Seria
Form of government : Monarchy (Sultanate)
Religion : Sunni Islam
Currency : Brunei dollar

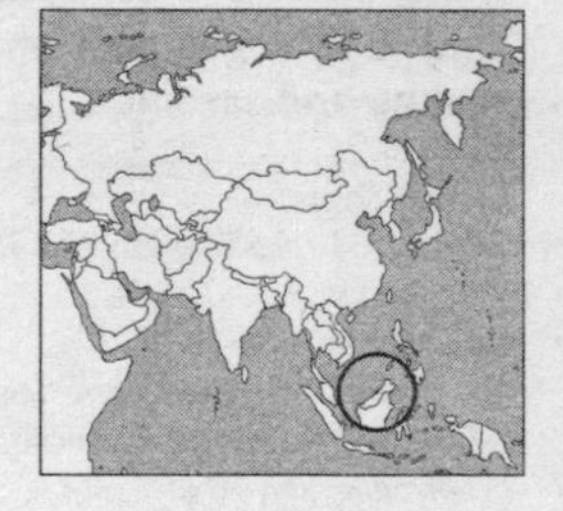

Bulgaria is a south-east European republic located on the east Balkan peninsula and has a coast on the Black Sea. It is bounded to the north by ROMANIA, west by SERBIA and THE FORMER YUGOSLAV REPUBLIC OF MACEDONIA and south by GREECE and TURKEY. The centre of Bulgaria is crossed from west to east by the Balkan Mountains. The south of the country has a Mediterranean climate with hot dry summers and mild winters. Further north the temperatures become more extreme and rainfall is higher in summer. The main river in Bulgaria is the Danube and about a third of the country is covered with forests. Traditionally Bulgaria is an agricultural country and a revolution in farming during the 1950s has led to great increases in output. This was due to the collectivization of farms and the use of more machinery, fertilizers and irrigation. Each agricultural region now has its own specialized type of farming. Increased mechanization led to more of the workforce being available to work in mines and industry. However, the country has suffered very high rates of inflation and unemployment in the early 1990s since the break up of the former Soviet Union, with whom Bulgaria had very close trade links. Tourism flourishes with over 10,000,000 people visiting the Black Sea resorts annually.

Quick facts:
Area : 110,912 sq km (42,823 sq miles)
Population : 8,472,000
Capital : Sofia (Sofiya)
Other major cities : Burgas, Plovdiv, Ruse, Varna
Form of government : Republic
Religion : Eastern Orthodox
Currency : Lev

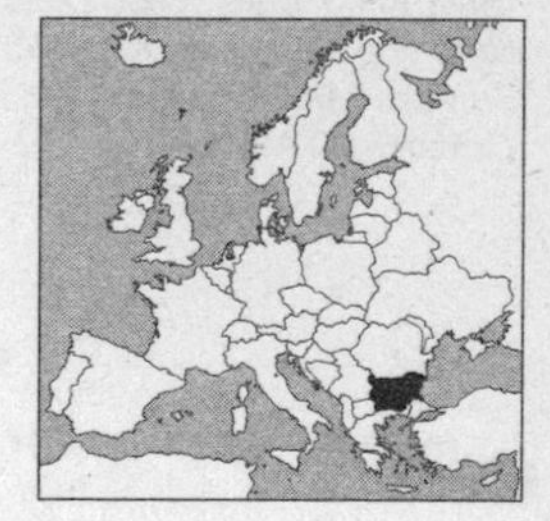

Burkina Faso (Burkina) a landlocked state in West Africa, Burkina lies on the fringe of the Sahara, to the north. The country is made up of vast monotonous plains and low hills which rise to 700 m (2297 ft) in the south-west. Precipitation is generally low, the heaviest rain falling in the south-west, while the rest of the country is semi-desert. In the last two decades the country has been stricken by drought. The dusty grey plains in the north and west have infertile soils which have been further impoverished by overgrazing and over cultivation. About 85% of the people live by subsistence farming, and food crops include sorghum, millet, pulses, corn and rice. Cotton is the main export along with minerals such as gold, and animal products. There is great poverty and shortage of work and many of the younger population go to GHANA and CÔTE D'IVOIRE for employment. The main industries are textiles, metal products and the processing of agricultural products and production of consumer items such as footwear and soap.

Quick facts:
Area : 274,200 sq km (105,869 sq miles)
Population : 10,103,000
Capital : Ouagadougou
Other major cities : Bobo-Dioulasso, Koudougou
Form of government : Republic
Religions : Animism, Sunni Islam
Currency : CFA Franc

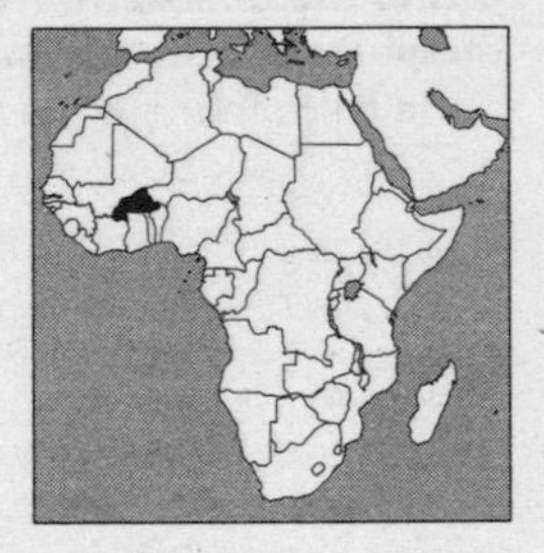

Burundi is a small, densely-populated country in central east Africa, bounded by RWANDA to the north, TANZANIA to the east and south, and DEMOCRATIC REPUBLIC OF CONGO to the west. It is one of the poorest nations in the world and has a mountainous terrain, with much of the country above 1500 m (4921 ft). The climate is equatorial but modified by altitude. The savanna in the east is several degrees hotter than the plateau and there are two wet seasons. The soils are not rich but there is enough rain to grow crops in most areas for subsistence farming. The main food crops are bananas, sweet potatoes, peas, lentils and beans. Cassava is grown near the shores of Lake Tanganyika which is in the Great Rift Valley. The main cash crop is coffee, which accounts for 90% of Burundi's export earnings. Cotton and tea are also cultivated for export. There is a little commercial fishing on Lake Tanganyika, otherwise industry is very basic. Since 1994 Burundi has been afflicted by ethnic conflict between the majority Hutu and minority Tutsi. Between 1994 and 1995 it is estimated that 150,000 were killed as a result of ethnic violence and the political situation remains highly volatile.

Quick facts:
Area : 27,834 sq km (10,747 sq miles)
Population : 6,105,000
Capital : Bujumbura
Form of government : Republic
Religion : RC
Currency : Burundi franc

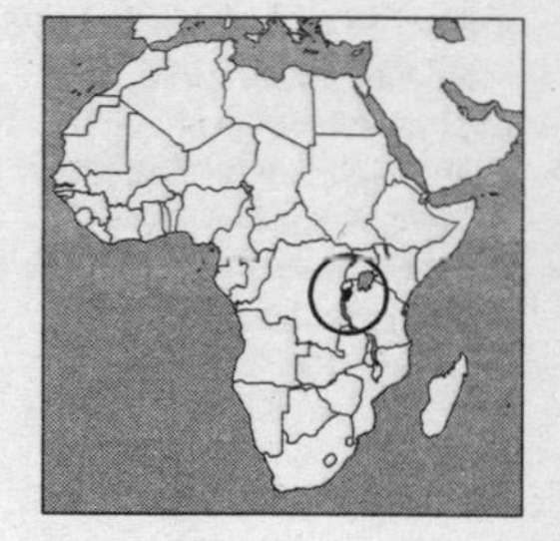

Cambodia is a South-East Asian state bounded by THAILAND, LAOS and VIETNAM and its southern coast lies on the Gulf of Thailand. The heart of the country is saucer-shaped, and gently rolling alluvial plains are drained by the Mekong river. The Dangrek Mountains form the frontier with Thailand in the north-west. In general Cambodia has a tropical monsoon climate and about half of the land is tropical forest. During the rainy season the Mekong swells and backs into the Tonle Sap (Great Lake), increasing its size threefold to about 10,400 km (4015 sq miles). This seasonal flooding means the area is left with rich silt when the river recedes. Crop production depends entirely on the rainfall and floods but production was badly disrupted during the civil war when there was widespread famine and yields still remain low. The cultivation of rice accounts for about 80% of agricultural land and the other main crop is rubber which grows in the eastern plateau. Despite the gradual rebuilding of the infrastructure in the early 1990s, Cambodia remains one of the world's poorest nations.

Quick facts:
Area : 181,035 sq km (69,898 sq miles)
Population : 9,387,000
Capital : Phnom-Penh
Other major cities : Battambang, Kampong Cham, Kampot
Form of government : People's Republic
Religion : Buddhism
Currency : Riel

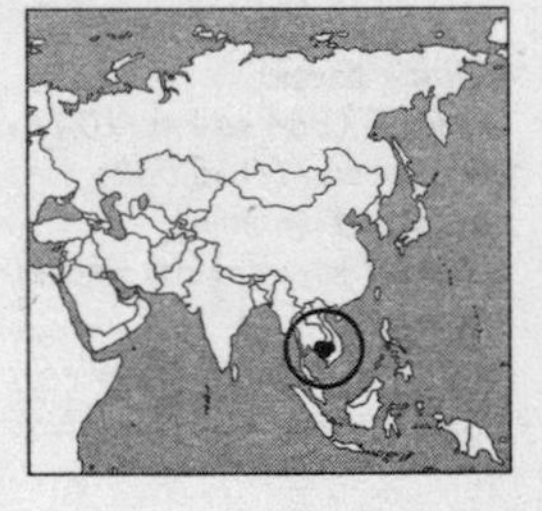

Cameroon is a triangular-shaped country of diverse landscapes in west central Africa. It stretches from Lake Chad at its apex to the northern borders of EQUATORIAL GUINEA, GABON and the CONGO in the south. The landscape ranges from low-lying lands, through the semi-desert Sahel, to dramatic mountain peaks and then to the grassy savanna, rolling uplands, steaming tropical forests and hardwood plantations. Further south are the volcanoes, including Mount Cameroon, an active volcano and the highest peak at 4095 m (14,435 ft) in western Africa, and the palm beaches at Kribi and Limbe. The climate is equatorial with high temperatures and plentiful rain. The majority of the population are farmers who live in the south and central Cameroon where they grow maize, millet, cassava and vegetables. In the drier north where drought and hunger are well-known, life is harder and this area is populated by semi-nomadic herders. Bananas, coffee and cocoa are the major exports although oil, gas and aluminum are becoming increasingly important.

Quick facts:
Area : 475,442 sq km (183,568 sq miles)
Population : 13,065,000
Capital : Yaoundé
Other major city : Douala
Form of government : Republic
Religions : Animism, RC, Sunni Islam
Currency : CFA Franc

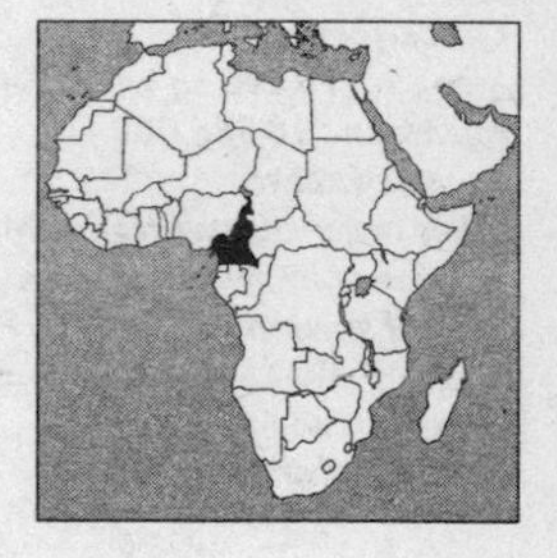

Canada is the second largest country in the world, and the largest in North America. Canada is a land of great climatic and geographical extremes. It lies to the north of the USA and has Pacific, Atlantic and Arctic coasts. The country has the highest number of inland waters and lakes in the world, including the Great Lakes on the border with the USA. The Rocky Mountains and Coast Mountains run down the west side, and the highest point, Mount Logan (5951 m/19,524 ft), is in the Yukon. Climates range from polar conditions in the north, to cool temperate in the south with considerable differences from west to east. More than 80% of its farmland is in the prairies that stretch from Alberta to Manitoba. Wheat and grain crops cover three-quarters of the arable land. Canada is rich in forest reserves which cover more than half the total land area. The most valuable mineral deposits (oil, gas, coal and iron ore) are found in Alberta. Most industry in Canada is associated with processing its natural resources and it is one of the main exporters of food products.

Quick facts:

Area : 9 ,970,610 sq km (3,849,663 sq miles)
Population : 28,386,000
Capital : Ottawa
Other major cities : Calgary, Montréal, Québec City, Toronto, Vancouver, Winnipeg
Form of government : Federal Parliamentary State
Religions : RC, United Church of Canada, Anglicanism
Currency : Canadian dollar

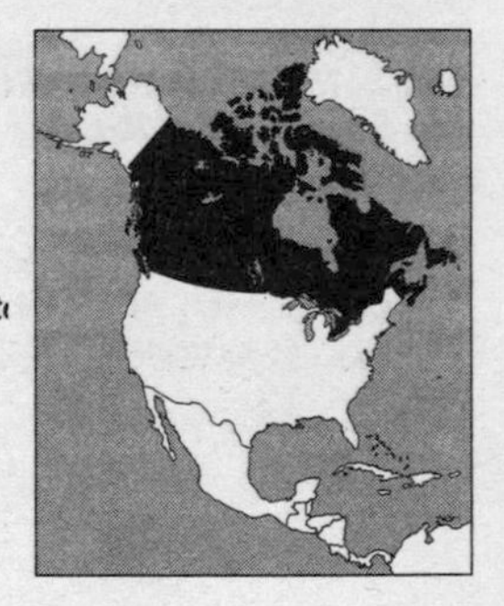

Cape Verde, one of the world's smallest nations, is situated in the Atlantic Ocean, about 640 km (400 miles) north-west of SENEGAL. It consists of 10 islands and 5 islets and there is an active volcano on Fogo, one of the islands. The islands are divided into the Windward group and the Leeward group. Over 50% of the population live on São Tiago on which is Praia, the capital. The climate is arid with a cool dry season from December to June and warm dry conditions for the rest of the year. Rainfall is sparse and the islands suffer from periods of severe drought. Agriculture is mostly confined to irrigated inland valleys and the chief crops are coconuts, sugar cane, potatoes, cassava and dates. Bananas and some coffee are grown for export. Fishing for tuna and lobsters is an important industry but in general the economy is shaky and Cape Verde relies heavily on foreign aid. Due to its lack of natural resources and droughts, large numbers of its people have emigrated for many years. Tourism is being encouraged although the number of visitors is at present relatively low.

Quick facts:
Area : 4033 sq km (1575 sq miles)
Population : 402,000
Capital : Praia
Form of government : Republic
Religion : RC
Currency : Cape Verde escudo

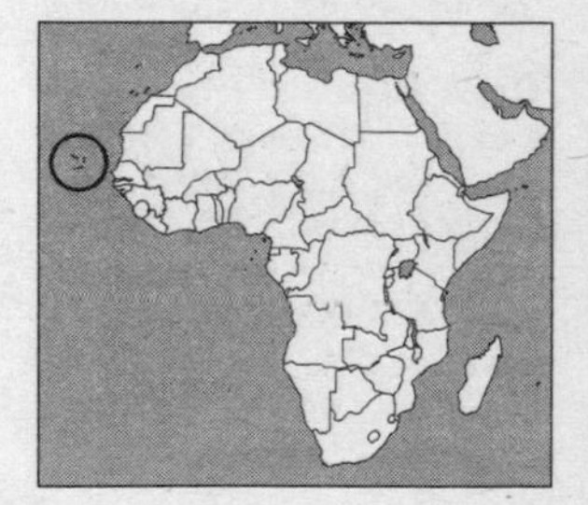

Central African Republic is a landlocked country in central Africa bordered by CHAD in the north, CAMEROON in the west, SUDAN in the east and the CONGO and DEMOCRATIC REPUBLIC OF CONGO in the south. The terrain consists of a 610–915 m (2000–3000 ft) high undulating plateau with dense tropical forest in the south and a semi-desert area in the east. The climate is tropical with little variation in temperature throughout the year. The wet months are May, June, October and November. Floods and tornadoes can occur at the beginning of the rainy season. Most of the population live in the west and in the hot, humid south and south-west. Over 86% of the working population are subsistence farmers and the main crops grown are cassava, groundnuts, bananas, plantains, millet and maize. Livestock rearing is small-scale because of the prevalence of the tsetse fly. Gems and industrial diamonds are mined and deposits of uranium, iron ore, lime, zinc and gold have been discovered although they remain relatively undeveloped. The country's main exports are coffee, diamonds, cotton, tobacco and timber although this is hampered by the distance from a port.

Quick facts:
Area : 622,984 sq km (240,535 sq miles)
Population : 3,284,000
Capital : Bangui
Form of government : Republic
Religions : Animism, RC
Currency : CFA Franc

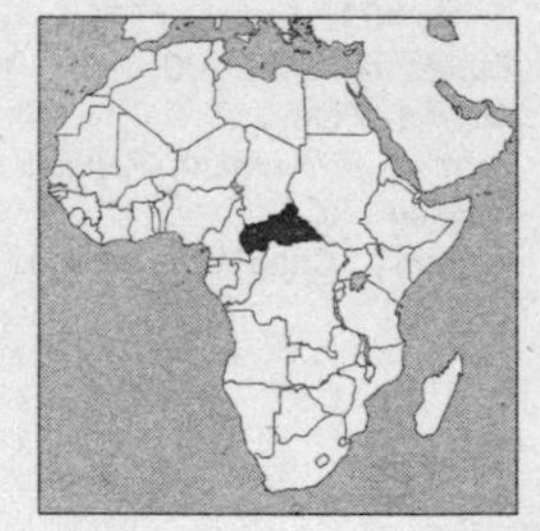

Chad, a landlocked country in the centre of northern Africa, extends from the edge of the equatorial forests in the south to the middle of the Sahara Desert in the north. It lies more than 1600 km (944 miles) from the nearest coast. The climate is tropical with adequate rainfall in the south but the north experiences semi-desert conditions. In the far north of the country the Tibesti Mountains rise from the desert sand more than 3000 m (9843 ft). The southern part of Chad is the most densely populated and its relatively well-watered savanna has always been the country's most arable region. Unless there is drought, this area is farmed for cotton (the main cash crop along with livestock exports), millet, sorghum, groundnuts, rice and vegetables. Fishing is carried out in the rivers and in Lake Chad. Cotton ginning and manufacture of peanut oil are the principal industries. Chad remains one of the poorest countries in the world, a result of drought and the civil war, which lasted from 1960 to 1988. Some unrest continues in the country.

Quick facts:
Area : 1,284,000 sq km (495,750 sq miles)
Population : 6,236,000
Capital : N'Djamena
Other major cities : Sarh, Moundou, Abéché
Form of government : Republic
Religions : Sunni Islam, Animism
Currency : CFA Franc

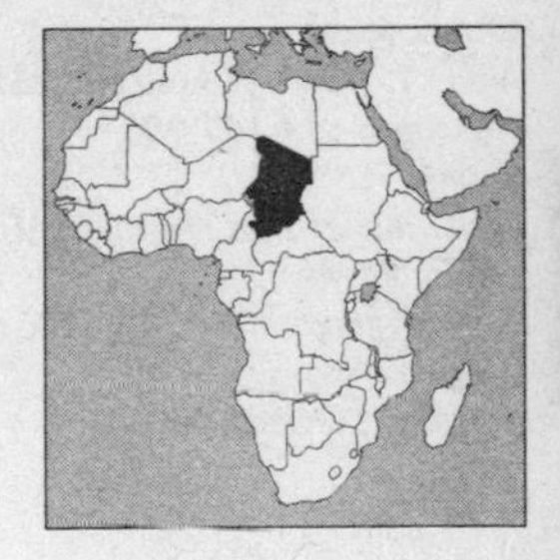

Chile lies like a backbone down the Pacific coast of the South American continent with the Andes Mountains extending the length of the country. Its Pacific coastline is 4200 km (2610 miles) long and the country is liable to volcanic explosions and earthquakes. Because of its enormous range in latitude it has almost every kind of climate from desert conditions to icy wastes. The north, in which lies the Atacama Desert, is extremely arid. The Atacama Desert is rich in mineral deposits and has large quantities of nitrates. The climate of the central region is Mediterranean and that of the south cool temperate. 60% of the population lives in the central valley where the climate is similar to southern California. The land here is fertile and the principal crops grown are grapes, wheat, apples, sugar beet, maize, tomatoes and potatoes. It is also in the central valley that the vast copper mine of El Teniente is located. This is one of the largest copper mines in the world and accounts for Chile's most important source of foreign exchange.

Quick facts:
Area : 756,945 sq km (292,258 sq miles)
Population : 14,107,000
Capital : Santiago
Other major cities : Arica, Concepcion, Valparaiso, Viña del Mar
Form of government : Republic
Religion : RC
Currency : Chilean peso

China, the third largest country in the world, covers a large area of East Asia and also includes over 3000 islands. In western China most of the terrain is inhospitable – in the north-west there are deserts that extend into MONGOLIA and the RUSSIAN FEDERATION, and much of the south-west consists of the ice-capped peaks of TIBET. The south-east has a green and well-watered landscape comprising terraced hillsides and paddy fields and its main rivers are the Yangtze, Huang He and Xi Jiang. Most of China has a temperate climate but in such a large country wide ranges of latitude and altitudes produce local variations. It is an agricultural country, and intensive cultivation and horticulture is necessary to feed its population of over one billion. Under the leadership of Deng Xiao Ping, China has experienced a huge modernization of agriculture and industry because of the supply of expertise, capital and technology from Japan and the West. The country has been opened up to tourists and to a degree has adopted the philosophy of free enterprise, resulting in a dramatic improvement in living standards. However, the change towards a market economy has created internal political problems. Pro-democracy demonstrations in 1989 resulted in the Tiananmen Square massacre, which was condemned throughout the world and raised questions regarding China's approach to human rights. Deng Xiao Ping had been *de facto* leader since announcing his retirement in 1989, but his influence on the country was profound until his death in February 1997.

Quick facts:
Area : 9,571,300 sq km (3,695,500 sq miles)
Population : 1,196,327,000
Capital : Beijing (Peking)
Other major cities: Chengdu, Guangzhou, Harbin, Shanghai, Tianjin, Wuhan
Form of government: People's Republic
Religions : Buddhism, Confucianism, Taoism
Currency : Yuan

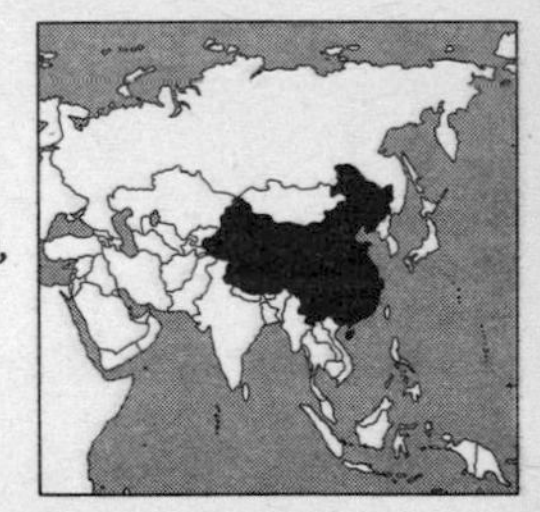

Colombia is situated in the north of South America and most of the country lies between the equator and 10° north. The Andes, which split into three ranges (the Cordilleras) in Colombia, run north along the west coast and gradually disappear toward the Caribbean Sea. Half of Colombia lies east of the Andes and much of this region is covered in tropical grassland. Toward the Amazon Basin the vegetation changes to tropical forest. The climates in Colombia include equatorial and tropical according to altitude. Very little of the country is under cultivation although much of the soil is fertile. The range of climates result in an extraordinary variety of crops of which coffee is the most important and includes cocoa beans, sugar cane, bananas, cotton and tobacco. Colombia is rich in minerals such as gold, silver, platinum and copper and produces about half of the world's emeralds. It is South America's leading producer of coal, and petroleum is the country's most important foreign revenue earner.

Quick facts:
Area : 1,141,748 sq km (440,831 sq miles)
Population : 35,983,000
Capital : Bogotá
Other major cities : Barranquilla, Cali, Cartagena, Medellin
Form of government : Republic
Religion : RC
Currency : Colombian peso

Comoros, The consist of three volcanic islands in the Indian Ocean situated between mainland Africa and MADAGASCAR. Physically four islands make up the group but the island of Mayotte remained a French dependency when the three western islands became a federal Islamic republic in 1975. The islands are mostly forested and the tropical climate is affected by Indian monsoon winds from the north. There is a wet season from November to April which is accompanied by cyclones. Only small areas of the islands are cultivated and most of this land belongs to foreign plantation owners. The chief product was formerly sugar cane, but now vanilla, copra, maize, cloves and essential oils are the most important products. The forests provide timber for building and there is a small fishing industry. The coelacanth, previously thought to have been extinct for millions of years, was discovered living in the seas off the Comoros.

Quick facts:
Area : 1865 sq km (720 sq miles) excluding Mayotte
Population : 538,000
Capital : Moroni
Other principal cities : Dornoni, Fomboni, Mutsamudu, Mitsamiouli
Form of government : Federal Islamic Republic
Religion : Sunni Islam
Currency : Comorian franc

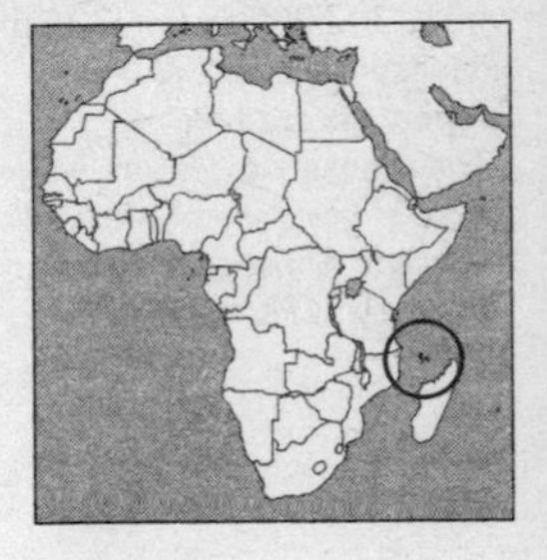

Congo formerly a French colony, the Republic of the Congo is situated in west central Africa where it straddles the Equator. The climate is equatorial, with a moderate rainfall and a small range of temperature. The Bateke Plateau has a long dry season but the Congo Basin is more humid and rainfall approaches 2500 mm (9.8 inches) each year. About 62% of the total land area is covered with equatorial forest from which timbers such as okoume and sapele are produced. Valuable hardwoods such as mahogany are exported. Cash crops such as coffee and cocoa are mainly grown on large plantations but food crops are grown on small farms usually worked by the women. A manufacturing industry is now growing and oil discovered offshore accounts for about 90% of the Congo's revenues and exports. The remaining exports are wood, cocoa, sugar, coffee and diamonds.

Quick facts:

Area : 342,000 sq km (132,046 sq miles)
Population : 2,527,750
Capital : Brazzaville
Other major city : Pointe-Noire
Form of government : Republic
Religion : Christian, Animism
Currency : CFA Franc

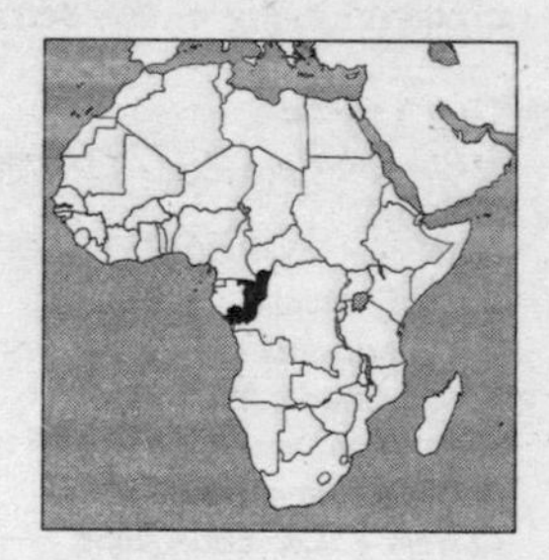

Congo, Democratic Republic of (formerly Zaïre) situated in west central Africa, it is a vast country with a short coastline of only 40 km (25 miles) on the Atlantic Ocean. Rain forests, which cover about 55% of the country, contain valuable hardwoods such as mahogany and ebony. The country is drained by the river Zaïre, which is largely navigable, and its main tributaries. There is enormous potential for hydroelectricity, but this is not yet exploited. Mountain ranges and plateaux surround the Zaïre Basin, and in the east the Ruwenzori Mountains overlook the lakes in the Great Rift Valley. In the central region the climate is hot and wet all year but elsewhere there are well-marked wet and dry seasons. Agriculture employs 75% of the population yet less than 3% of the country can be cultivated. Grazing land is limited by the infestation of the tsetse fly. Cassava is the main subsistence crop, and coffee, tea, cocoa, rubber and palms are grown for export. The country has huge mineral resources, particularly cobalt (around 65% of the world's deposits), with copper, uranium, gold and diamonds being exported. Other natural resources include silver, iron ore and coal. The population figure is very volatile as it is affected by tribal fighting in neighbouring countries leading to an influx of refugees from Rwanda and Burundi.

Quick facts:
Area : 2,344,860 km (905,350 miles)
Population : 46,498,550
Capital : Kinshasa
Other major cities : Bukavu, Kananga, Kisangani, Lubumbashi, Matadi, Mbuji-Mayi
Form of government : Republic
Religion : RC, Protestantism, Muslim, Kimbanguist
Currency : New zaire

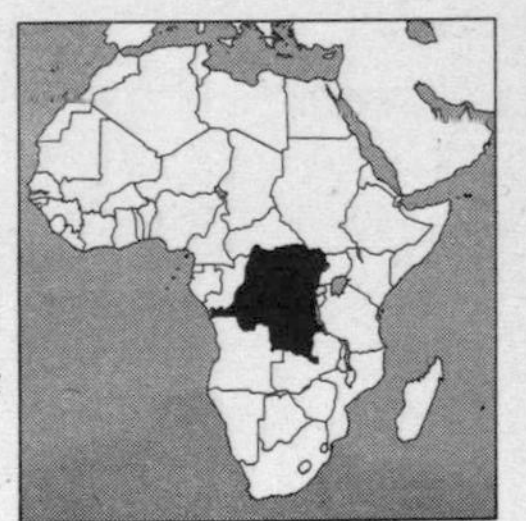

Costa Rica with the Pacific Ocean to the south and west and the Caribbean Sea to the east, Costa Rica is sandwiched between the central American countries of NICARAGUA and PANAMA. Much of the country consists of volcanic mountain chains which run north-west to south-east. The climate is tropical with a small temperature range and abundant rain. The dry season is from December to April. The most populated area is the Valle Central in which the Spanish settled in the 16th century. The upland areas have rich volcanic soils which are good for coffee growing and the slopes provide lush pastures for cattle. Coffee and bananas are grown commercially and are the major agricultural exports. Costa Rica's mountainous terrain provides hydroelectric power, which makes it almost self-sufficient in electricity, and attractive scenery for its growing tourist industry. The country has a high literacy rate (around 92%) and culture reflects its Spanish heritage.

Quick facts:
Area : 51,100 sq km (19,730 sq miles)
Population : 3,323,000
Capital : San José
Other major cities : Alajuela, Límon, Puntarenas
Form of government : Republic
Religion : RC
Currency : Colon

Côte d'Ivoire, a former French colony in west Africa, Côte d'Ivoire is located on the Gulf of Guinea with GHANA to the east and LIBERIA and GUINEA to the west. The south-west coast has rocky cliffs but further east there are coastal plains which are the country's most prosperous region. The climate is tropical and affected by distance from the sea. The coastal area has two wet seasons but in the north, there is only the one. Côte d'Ivoire is basically an agricultural country which produces cocoa, coffee, rubber, bananas and pineapples and employs about 55% of the workforce. It is the world's largest producer of cocoa and the fourth largest producer of coffee. These two crops bring in half the country's export revenue although timber production is also of economic importance. Since independence industrialization has developed rapidly, particularly food processing, textiles and sawmills. Oil was discovered offshore in the late 1970s and there is mining for gold and diamonds.

Quick facts:
Area : 322,463 sq km (124,503 sq miles)
Population : 14,137,000
Capital : Yamoussoukro (official capital)
Other major cities : Abidjan (actual capital), Bouaké, Daloa
Form of government : Republic
Religions : Animism, Sunni Islam, RC
Currency : CFA Franc

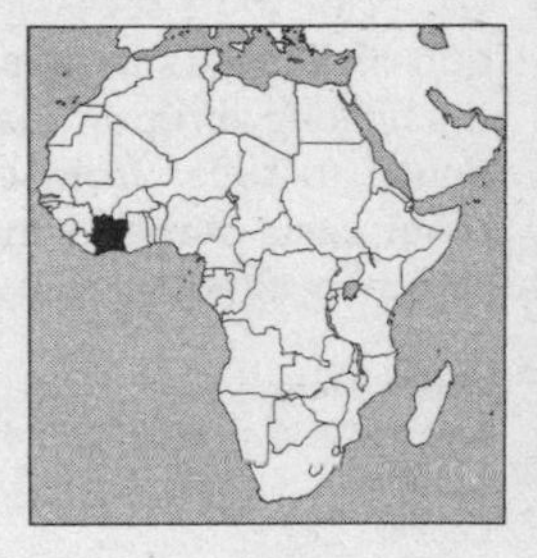

Croatia (Hrvatska), a republic of former YUGOSLAVIA, made a unilateral declaration of independence on 25 June, 1991. Sovereignty was not formally recognized by the international community until early in 1992. Located in south-east Europe, it is bounded to the west by the Adriatic Sea, to the north by SLOVENIA and ROMANIA, and to the south by BOSNIA & HERZEGOVINA. Western Croatia lies in the Dinaric Alps. The eastern region, drained by the rivers Sava and Drava which both flow into the Danube, is low-lying and agricultural. The chief farming region is the Pannonian Plain. Over one third of the country is forested with beech and oak trees being predominant, and timber is a major export. Deposits of coal, bauxite, copper, petroleum, oil and iron ore are substantial, and most of the republic's industry is based on their processing. In Istria in the north-west and on the Dalmatian coast tourism was a major industry until the Croatia became embroiled in the Serbo-Croat war prior to its secession in 1992. Following the formal recognition of Croatia's independence by the international community, the fighting abruptly ceased; however, the tourism industry continued to suffer from the effects of the on-going hostilities in other parts of the former Yugoslavia. More recently, tourists are returning although there is a need to rebuild the infrastructure.

Quick facts:
Area : 56,538 sq km (21,824 sq miles)
Population : 4,665,810
Capital : Zagreb
Other major cities : Osijek, Rijeka, Split
Form of government : Republic
Religions : RC, Eastern Orthodox
Currency : Kuna

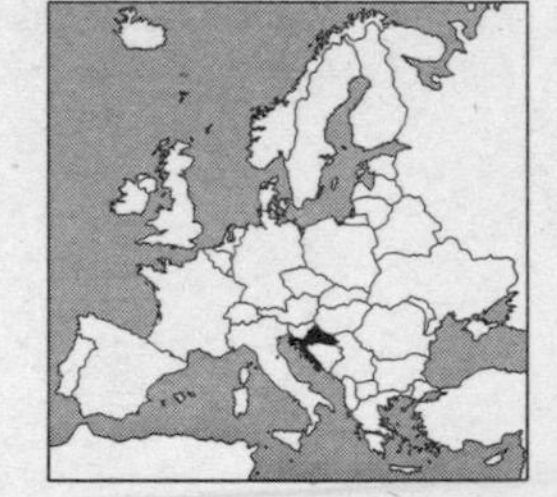

Cuba is the largest and most westerly of the Greater Antilles group of islands in the West Indies. It is strategically positioned at the entrance to the Gulf of Mexico and lies about 140 km (87 miles) south of the tip of Florida. Cuba is as big as all other Caribbean islands put together and is home to a third of the whole West Indian population. The climate is warm and generally rainy and hurricanes are liable to occur between June and November. It possesses unusual natural subsurface limestone caverns and its rivers tend to be short and unnavigable. The island consists mainly of extensive plains and the soil is fertile. The most important agricultural product is sugar and its by-products, and the processing of these is the most important industry. Tobacco is also of commercial significance, with Havana cigars being known internationally. Most of Cuba's trade was with other communist countries, particularly the former USSR, and the country's economy has suffered as a result of a US trade embargo.

Quick facts:

Area : 110,861 sq km (42,803 sq miles)
Population : 10,986,000
Capital : Havana (La Habana)
Other major cities : Camaguey, Holguin, Santa Clara, Santiago de Cuba
Form of government : Socialist Republic
Religion : RC
Currency : Cuban peso

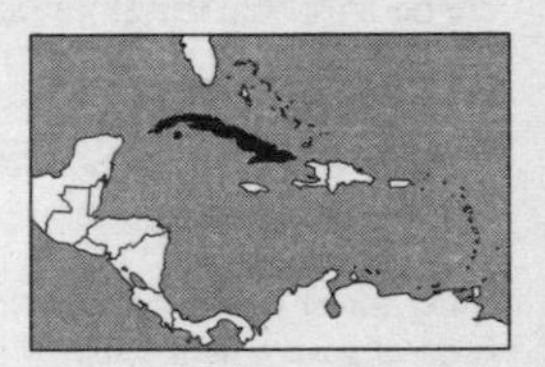

Cyprus is an island which lies in the eastern Mediterranean about 85 km (53 miles) south of TURKEY. It has a long thin panhandle and is divided from west to east by two parallel ranges of mountains which are separated by a wide central plain open to the sea at either end. The highest point is Mount Olympus (1951 m/6401 ft) in the south-west. The climate is Mediterranean with very hot dry summers and warm damp winters. This contributes towards the great variety of crops grown e.g. early potatoes, vegetables, cereals, tobacco, olives, bananas and grapes and this accounts for about 17% of the land. The grapes are used for the strong wines and sherries for which Cyprus is famous. The main mineral found is copper while asbestos, gypsum and iron pyrites are also found. Fishing is a significant industry, but above all the island depends on visitors and it is the tourist industry which has led to a recovery in the economy since 1974. There are no railways on the island although it does possess three international airports.

Quick facts:

Area : 9251 sq km (3572 sq miles)
Population : 732,000
Capital : Nicosia
Other major cities : Famagusta, Limassol, Larnaca
Form of government : Republic
Religions : Greek Orthodox, Sunni Islam
Currency : Cyprus pound

Czech Republic, The, was newly constituted on 1 January, 1993 with the dissolution of the 74 year-old federal republic of Czechoslovakia. It is landlocked at the heart of central Europe, bounded by SLOVAKIA, GERMANY, POLAND and AUSTRIA. Natural boundaries are formed by the Sudeten Mountains in the north, the Erzgebirge, or Ore Mountains, to the north-west, and the Bohemian Forest in the south-west. The climate is humid continental with warm summers and cold winters. Most rain falls in summer and thunderstorms are frequent. Agriculture, although accounting for only a small percentage of the national income, is highly developed and efficient. Major crops are sugar beet, wheat and potatoes. Over a third of the labour force is employed in industry which has to import its raw materials and energy. The most important industries are iron and steel, coal, machinery, cement and paper but industrialization has caused serious environmental problems. Recently investment has gone into electronic factories and research establishments. Tourism has increased post-Communism with the country's many resorts, historic cities and winter sports facilities attracting visitors.

Quick facts:
Area : 78,864 sq km (30,449 sq miles)
Population : 10,430,770
Capital : Prague (Praha)
Other major cities : Brno, Olomouc, Ostrava, Plze
Form of government : Republic
Religions : RC, Protestantism
Currency : Koruna

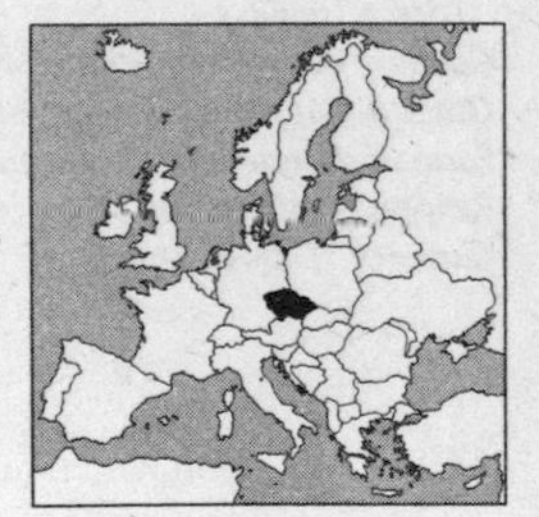

Denmark is a small European state lying between the North Sea and the entrance to the Baltic. It consists of a western peninsula and an eastern archipelago of 406 islands only 89 of which are populated. The country is very low lying and the proximity of the sea combined with the effect of the Gulf Stream result in warm sunny summers and cold cloudy winters. The scenery is very flat and monotonous but the acidic soils need a great deal of fertilization for a wide variety of crops to be grown. It is an agricultural country and three-quarters of the land is cultivated mostly by the rotation of grass, barley, oats and sugar beet. Animal husbandry is, however, the most important activity, its produce including the famous bacon and butter. It is estimated that 85% of the population lives in the towns and cities. Despite Denmark's limited range of raw materials it produces a wide range of manufactured goods and is famous for its imaginative design of ceramics, furniture, silverware and porcelain, there being a permanent exhibition of these in its capital.

Quick facts:
Area : 43,077 sq km (16,632 sq miles)
Population : 5,192,710 (excluding the Faeroe Islands)
Capital : Copenhagen (København)
Other major cities : Ålborg, Århus, Odense
Form of government : Constitutional Monarchy
Religion : Lutheranism
Currency : Danish krone

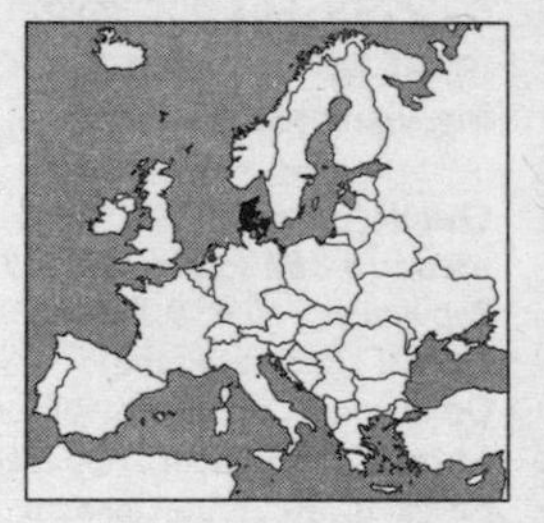

Djibouti is situated in north-east Africa and is bounded almost entirely by ETHIOPIA except in the south-east where it shares a border with SOMALIA and in the north-west where it shares a border with ERITREA. Its coastline is on the Gulf of Aden. The land which is mainly basalt plains has some mountains rising to over 1500 m (4922 ft). The climate is hot, among the world's hottest, and extremely dry. Less than a tenth of the land can be farmed even for grazing so it has great difficulty supporting its modest population. The native population is mostly nomadic, moving from oasis to oasis or across the border to Ethiopia in search of grazing land. Crops raised include fruits, vegetables and dates. Most foodstuffs for the urban population in Djibouti city are imported. The capital is linked to Addis Ababa by a railway. Cattle, hides and skins are the main exports. There are small deposits of copper, iron ore and gypsum but these are not mined.

Quick facts:
Area : 23,200 sq km (8958 sq miles)
Population : 516,000
Capital : Djibouti (population 340,700)
Form of government : Republic
Religion : Sunni Islam
Currency : Djibouti franc

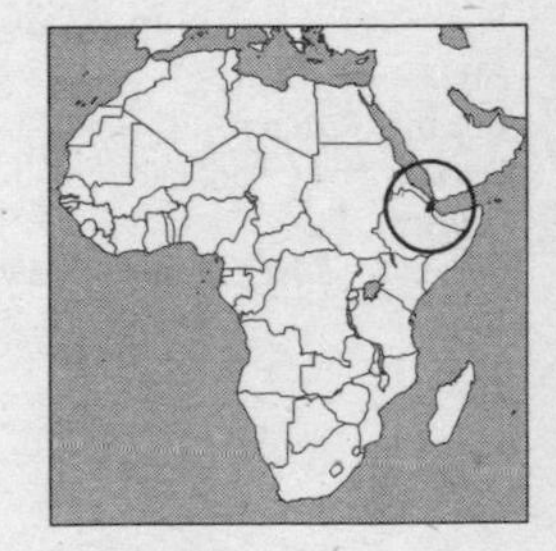

Dominica discovered by Columbus, Dominica is the most northerly of the Windward Islands in the West Indies. It is situated between the islands of Martinique and Guadeloupe. The island is very rugged and with the exception of 225 sq km (87 sq miles) of flat land, it consists of three inactive volcanoes, the highest of which is 1447 m (4747 ft). There are many unnavigable rivers and Boiling Lake is situated in the south which often gives off sulphurous gases. The climate is tropical and even on the leeward coast it rains two days out of three. The wettest season is from June to October when hurricanes often occur. The steep slopes are difficult to farm but agriculture provides almost all Dominica's exports. Bananas are the main agricultural export but copra, citrus fruits, cocoa, coconuts, bay leaves, cinnamon and vanilla are also revenue earners. Industry is mostly based on the processing of the agricultural products.

Quick facts:
Area : 751 sq km (290 sq miles)
Population : 82,430
Capital : Roseau
Form of govt : Republic
Religion : RC
Currency : East Caribbean dollar

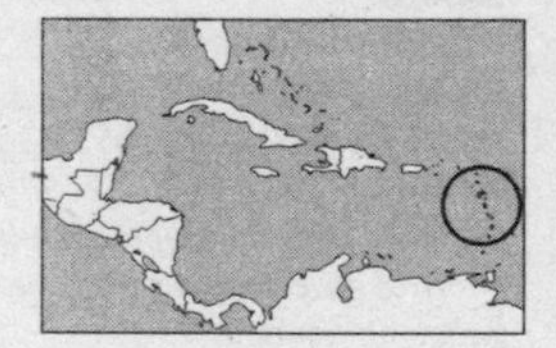

Dominican Republic forms the eastern portion of the island of Hispaniola in the West Indies. It covers two-thirds of the island, the smaller portion consisting of HAITI. The climate is semi-tropical and occasionally hurricanes occur causing great destruction, the last being Hurricane David in 1979. The west of the country is made up of four almost parallel mountain ranges and between the two most northerly is the fertile Cibao valley. The south-east is made up of fertile plains. Although well endowed with fertile land, only about 30% is cultivated. Sugar is the main crop and mainstay of the country's economy and is grown mainly on plantations in the south-east plains. Other crops grown are rice, coffee, bananas, cocoa and tobacco. Mining of gold, silver, platinum, nickel and aluminium is carried out but the main industries are food processing and making consumer goods. Fishing is also carried out but not to any great extent due to lack of equipment and refrigeration facilities. The island has fine beaches and the tourism industry is now very important to the economy.

Quick facts:
Area : 48,734 sq km (18,816 sq miles)
Population : 7,863,000
Capital : Santo Domingo
Other major cities : Barahona, Santiago, San Pedro de Macoris
Form of government : Republic
Religion : RC
Currency : Dominican peso

Ecuador is an Andean country situated in the north-west of the South American continent. It is bounded to the north by COLOMBIA and to the east and south by PERU. It also includes the Galapagos Islands which are located about 965 km (600 miles) west of the mainland. The country contains over 30 active volcanoes. Running down the middle of Ecuador are two ranges of the Andes which are divided by a central plateau. The coastal area consists of plains and the eastern area is made up of tropical jungles. The climate varies from equatorial through warm temperate to mountain conditions according to altitude. It is in the coastal plains that plantations of bananas, cocoa, coffee and sugar cane are found. In contrast to this the highland areas are adapted to grazing, dairying and cereal growing. The fishing industry is important on the Pacific Coast and processed fish such as tuna and shrimp is one of the main exports. Ecuador is one of the world's leading producers of balsa wood. Oil is produced in the eastern region and crude oil is Ecuador's most important export. The official language is Spanish although many people in rural areas speak Quecha, the Incan language.

Quick facts:

Area : 283,561 sq km (109,484 sq miles)
Population : 11,592,300
Capital : Quito
Other major cities : Ambato, Cuenca, Guayaquil, Machala
Form of government : Republic
Religion : RC
Currency : Sucre

Egypt is situated in north-east Africa, acting as the doorway between Africa and Asia. Its outstanding physical feature is the river Nile, the valley and delta of which cover about 35,580 sq km (13,737 sq miles). The climate is mainly dry but there are winter rains along the Mediterranean coast. The temperatures are comfortable in winter but summer temperatures are extremely high particularly in the south. The rich soils deposited by floodwaters along the banks of the Nile can support a large population and the delta is one of the world's most fertile agricultural regions. Around 99% of the population lives in the delta and Nile valley where the main crops are rice, cotton, sugar cane, maize, tomatoes and wheat. This concentration makes it one of the most densely populated areas in the world. The main industries are food processing and textiles. The economy has been boosted by the discovery of oil and is enough to supply the country's needs and leave surplus for export. Natural gas production is increasing for domestic use and Egypt has a significant fishing industry, mainly in the shallow lakes and Red Sea. The Suez Canal, shipping and tourism connected with the ancient sites are also important revenue earners.

Quick facts:
Area : 1,001,449 sq km (386,662 sq miles)
Population : 58,732,000
Capital : Cairo (El Qahira)
Other major cities : Alexandria, Giza, Port Said, Suez
Form of government : Republic
Religions : Sunni Islam, Christianity
Currency : Egyptian pound

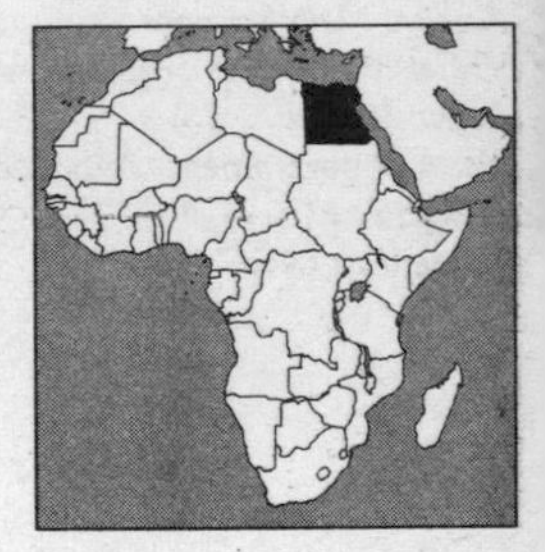

El Salvador is the smallest and most densely populated state in Central America. It is bounded north and east by HONDURAS and has a Pacific coast to the south. Two volcanic ranges run from east to west across the country. The Lempa river cuts the southern ranges in the centre of the country and opens as a large sandy delta to the Pacific Ocean. Although fairly near to the equator, the climate tends to be warm rather than hot and the highlands have a cooler temperate climate. The country is predominantly agricultural and 32% of the land is used for crops such as coffee (the major crop and revenue earner), cotton, maize, beans, rice and sorghum, and a slightly smaller area is used for grazing cattle, pigs, sheep and goats. Fishing is carried out, the most important being shrimp, although tuna, mackerel and swordfish are caught. A few industries such as food processing, textiles and chemicals are found in the major towns. The country suffers from a high rate of inflation and unemployment and is one of the poorest countries in the west.

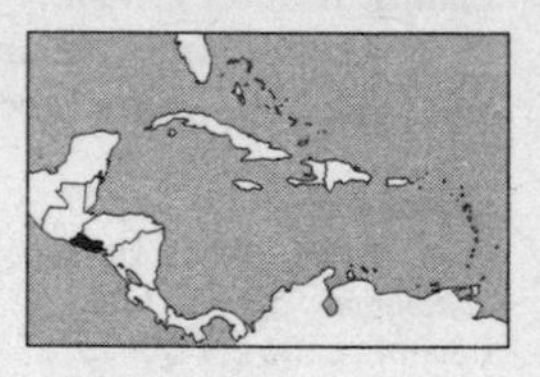

Quick facts:
Area : 21,041 sq km (8124 sq miles)
Population : 5,752,600
Capital : San Salvador
Other major cities : Mejicanos, Santa Ana, San Miguel
Form of government : Republic
Religion : RC
Currency : Colón

Equatorial Guinea lies about 200 km (124 miles) north of the Equator on the hot humid coast of West Africa. The country consists of a square-shaped mainland area (Mbini) with its few small offshore islets, and the islands of Bioko and Pagalu. The climate is tropical and the wet season in Bioko and Pegalu lasts from December to February. Bioko is a very fertile volcanic island and it is here the capital Malabo is sited beside a volcanic crater flooded by the sea. It is also the centre of the country's cocoa production. The country now relies heavily on foreign aid. Coffee is grown for export on the mainland which also produces timber – the highest value export. Spanish is the official language although a variant of Bantu, Fang, is most commonly used. There is, however, much potential for a tourist industry.

Quick facts:
Area : 28,051 sq km (10,830 sq miles)
Population : 432,840
Capital : Malabo
Other major city : Bata
Form of government : Republic
Religion : RC
Currency : CFA Franc

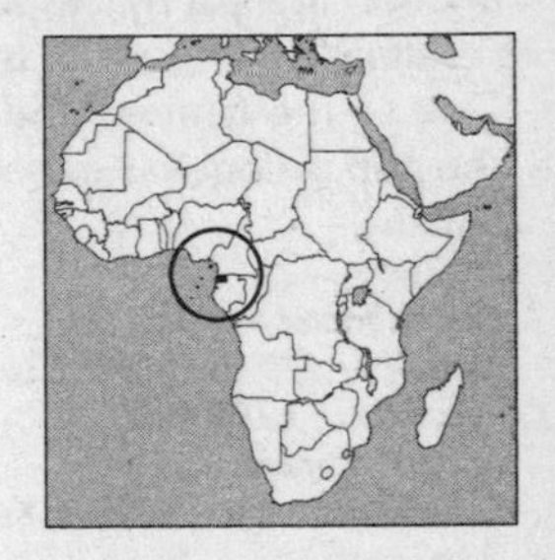

Eritrea, formerly an autonomous province of ETHIOPIA, gained independence in May 1993 shortly after a landslide vote in favour of sovereignty. Bounded by DJIBOUTI, SUDAN and ETHIOPIA, Eritrea has acquired Ethiopia's entire coastline along the Red Sea. The small Eritrean port of Aseb, in the southeast corner of the country has, however, been designated a 'free port' guaranteeing the right of access for the now landlocked Ethiopia. Eritrea's climate is hot and dry along its desert coast but is colder and wetter in its central highland regions. Most of the population depend on subsistence farming. Future revenues may come from developing fishing, tourism and oil industries. Eritrea's natural resources include gold, potash, zinc, copper, salt, fish and probably oil. Deforestation and the consequent erosion are partly responsible for the frequent droughts and resultant famines that have blighted this area in recent years. Due to the famines and war with Ethiopia, a great number of the population was either displaced or were living as refugees in Sudan.

Quick facts:
Area : 121,140 sq km (46,850 sq miles)
Population : 3,703,400
Capital : Asmara
Other major cities : Mitsiwa, Keren, Nak'fa, Ak'ordat
Form of government : Republic
Religion : Sunni Islam, Christianity
Currency : Ethiopian birr

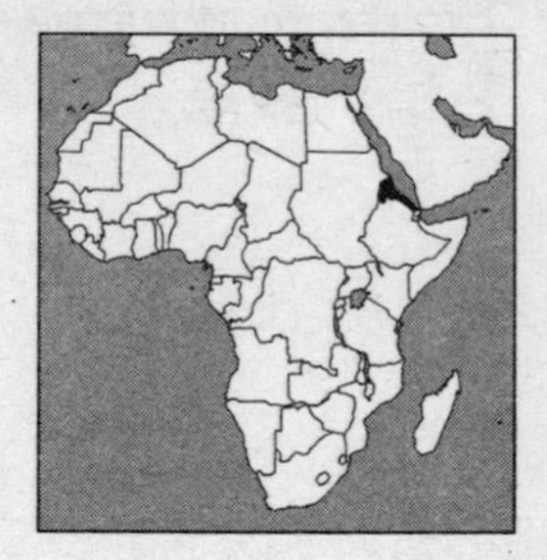

Estonia, which has over 1500 islands, lies to the north-west of the RUSSIAN FEDERATION and is bounded to the north by the Gulf of Finland, to the west by the Baltic Sea and to the south by LATVIA. It is the smallest of the three previous Soviet Baltic Republics. Agriculture and dairy farming are the chief occupations and there are nearly three hundred agricultural collectives and state farms. The main products are grain, potatoes, flax, vegetables, meat, milk and eggs. Livestock includes cattle, sheep, goats and pigs. Almost 22% of Estonia is forested, mainly with aspen, pine, birch and fir and this provides material for sawmills, furniture, match and pulp industries. The country has rich, high quality shale deposits and phosphorous has been found near Tallinn. Peat deposits are substantial and supply some of the electric power stations. Estonia has about 72% of its population living in urban areas with almost a third living in the capital city. The economy is currently undergoing a major transformation to a free market system. Tourism and investment from the West have greatly contributed to the country's economy.

Quick facts:
Area : 45,100 sq km (17,413 sq miles)
Population : 1,571,600
Capital : Tallinn
Other major cities : Tartu, Narva, Pärnu
Form of government : Republic
Religion : Eastern Orthodox, Lutheranism
Currency : Kroon

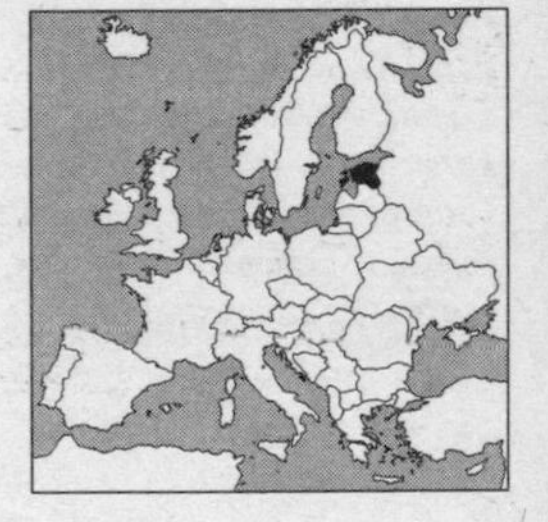

Ethiopia is a landlocked, east African country with borders on SUDAN, KENYA, SOMALIA, DJIBOUTI and ERITREA. Most of the country consists of highlands which drop sharply toward Sudan in the west. Because of the wide range of latitudes, Ethiopia has many climatic variations between the high temperate plateau and the hot humid lowlands. The country is very vulnerable to drought but in some areas thunderstorms can erode soil from the slopes reducing the area available for crop planting. Around 80% of the population is subsistence farmers and there are mineral deposits of copper, iron, petroleum, platinum and gold which have been exploited. Coffee is the main source of rural income and teff is the main food grain. The droughts in 1989–90 have brought much famine. Employment outside agriculture is confined to a small manufacturing sector in Addis Ababa. The country is wrecked with environmental, economic and political problems that culminated in May 1993 when one of Ethiopia's provinces, Eritrea, became independent.

Quick facts:
Area : 1,221,900 sq km (471,778 sq miles)
Population : 56,370,400
Capital : Addis Ababa (Adis Abeba)
Other major cities : Dire Dawa, Nazret
Form of government : In transition
Religion : Ethiopian Orthodox, Sunni Islam
Currency : Ethiopian birr

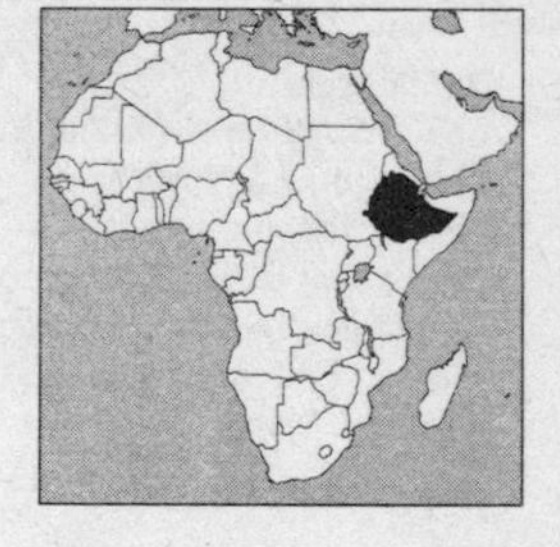

Faeroe (Faroe) Islands (Føroyar) have been a self-governing part of the Danish realm since 1948. They consist of a group of 18 basaltic islands and are situated in the North Atlantic, approximately halfway between the Shetland Islands and Iceland. The landscape of these islands is characterised by steep, stepped peaks rising out of the sea to nearly 900 m (3000 ft) and glaciated, trough-shaped valleys. Although the islands are inhabited, poor agricultural conditions compel the population to seek their living at sea. Fishing, including some whaling, is the main occupation and exports comprise fish and associated products.

Quick facts:
Area : 1,399 sq km (540 sq miles)
Population : 46,390
Capital : Tørshavn
Other major cities : Dire Dawa, Nazret
Form of government : self-governing part of Danish realm
Religion : Lutheranism
Currency : Danish krone

Falkland Islands (Islas Malvinas), situated in the South Atlantic, they are a British Crow Colony consisting of two large islands (West and East Falkland), separated by the 16 km (10 miles) wide Falkland Sound, and surrounded by some 200 smaller islands. Lying about 650 km (410 miles) east of southern Argentina, these islands were invaded by Argentina in 1982. Argentina had long laid claim to these 'Islas Malvinas' only to be recaptured by a British marine task force a few months later. The main economic activity is sheep farming, with open grazing on the wind-swept, treeless, rugged moorland that rises to over 700 m (2295 ft) on both main islands. The highest point is Mount Usborne at 705 m. Over recent years, substantial income has been gained from the sales of licences to permit foreign trawlers to fish in the Falklands exclusion zone. There are also considerable offshore oil reserves available.

Quick facts:
Area : 12,173 sq km (4700 sq miles)
Population : 2370
Capital : Stanley
Form of government : colony under British administration
Religion : Christianity
Currency: Falkland Islands pound

Fiji is one of the largest nations in the western Pacific and consists of some 320 islands and atolls, but only 150 are inhabited. It is situated around the 180° International Date Line and lies about 17° south of the Equator. Fiji has high rainfall, high temperatures and plenty of sunshine all year round. The two main islands, Viti Levu and Vanua Levu, are extinct volcanoes and most of the islands in the group are fringed with coral reefs. The south-east of the islands have tropical rain forests but a lot of timber has been felled and soil erosion is a growing problem. The main cash crop is sugar cane although copra, ginger and fish are also exported. Tourism is now a major industry and source of revenue although it was adversely affected by political coups in the late 80s. However, in 1993, great destruction was caused by Cyclone Kina to agriculture and the general infrastructure.

Quick facts:
Area : 18,274 sq km (7056 sq miles)
Population : 769,800
Capital : Suva
Other major cities: Lautoka, Nadi
Form of government : Republic
Religion : Christianity, Hinduism
Currency : Fijian dollar

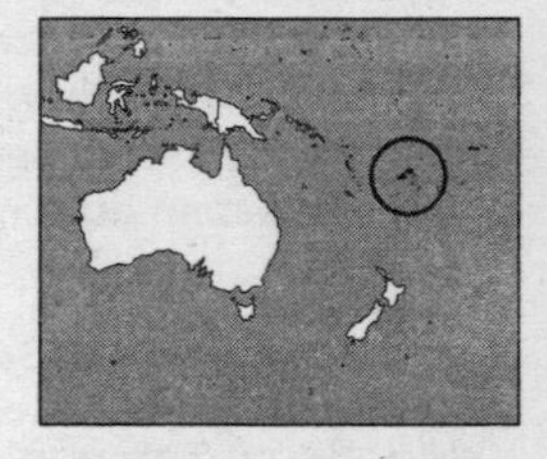

Finland lies at the eastern limit of western Europe with the RUSSIAN FEDERATION to the east and the Gulf of Bothnia to the west. Most of the country is low lying except for the north which rises to over 1000 m (3281 ft) in Lapland. Almost three-quarters of the country is forested comprising mainly coniferous trees such as spruce and pine and many thousands of lakes. The climate has great extremes between summer and winter. Winter is very severe and lasts about six months but only for three months in the south. Summers are short but quite warm with light rain throughout the country. Finland is largely self-sufficient in food and produces great surpluses of dairy produce. Most crops are grown in the south-west. In the north reindeer are herded and forests yield great quantities of timber for export. Just under 20% of the country's electricity was supplied by its hydroelectric power stations in the early 1990s. Major industries are timber products, wood pulp and paper, machinery and shipbuilding, which has developed due to the country's great need for an efficient fleet of ice breakers. Finland has an efficient transport system utilizing canals, road, rail and air services.

Quick facts:
Area : 338,000 sq km (130,500 sq miles)
Population : 5,120,000
Capital : Helsinki (Helsingfors)
Other major cities : Turku, Tampere
Form of government : Republic
Religion : Lutheranism
Currency : Markka

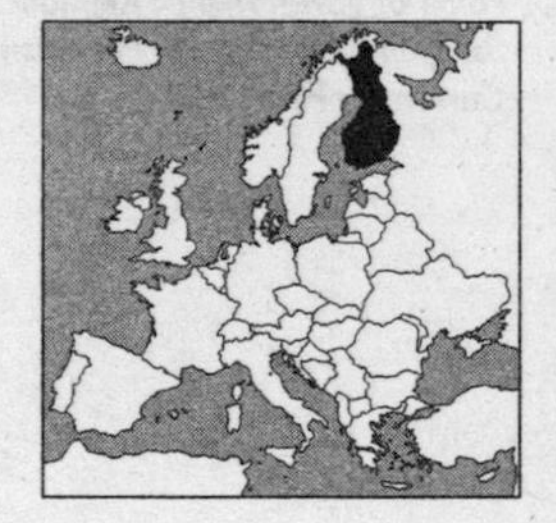

France is the largest country in western Europe and has a coastline on the English Channel, the Mediterranean Sea and on the Atlantic Ocean. The lowest parts of the country are the great basins of the north and south-west from which it rises to the Massif Central and the higher Alps, Jura and Pyrénées. Climate ranges from moderate maritime in the north-west to Mediterranean in the south. Farming is possible in all parts of France with forestry and fishing also providing some employment. The western shores are ideal for rearing livestock, while the Paris Basin is good arable land. It is in the south-west around Bordeaux that the vineyards produce some of the world's best wines and in the 1990s France's production was the world's highest. The main industrial area of France is in the north and east, and the main industries are iron and steel, engineering, chemicals, textiles and electrical goods. France has a long cultural history of art, literature, sculpture, music and is famous for its immense Gothic churches.

Quick facts:
Area : 547,026 sq km (211,208 sq miles)
Population : 58,207,300
Capital : Paris
Other major cities : Bordeaux, Lyon, Marseille, Nantes, Nice, Toulouse, Strasbourg
Form of government : Republic
Religion : RC
Currency : Franc

Gabon is a small country in west-central Africa which straddles the Equator. It has a low narrow coastal plain and the rest of the country comprises a low plateau. Three quarters of Gabon is covered with dense tropical forest. The climate is hot, humid and typically equatorial with little seasonal variation. It was in Lambaréné that Albert Schweitzer, the medical missionary, had his hospital. Until the 1960s timber was virtually Gabon's only resource and then oil was discovered. By the mid-1980s it was Africa's sixth largest oil producer and other minerals such as manganese, uranium and iron ore were being exploited. Deposits of lead and silver have also been discovered. Much of the earnings from these resources was squandered and around two-thirds of the Gabonese people remain subsistence farmers growing cassava, sugar cane, plantains and yams. It is believed that the original inhabitants of the country were Pygmies but only a small number of them remain. The country has great tourist potential but because of the dense hardwood forests transport links with the uninhabited interior are very difficult.

Quick facts:
Area : 267,667 sq km (103,346 sq miles)
Population : 1,348,700
Capital : Libreville
Other major city : Port Gentile
Form of government : Republic
Religion : RC, Animism
Currency : CFA Franc

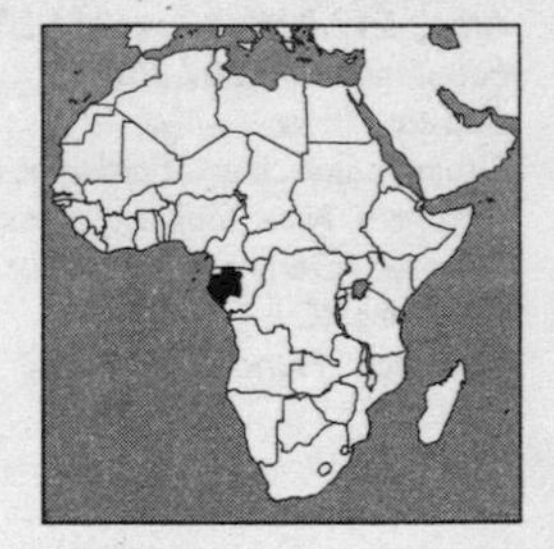

Gambia, the smallest country in Africa, pokes like a crooked finger into SENEGAL. The country is divided along its entire length by the river Gambia which can only be crossed at two main ferry crossings. Gambia has two very different seasons. In the dry season there is little rainfall, then the south-west monsoon sets in with spectacular storms producing heavy rain for four months. Most Gambians live in villages with a few animals, and grow enough millet and sorghum to feed themselves. Groundnuts are the main and only export crop of any significance. The river provides a thriving local fishing industry and the white sandy beaches on the coast are becoming increasingly popular with foreign tourists, although a military takeover in 1994 dealt tourism and trade a severe blow.

Quick facts:
Area : 11,295 sq km (4361 sq miles)
Population : 1,205,000
Capital : Banjul
Form of government : Republic
Religion : Sunni Islam, some Christian
Currency : Dalasi

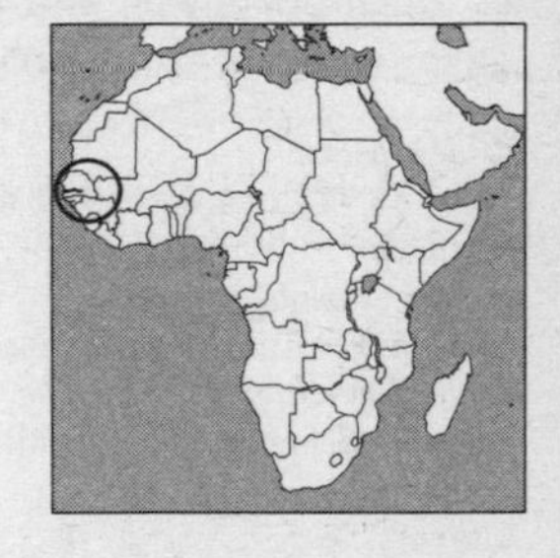

Georgia is a republic in the south-west of the former USSR occupying the central and western parts of the Caucasus. It shares borders with TURKEY, ARMENIA, AZERBAIJAN and the RUSSIAN FEDERATION. It is bounded to the west by the Black Sea. Almost 40% of the country is covered with forests. Agriculture, which is the main occupation of the population, includes tea cultivation and fruit growing, especially citrus fruits and viticulture. The republic is rich in minerals, especially manganese but imports the majority of its energy needs. Industries include coal, timber, machinery, chemicals, silk, food processing and furniture. The Black Sea tourist trade was in the past and should again become an economic mainstay. Georgia declared itself independent in 1991. A struggle for regional autonomy by ethnic minorities led to much disruption and violent conflict. Elections were held in 1995 heralding some progress and reform.

Quick facts:
Area : 69,773 sq km (26,911 sq miles)
Population : 5,219,800
Capital : T'bilisi
Other major cities : Kutaisi, Rustavi, Batumi
Form of government : Republic
Religion : Georgian and Russian Orthodox, Muslim
Currency : Lari

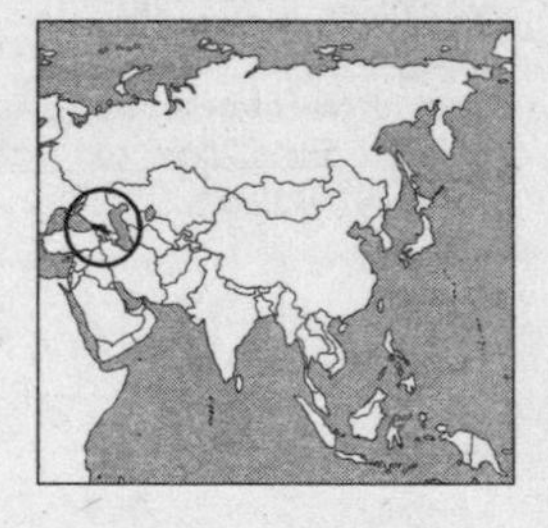

Germany is a large populous country in northern central Europe which comprises the former East and West German republics, reunified in 1990. In the north is the North German Plain which merges with the North Rhinelands in the west. Further south, a plateau which stretches across the country from east to west, is divided by the river Rhine. In the south-west the Black Forest separates the Rhine Valley from the fertile valleys and scarplands of Swabia. More recently coniferous forests have suffered from acid rain, due to industrial pollution. The Bohemian Uplands and Erz Mountains mark the border with the CZECH REPUBLIC. Generally the country has warm summers and cold winters. Agricultural products include wheat, rye, barley, oats, potatoes and sugar beet, although agriculture accounts for only a small percentage of employment and a third of the country's food has to be imported. The main industrial and most densely populated areas are in the Ruhr Valley. Principal manufacturing industries are chemical products, vehicles, electrical and non-electrical machinery, food products, metals and metal products. Chemical and textile industries are found in the cities along the Rhine and motor vehicle industry in the large provincial cities. The country depends heavily on imports.

Quick facts:
Area : 365,755 sq km (137,738 sq miles)
Population : 81,200,600
Capital : Berlin, Bonn (Seat of government)
Other major cities : Cologne, Dortmund, Düsseldorf, Essen, Frankfurt, Hamburg, Leipzig, Munich, Stuttgart
Form of government : Republic
Religions : Lutheranism, RC
Currency : Deutsche Mark

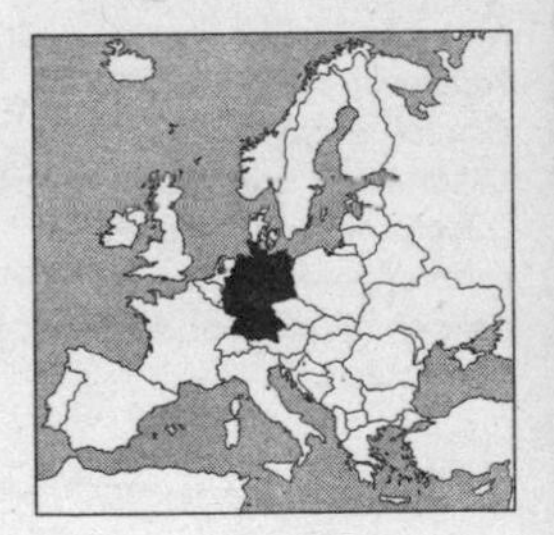

Ghana is located on the southern coast of West Africa between CÔTE D'IVOIRE and TOGO. In 1957, as the former British Gold Coast, it became the first black African state to achieve independence from European colonial rule. It has palm-fringed beaches of white sand along the Gulf of Guinea and where the great river Volta meets the sea there are peaceful blue lagoons. The climate on the coast is equatorial and towards the north there are steamy tropical evergreen forests which give way in the far north to tropical savanna. The landscape becomes harsh and barren near the border with BURKINA FASO. Most Ghanaians are village dwellers whose homes are made of locally available materials. The south of the country has been most exposed to European influence and it is here that cocoa, rubber, palm oil and coffee are grown. Ghana's most important crop is cocoa and others include coffee, palm kernels, coconut oil, copra, shea nuts and bananas which are all exported. Fishing is also of major importance and has increased in recent years. Ghana has important mineral resources such as manganese and bauxite. Most of Ghana's towns are in the south but rapid growth has turned many of them into unplanned sprawls.

Quick facts:
Area : 238,537 sq km (92,100 sq miles)
Population : 17,459,350
Capital : Accra
Other major cities : Cape Coast, Kumasi, Tamale, Tema, Sekondi-Takoradi
Form of government : Republic
Religion : Protestant, Animism, RC
Currency : Cedi

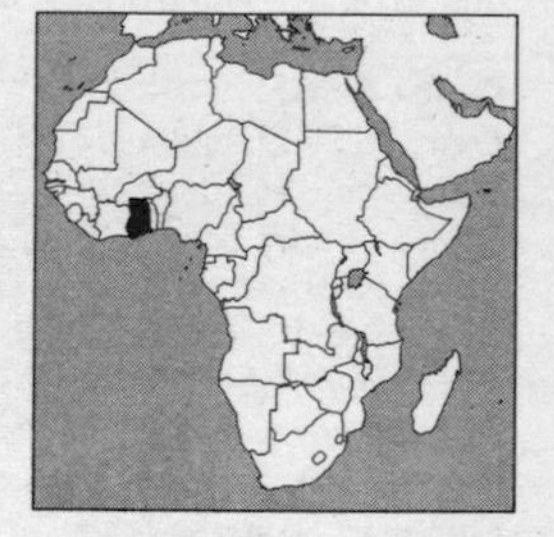

Greece the Greek peninsula is the most south-easterly extension of Europe. The Pindus Mountains divide Greece from the Albanian border in the north to the Gulf of Corinth in the south. About 70% of the land is hilly with harsh mountain climates and poor soils and there are few natural resources of economic value although there are deposits of petroleum and natural gas found under the Aegean Sea. The Greek islands and coastal regions have a typical Mediterranean climate with mild rainy winters and hot dry summers. Winter in the northern mountains is severe with deep snow and heavy precipitation. Agriculture is the chief activity and large scale farming is concentrated on the east coasts. The main industries are small processing plants for tobacco, food and leather. Fishing is an important activity around the 2000 islands which lie off the mainland. Tourists visit the country in the summer for the sun and in winter for its spectacular ancient ruins and provide a major source of revenue for the country along with shipping.

Quick facts:
Area : 131,958 sq km (50,948 sq miles)
Population : 10,540,800
Capital : Athens (Athinai)
Other major cities : Iraklian, Lárisa, Patras, Piraeus, Thessaloníki
Form of government : Republic
Religion : Greek Orthodox
Currency : Drachma

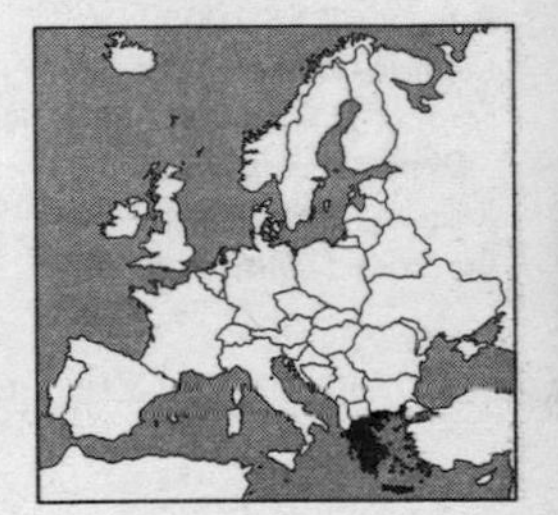

Greenland (Kalaallit Nunaat) is the largest island in the world (discounting continental land masses). It lies mainly within the Arctic Circle, off the northeast coast of CANADA. Its vast interior is mostly covered with a permanent ice cap that has a known thickness of up to 3300 m (11,000 ft). The ice-free coastal strips are characterised by largely barren mountains, rising to Gunnbjorn at 3700 m (12,140 ft) in the south-east, glaciers flowing into deeply indented fjords, fringed by many islands, islets and icebergs. Of the small ice-free fringe, only about a third (150,000 sq km/58,000 sq miles) can be classed as being inhabited — mainly in the south-west. The largely Eskimo (Inuit) population is heavily dependent on fishing for its livelihood and fish account for 95% of exports. There is some sheep farming and mining of coal and mineral resources include iron ore, lead, zinc, uranium and molybdenum.

Quick facts:
Area: 2,175,600 sq km (840,000 sq miles)
Population: 58,200
Capital: Gothåb (Nuuk)
Form of government: Self-governing part of the Danish realm
Religion: Lutheranism
Currency: Danish krone

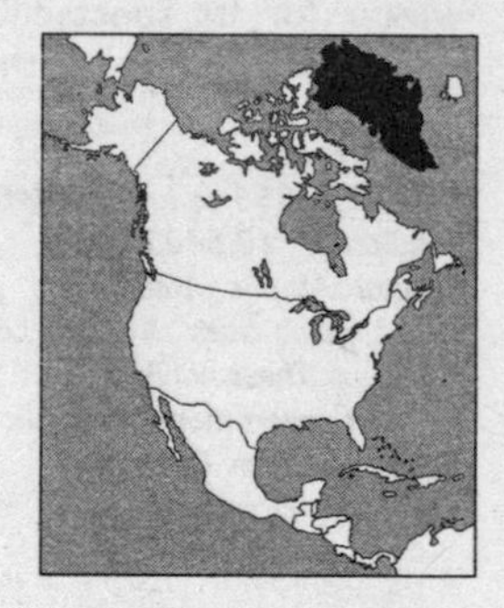

Grenada is the most southerly of the Windward Island chain in the Caribbean and its highest peak at 838 m (2,750 ft) is Mount St Catherine. Its territory includes the southern Grenadine Islands to the north. The main island consists of the remains of extinct volcanoes and has an attractive wooded landscape. In the dry season its typical climate is very pleasant with warm days and cool nights but in the wet season it is hot day and night. Agriculture is the island's main industry and the chief crops grown for export are citrus fruits, cocoa, nutmegs, bananas and mace. Other crops grown are cloves, cotton, coconuts and cinnamon. Apart from the processing of its crops Grenada has little manufacturing industry although tourism is an important source of foreign revenue. It is a popular port of call for cruise ships.

Quick facts:
Area : 344 sq km (133 sq miles)
Population : 94,373
Capital : St Georges
Form of government : Constitutional Monarchy
Religion : RC, Anglicanism, Methodism
Currency : East Caribbean dollar

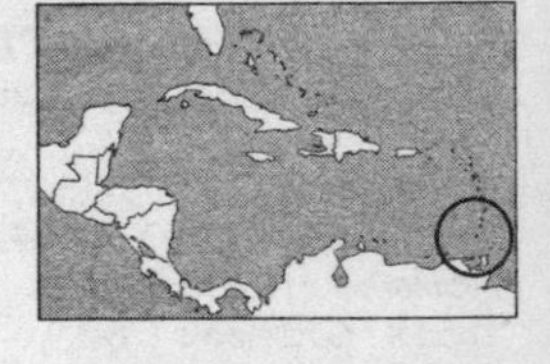

Guatemala is situated between the Pacific Ocean and the Caribbean Sea where North America meets Central America. It is a mountainous country with a ridge of volcanoes running parallel to the Pacific coast. It has a tropical climate with little or no variation in temperature and a distinctive wet season. The Pacific slopes of the mountains are exceptionally well watered and fertile and it is here that most of the population is settled. Coffee growing on the lower slopes dominates the economy although bananas, sugar, cardamom, petroleum and shellfish are exported. The forested area of the country, about 36%, plays an important part in the country's economy and produces balsam, cabinet woods, chicle and oils. There are also deposits of petroleum and zinc, while lead and silver are mined. Industry is mainly restricted to the processing of the agricultural products. Guatemala is politically a very unstable country and civil conflict has practically destroyed tourism.

Quick facts:

Area : 108,889 sq km (42,042 sq miles)
Population : 10,813,000
Capital : Guatemala City
Other major cities : Antigua, Mazatenango, Puerto Barrios, Quezaltenango
Form of government : Republic
Religion : RC
Currency : Quetzal

Guiana (French) *or* **Guyane** is situated on the north-east coast of South America and is still an overseas department of FRANCE. It is bounded to the south and east by BRAZIL and to the west by SURINAME. The climate is tropical with heavy rainfall. Guiana's economy relies almost completely on subsidies from France. It has little to export apart from shrimps and the small area of land which is cultivated produces rice, manioc and sugar cane. Recently the French have tried to develop the tourist industry and exploit the extensive reserves of hardwood in the jungle interior. This has led to a growing sawmill industry and the export of logs. Natural resources, in addition to timber, include bauxite, cinnabar (mercury ore) and gold (although this is in scattered deposits). The Ariane rocket launch site of the European Space Agency is located at Kourou.

Quick facts:
Area : 91,000 sq km (35,135 sq miles)
Population : 151,200
Capital : Cayenne
Form of government : French overseas department
Religion : RC
Currency : Franc

Guinea, formerly a French West African territory, is located on the coast at the 'bulge' in Africa. It is a lush green beautiful country about the same size as the UNITED KINGDOM. It has a tropical climate with constant heat and a high rainfall near the coast. Its principal rivers are the Gambia and the Bafing while the Niger rises in the forests of the Guinea highlands. Guinea has great agricultural potential and many of the coastal swamps and forested plains have been cleared for the cultivation of rice, cassava, yams, maize and vegetables. Around 80% of the population are subsistence farmers. Although the country has eight national languages, the official language is French. Further inland on the plateau of Futa Jalon dwarf cattle are raised and in the valleys bananas and pineapples are grown. Coffee and kola nuts are important cash crops grown in the Guinea highlands to the southwest. Minerals such as bauxite, of which there are substantial reserves, iron ore, diamonds, gold and uranium are mined but development is hampered by lack of transport.

Quick facts:
Area : 245,857 sq km (94,925 sq miles)
Population : 6,913,400
Capital : Conakry
Other major cities : Kankan, Kindia, Labé
Form of government : Republic
Religion : Sunni Islam
Currency : Guinea franc

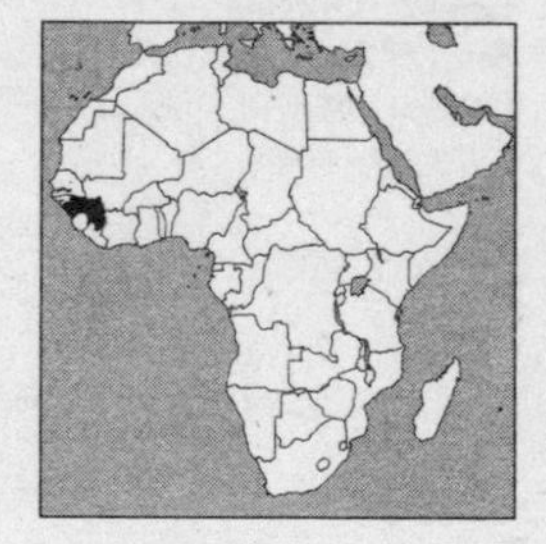

Guinea-Bissau formerly a Portuguese territory but granted independence in 1974, Guinea-Bissau is located south of SENEGAL on the Atlantic coast of West Africa. It is a country of stunning scenery and rises from a deeply indented and island-fringed coastline to a low inland plateau. The adjacent Bijagos archipelago forms part of its territory. The climate is tropical with abundant rain from June to November but hot dry conditions for the rest of the year. Years of Portuguese rule and civil war have left Guinea-Bissau impoverished, and it is one of the poorest West African states. The country's main aim is to become self-sufficient in food, and the main crops grown by the subsistence farmers are rice, groundnuts, cassava, sugar cane, plantains, maize, and coconuts. Fishing is an important export industry although cashew nuts are the principal export. Peanuts, palm products and cotton are also a source of export revenue.

Quick facts:
Area : 36,125 sq km (13,948 sq miles)
Population : 1,066,400
Capital : Bissau
Form of government : Republic
Religion : Animism, Sunni Islam
Currency : Peso

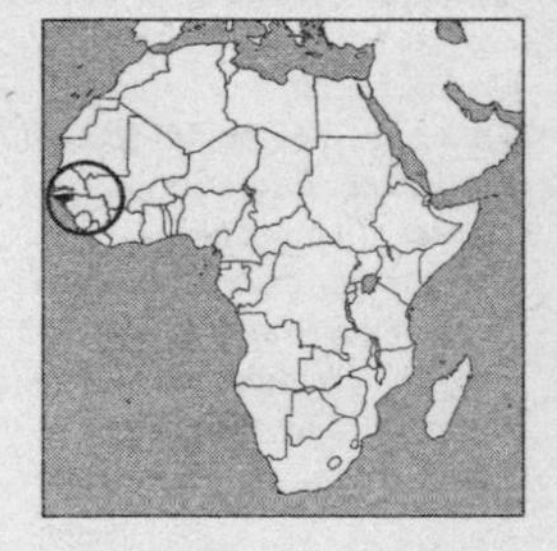

Guyana, the only English-speaking country in South America, is situated on the north-east coast of the continent on the Atlantic Ocean. The country is intersected by many rivers and the coastal area comprises tidal marshes and mangrove swamps. It is on this narrow coastal area that rice is grown and vast plantations produce sugar. The jungle in the south-west has potential for the production of minerals, hardwood and hydroelectric power, but 90% of the population live in the coastal area where the climate is moderated by sea breezes. The country became independent in 1966. Sugar and its by-products and rice are the mainstay of the country's economy, while tropical fruits and vegetables such as coconuts, citrus, coffee and corn are grown mainly for home consumption. Large numbers of livestock including cattle, sheep, pigs and chickens are also raised. Guyana's principal mineral is bauxite with gold, manganese and diamonds being produced.

Quick facts:
Area : 214,969 sq km (83,000 sq miles)
Population : 836,400
Capital : Georgetown
Other major cities : Linden, New Amsterdam
Form of government : Cooperative Republic
Religion : Hinduism, Protestantism, RC
Currency : Guyana dollar

Haiti occupies the western third of the large island of Hispaniola in the Caribbean. It is a mountainous country consisting of five different ranges, the highest point reaching 2680 m (8793 ft) at Pic La Selle. The mountain ranges are separated by deep valleys and plains. The climate is tropical but semi-arid conditions can occur in the lee of the central mountains. Hurricanes and severe thunderstorms are a common occurrence. Only a third of the country is arable, yet agriculture is the chief occupation with around 80% of the population concentrated in rural areas. Many farmers grow only enough to feed their own families, and the export crops – coffee, sugar and sisal – are grown on large estates. Severe soil erosion caused by extensive forest clearance has resulted in a decline in crop yields and environmental damage has been caused. The country has only limited amounts of natural resources, bauxite not now being commercially profitable, although deposits of salt, copper and gold exist. Haiti is the poorest country in the Americas and has experienced many uprisings and attempted coups.

Quick facts:
Area : 27,750 sq km (10,714 sq miles)
Population : 7,180,000
Capital : Port-au-Prince
Other major cities : Cap-Haïtien, Gonaïves, Jérémie, Les Cayes
Form of government : Republic
Religion : RC, Voodooism
Currency : Gourde

Honduras is a fan-shaped country in Central America which spreads out toward the Caribbean Sea at the Gulf of Honduras. Four-fifths of the country is covered in mountains which are indented with river valleys running toward the very short PACIFIC coast. There is little change in temperatures throughout the year and rainfall is heavy, especially on the Caribbean coast where temperatures are also higher than inland. The highlands are covered with forests, mainly of oak and pine, while palms and mangroves grow in the coastal areas. The country is sparsely populated and although agricultural, only about 25% of the land is cultivated. Honduras was once the world's leading banana exporter and although that fruit is still its main export, agriculture is now more diverse. Grains, coffee and sugar are important crops, and these are grown mainly on the coastal plains of the Pacific and Caribbean. Forestry is one of the principal industries producing mahogany, pine, walnut, ebony and rosewood. Industry has increased in recent years, producing cotton, cement and sugar products for export.

Quick facts:
Area : 112,088 sq km (43,277 sq miles)
Population : 5,967,450
Capital : Tegucigalpa
Other major cities : La Ceiba, Puerto Cortés, San Pedro Sula
Form of government : Republic
Religion : RC
Currency : Lempira

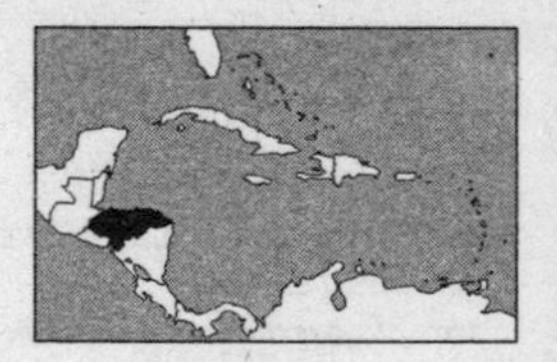

Hong Kong is a Special Autonomous Province of China. It is located in the South China Sea and consists of Hong Kong Island (once a barren rock), the peninsula of Kowloon and about 1000 sq km (386 sq miles) of adjacent land known as the New Territories. Hong Kong is situated at the mouth of the Pearl River about 130 km (81 miles) south-east of Guangzhou (Canton). The climate is warm subtropical with cool dry winters and hot humid summers. Hong Kong has no natural resources, even its water comes from reservoirs across the Chinese border. Its main assets are its magnificent natural harbour and its position close to the main trading routes of the Pacific. Hong Kong's economy is based on free enterprise and trade, an industrious work force and an efficient and aggressive commercial system. Hong Kong's main industries are textiles, clothing, tourism and electronics.

Quick facts:
Area : 1074 sq km (416 sq miles)
Population : 6,305,400
Form of government : under Chinese control from 1st July, 1997
Religion : Buddhism, Taoism, Christianity
Currency : Hong Kong dollar

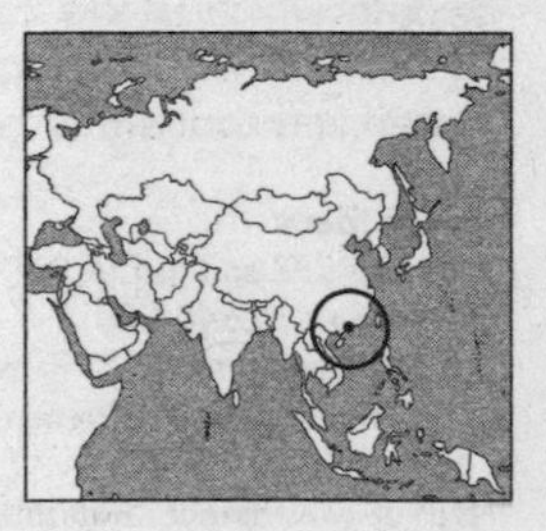

Hungary landlocked in the heartland of Europe, Hungary is dominated by the great plain to the east of the river Danube which runs north-south across the country and its tributaries include the Tisza, the longest river. In the west lies the largest lake in Central Europe, Lake Balaton. Winters are severe, but the summers are warm and although wet in the west, summer droughts often occur in the east. Hungary experienced a modest boom in its economy in the 1970s and 1980s. The government invested money in improving agriculture by mechanizing farms, using fertilizers and bringing new land under cultivation. Yields of cereals for bread making and rice have since soared and large areas between the Danube and Tisza rivers are now used to grow vegetables. However, the use of these artificial fertilizers has caused water pollution. Industries have been carefully developed where adequate natural resources exist such as bauxite which is the country's main resource. New industries like electrical and electronic equipment are now being promoted and tourism is fast developing around Lake Balaton.

Quick facts:
Area : 93,032 sq km (35,920 sq miles)
Population : 10,546,000
Capital : Budapest
Other major cities : Debrecen, Miskolc, Pécs, Szeged
Form of government : Republic
Religion : RC, Calvinism, Lutheranism
Currency : Forint

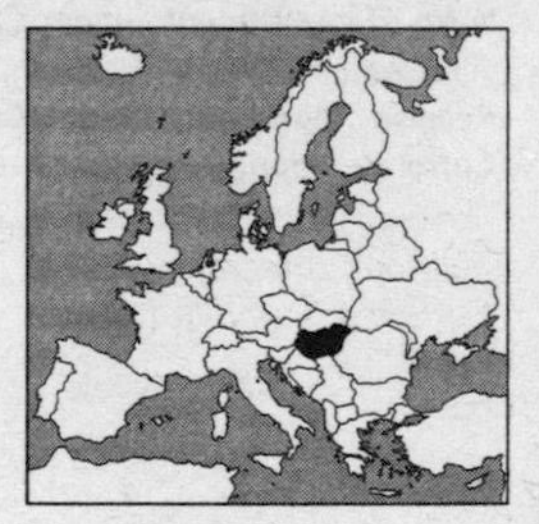

Iceland is a large island situated in a tectonically unstable part of the North Atlantic Ocean, just south of the Arctic Circle. The island has over 100 volcanoes, at least one of which erupts every five years. One ninth of the country is covered with ice and snowfields and there are about 700 hot springs which are an important source of central heating, particularly in the volcanic areas. In the capital city, the majority of homes and industries are heated by this method. The climate is cool temperate but because of the effect of the North Atlantic Drift it is mild for its latitude. The south-west corner is the most densely populated area as the coast here is generally free from ice. Less than 1% of the land is cultivated mostly for fodder and root crops to feed sheep and cattle, with about 5% of the workforce thus engaged. The island's economy is based on its sea fishing industry which accounts for 70% of exports. Wool sweaters and sheepskin coats are also exported. The use of hydroelectric power is being developed for industrial use.

Quick facts:
Area : 103,000 sq km (39,768 sq miles)
Population : 263,800
Capital : Reykjavík
Other major cities : Akureyri, Kópavogur
Form of government : Republic
Religion : Lutheranism
Currency : Icelandic króna

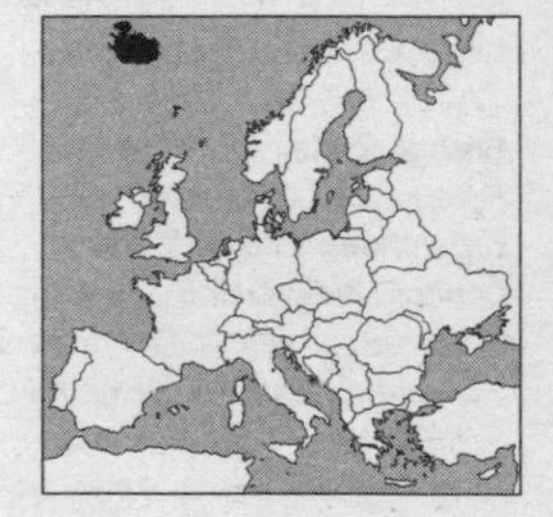

India is a vast country in South Asia which is dominated in the extreme north by the world's youngest and highest mountains, the Himalayas which extend about 2400 km (about 1500 miles) along India's northern and eastern borders. The range contains Mount Everest and K2. At the foot of the Himalayas, a huge plain, drained by the Indus and Ganges rivers, is one of the most fertile areas in the world and the most densely populated part of India. Further south the ancient Deccan plateau extends to the southern tip of the country. India generally has four seasons, the cool, the hot, the rainy and the dry. Rainfall varies from 100 mm (3.94 inches) in the north-west desert to 10,000 mm (394 inches) in Assam. About 70% of the population depend on agriculture for their living and the lower slopes of the Himalayas represent one of the world's best tea growing areas. Rice, sugar cane and wheat are grown in the Ganges plain and there is a comprehensive system of irrigation to aid agriculture. India is self-sufficient in all of its major food crops and main exports include precious stones and jewellery, engineering products, clothes and chemicals.

Quick facts:
Area : 3,287,590 sq km (1,269,346 sq miles)
Population : 928,658,000
Capital : New Delhi
Other major cities : Ahmadabad, Bangalore, Bombay, Calcutta, Delhi, Hyderabad, Kampur, Madras
Form of government : Federal Republic, Secular Democracy
Religion : Hinduism, Islam, Sikkism, Christianity, Jainism, Buddhism
Currency : Rupee

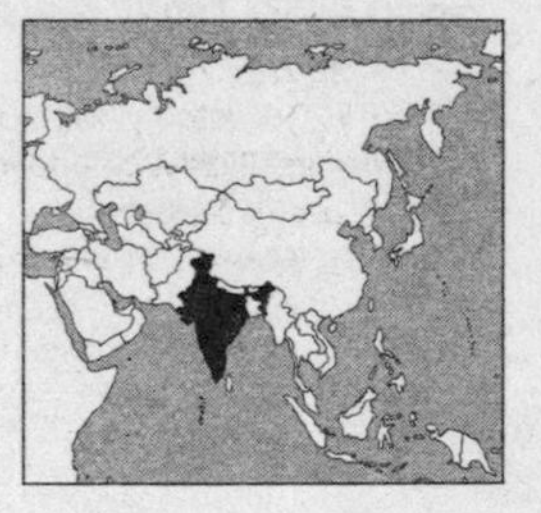

Indonesia is made up of 13,667 islands which are scattered across the Indian and Pacific Oceans in a huge crescent and is the world's fourth most highly populated country. Its largest landmass is the province of Kalimantan which is part of the island of Borneo. Sumatra is the largest individual island. Java, however, is the dominant and most densely populated island. The climate is generally tropical monsoon and temperatures are high all year round. The country has 100 volcanoes, and earthquakes are frequent in the southern islands. Overpopulation is a big problem especially in Java, where its fertile rust-coloured soil is in danger of becoming exhausted. Rice, maize and cassava are the main crops grown. Indonesia has the largest reserves of tin in the world and is one of the world's leading rubber producers. Other mineral resources found are bauxite, natural gas, nickel and copper. Oil production is also important. Indonesia's resources are not as yet fully developed but the country's economy is now expanding and needs to create over 2 million jobs annually to keep pace with the expanding population.

Quick facts:
Area : 1,904,570 sq km (735,358 sq miles)
Population : 197,366,000
Capital : Jakarta
Other major cities : Bandung, Medan, Palembang, Semarang, Surabaya
Form of government : Republic
Religion : Sunni Islam, Christianity, Hinduism
Currency : Rupiah

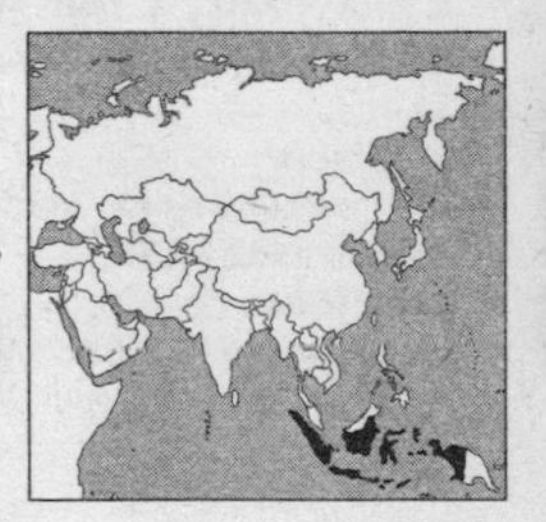

Iran lies across The Gulf from the Arabian peninsula and stretches from the Caspian Sea to the Arabian Sea. It is a land dominated by mountains in the north and west, with a huge expanse of desert in its centre. The climate is hot and dry, although more temperate conditions are found on the shores of the Caspian Sea. In winter, terrible dust storms sweep the deserts and almost no life can survive. Most of the population live in the north and west, where Tehran is situated. The only good agricultural land is on the Caspian coastal plains, where wheat, barley, potatoes and rice are grown. Fresh and dried fruit are the country's main exports apart from petroleum. About 5% of the population are nomadic herdsmen who wander in the mountains. Most of Iran's oil is in the south-west, and other valuable minerals include coal, iron ore, copper and lead. Precious stones are found in the north-east. Main exports are petrochemicals, carpets and rugs, textiles, raw cotton and leather goods. There was a rapid expansion in the economy from petroleum industry revenue. However, after the Islamic revolution in the late 1970s, a war with Iraq, the economy slowed dramatically but there is now an improvement.

Quick facts:
Area : 1,648,000 sq km (636,296 sq miles)
Population : 66,593,800
Capital : Tehran
Other major cities : Esfahan, Mashhad, Tabriz
Government : Islamic Republic
Religion : Shia Islam
Currency : Rial

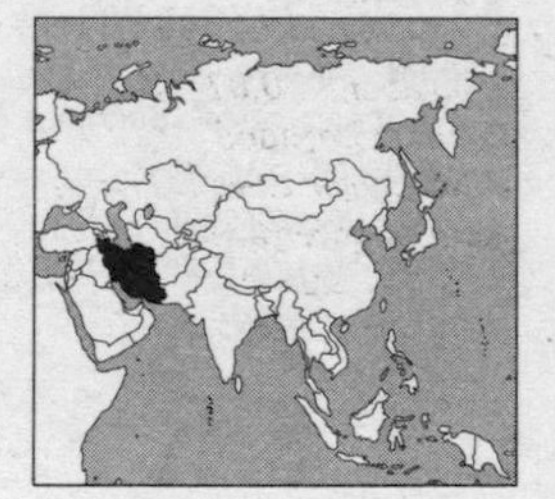

Iraq is located in south-west Asia, wedged between The Gulf and SYRIA. It is almost landlocked except for its outlet to The Gulf at Shatt al Arab. Its two great rivers, the Tigris and the Euphrates, flow from the north-west into The Gulf at this point. The climate is arid with very hot summers and cold winters. The high mountains on the border with TURKEY are snow covered for six months of the year, and desert in the south-west covers nearly half the country. The only fertile land in Iraq is in the basins of the Tigris and Euphrates where wheat, barley, rice, tobacco and cotton are grown with the country being primarily an agricultural one. The world's largest production of dates also comes from this area and is the country's main export product. A variety of other fruits is grown such as apples, olives, figs, grapes and pomegranates. Iraq profited from the great oil boom of the 1970s, but during the war with Iran oil terminals in The Gulf were destroyed and the Trans-Syrian Pipeline closed. The country is in a state of economic crisis with the health of the general population being low due to endemic diseases and poor sanitary conditions.

Quick facts:
Area : 434,924 sq km (167,925 sq miles)
Population : 20,877,400
Capital : Baghdad
Other major cities : Al-Basrah, Al Mawsil
Form of government : Republic
Religion : Shia Islam, Sunni Islam
Currency : Iraqi dinar

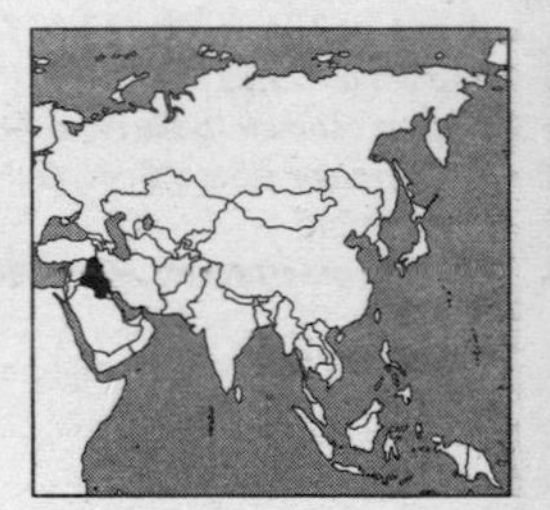

Ireland, Republic of is one of Europe's most westerly countries, situated in the Atlantic Ocean and separated from Great Britain by the Irish Sea. It has an equable climate, with mild south-west winds which makes temperatures uniform over most of the country.The Republic extends over four fifths of the island of Ireland and the west and south-west is mountainous, with the highest peak reaching 1041 m (3416 ft) at Carrauntoohil. The central plain is largely limestone covered in boulder clay which provides good farmland and pasture with about 80% of the land being under agriculture. The main rivers are the Erne and the Shannon. Livestock production is the most important including cattle, sheep, pigs and horses. The rural population tend to migrate to the cities, mainly Dublin, which is the main industrial centre and the focus of radio, television, publishing and communications. Lack of energy resources and remoteness from major markets has slowed industrial development, although the economy has improved in recent years with tourism showing a marked improvement.

Quick facts:
Area : 70,284 sq km (27,137 sq miles)
Population : 3,621,000
Capital : Dublin (Baile Atha Cliath)
Other major cities : Cork, Galway, Limerick, Waterford
Form of government : Republic
Religion : RC
Currency : Punt = 100 pighne

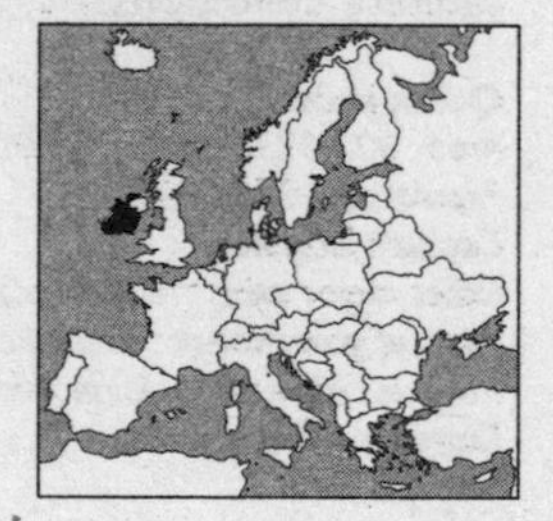

Israel occupies a long narrow stretch of land in the south-east of the Mediterranean. Its eastern boundary is formed by the Great Rift Valley, through which the river Jordan flows to the Dead Sea. The south of the country is made up of a triangular wedge of the Negev Desert which ends at the Gulf of Aqaba. The Negev desert has mineral resources such as copper, phosphates, manganese plus commercial amounts of natural gas and petroleum. Other assets are the vast amounts of potash, bromine and other minerals found in the Dead Sea. The climate in summer is hot and dry, in winter it is mild with some rain. The south of the country is arid and barren. Most of the population live on the coastal plain bordering the Mediterranean where Tel Aviv-Jaffa is the main commercial city. Israel's agriculture is based on collective settlements known as kibbutz. The country is virtually self-sufficient in foodstuffs and a major exporter of its produce. Jaffa oranges are famous throughout Europe. A wide range of products is processed or finished in the country, and main exports include finished diamonds, textiles, fruit, vegetables, chemicals, machinery and fertilizers.

Quick facts:
Area : 20,770 sq km (8019 sq miles)
Population : 5,732,000
Capital : Jerusalem
Other major cities : Tel Aviv-Jaffa, Haifa, Holon
Form of government : Republic
Religion : Judaism, Sunni Islam, Christianity
Currency : Shekel

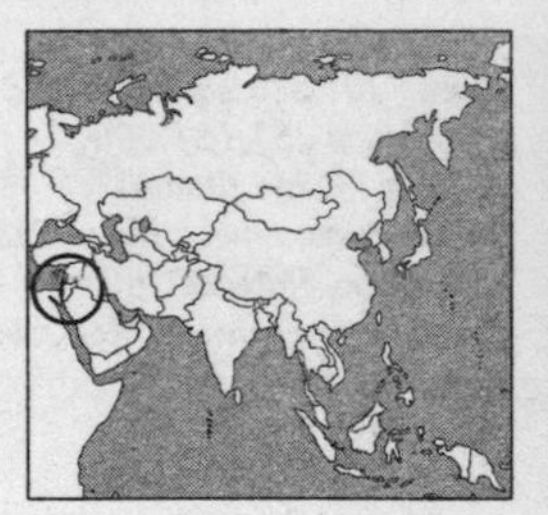

Italy is a republic in southern Europe, which comprises a large peninsula and the two main islands of Sicily and Sardinia. The Alps form a natural boundary with its northern and western European neighbours, and the Adriatic Sea to the east separates it from the countries of former YUGOSLAVIA. The Apennine Mountains form the backbone of Italy and extend the full length of the peninsula. Between the Alps and the Apennines lies the Po valley, a great fertile lowland. Sicily and Sardinia are largely mountainous. Much of Italy is geologically unstable and it has four active volcanoes, including Etna, Vesuvius and Stromboli. Italy enjoys warm dry summers and mild winters. In the south farms are small and traditional. Industries in the north include motor vehicles, textiles, clothing, leather goods, glass and ceramics. Although there is a lack of natural resources, almost 60% of the land is under crops and pasture and there is an abundance of building stone, particularly marble. The coastal waters are rich in marine life, with anchovy, sardine and tuna being of commercial importance. Tourism is an important source of foreign currency.

Quick facts:

Area : 301,225 sq km (116,304 sq miles)
Population : 57,181,000
Capital : Rome (Roma)
Other major cities : Milan, Naples, Turin, Genoa, Palermo, Florence
Form of government : Republic
Religion : RC
Currency : Lira

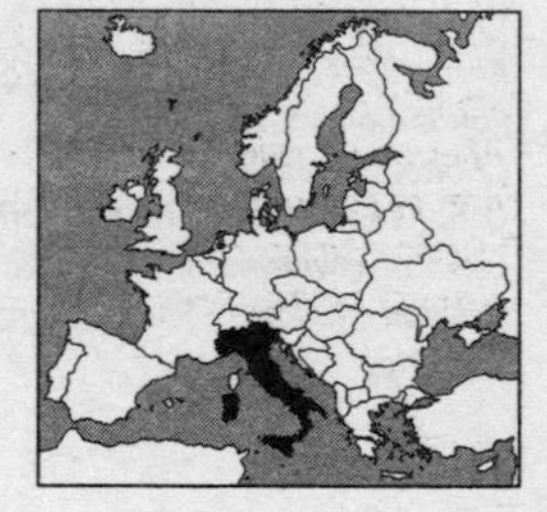

Jamaica is an island state in the Caribbean Sea about 150 km (93 miles) south of CUBA. The centre of the island comprises a limestone plateau and this is surrounded by narrow coastal flatlands and palm fringed beaches. The highest mountains, the Blue Mountains, are in the east of the island. The climate is tropical with high temperatures at the coast, with slightly cooler and less humid conditions in the highlands. Jamaica suffers from severe earthquakes and thermal springs can be found in areas of the country. The island lies right in the middle of the hurricane zone. The traditional crops grown are sugar cane, bananas, peppers, ginger, cocoa and coffee, and new crops such as winter vegetables, fruit and honey are being developed for export. The mining of bauxite and alumina plays a very important part in Jamaica's economy and accounts for around 60% of its total yearly exports. Industrialization has been encouraged and clothing, footwear, cement and agricultural machinery are now produced. Tourism is a particularly important industry with over 1 million visitors annually, as is the illegal trade in cannabis.

Quick facts:
Area : 10,990 sq km (4243 sq miles)
Population : 2,513,500
Capital : Kingston
Other major cities : Montego Bay, Spanish Town
Form of government : Constitutional Monarchy
Religion : Anglicanism, RC, other Protestantism
Currency : Jamaican dollar

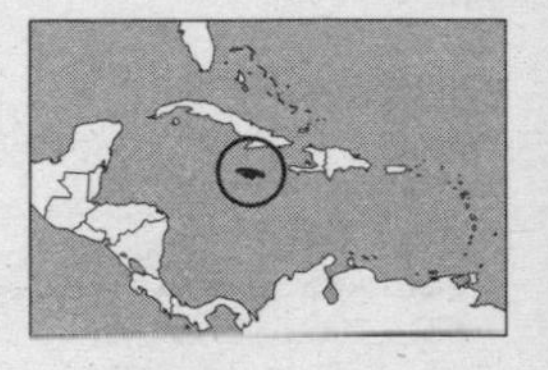

Japan is located on the eastern margin of Asia and consists of four major islands, Honshu, Hokkaido, Kyushu and Shikoku and many small islands. It is separated from the mainland of Asia by the Sea of Japan. The country is made up of six chains of steep serrated mountains, which contain about 60 active volcanoes. Earthquakes are frequent and widespread and often accompanied by giant waves (tsunami). A devastating earthquake occurred in 1995 when more than 5000 people died and over 300,000 were left homeless. Summers are warm and humid and winters mild, except on Hokkaido which is covered in snow in winter. Japan's agriculture is highly advanced with extensive use made of fertilizers and miniature machinery for the small fields. Fishing is important. Japan is the second largest industrial economy in the world and its heavy industries such as vehicles, machinery, electrical equipment and chemicals account for almost three-quarters of its export revenue. It is very dependent on imported raw materials, and its success is based on manufacturing industry, which employs about one third of the workforce.

Quick facts:
Area : 377,708 sq km (145,834 sq miles)
Population : 125,383,200
Capital : Tokyo
Other major cities : Osaka, Nagoya, Sapporo, Kobe, Kyoto, Yokohama
Form of government : Constitutional Monarchy
Religion : Shintoism, Buddhism, Christianity
Currency : Yen

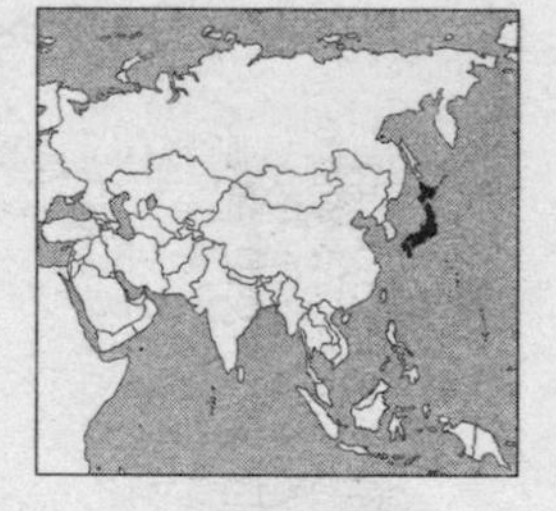

Jordan almost landlocked except for a short coastline on the Gulf of Aqaba, Jordan is bounded by SAUDI ARABIA, SYRIA, IRAQ and ISRAEL. Almost 80% of the country is desert and the rest comprises the East Bank Uplands and Jordan Valley, part of the Great Rift Valley. In general summers are hot and dry and winters cool and wet, with variations related to altitude. The east has a desert climate. Since under 5% of the land is arable, and only part of this is irrigated, production of grain is insufficient for the country's needs although some fruits and vegetables are grown for export. Amman is the main industrial centre of the country and the industries include phosphates, petroleum products, cement, iron and fertilizers. The rich Arab states such as Saudi Arabia give Jordan substantial economic aid and the country has a modern network of roads which link the major cities. In 1994 an historic peace agreement was signed with Israel which ended 46 years of hostilities.

Quick facts:
Area : 97,740 sq km (37,737 sq miles)
Population : 4,482,600
Capital : Amman
Other major cities : Aqaba, Irbid, Zarga
Form of government : Constitutional Monarchy
Religion : Sunni Islam
Currency : Jordanian dinar

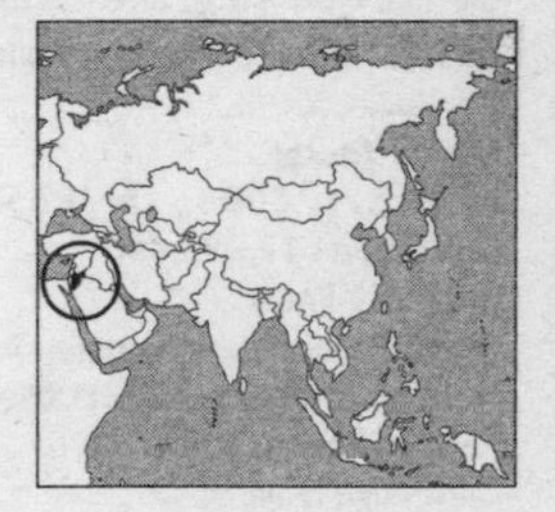

Kazakhstan, the second largest republic of the former USSR, extends approximately 3000 km (1864 miles) from the coast of the Caspian Sea to the north-west corner of MONGOLIA. The west of the country is low-lying, the east hilly, and in the south-east mountainous areas include parts of the Tian Shan and Altai ranges. The climate is continental and very dry with great extremes of temperature. Much of the country is desert and semi-desert with wastelands of stone, sand and salt. Crops can only be grown in the wetter north-west regions or on land irrigated by the Syrdar'ya river. Extensive pastoral farming is carried out, and cattle, sheep and goats are the main livestock reared. The country is rich in minerals, particularly copper, lead, zinc, coal, tungsten, iron ore, oil and gas. Kazakhstan declared itself independent in 1991, since when economic prospects have remained positive, although environmental problems have been left as a legacy of past Soviet exploitation, and these have still to be tackled (e.g. the over-draining of the Aral Sea). Exploitation of the vast Tengiz oil field is planned with foreign aid.

Quick facts:
Area : 2,717,300 sq km (1,050,000 sq miles)
Population : 17,193,400
Capital : Almaty
Other major cities : Karaganda, Semey, Shymkent
Form of government : Republic
Religion : Sunni Islam
Currency : Tenge

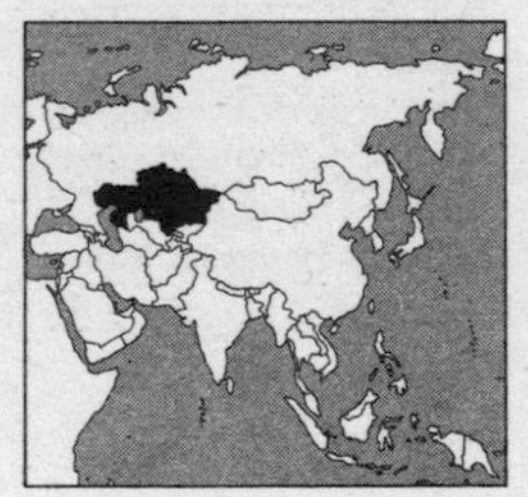

Kenya located in east Africa, Kenya straddles the Equator and extends from Lake Victoria in the south-west, to the Indian Ocean in the south-east. Highlands run north to south through central Kenya and are divided by the steep-sided Great Rift Valley. The coastal lowlands have a hot humid climate but in the highlands it is cooler and rainfall heavier. In the east it is very arid. The south-western region is well-watered with huge areas of fertile soil and this accounts for the bulk of the population and almost all its economic production. A wide variety of crops are grown for domestic consumption such as wheat, maize and cassava. Tea, coffee, sisal, sugar cane and cotton are grown for export. Oil refining at Mombasa is the country's largest single industry, and other industry includes food processing and textiles. Mining is carried out on a small scale for soda ash, gold and limestone but large quantities of silver and lead exist near Mombasa. Tourism is an important source of foreign revenue; the many wildlife and game reserves being a major attraction.

Quick facts:
Area : 580,367 sq km (224,080 sq miles)
Population : 28,091,700
Capital : Nairobi
Other major cities : Mombasa, Eldoret, Kisumu, Nakuru
Form of government : Republic
Religions : RC, Protestantism, other Christianity, Animism
Currency : Kenya shilling

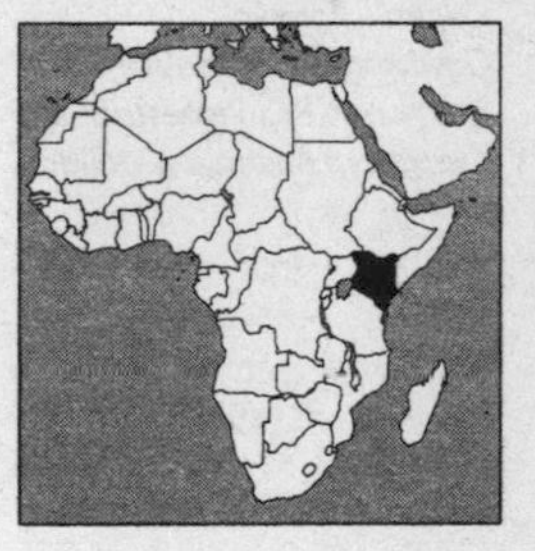

Kiribati (formerly known as the Gilbert Islands) comprises three groups of coral atolls and one isolated volcanic island spread over a large expanse of the central Pacific. The group includes Banaba Island, the Phoenix Islands and some of the Line Islands. The climate is maritime equatorial with a rainy season from October to March. Most islanders are involved in subsistence agriculture. The principal tree is the coconut which grows well on all the islands. There are palm, breadfruit trees, bananas and papaw to be found. Soil is negligible and the only vegetable which can be grown is calladium. Tuna fishing is an important industry with coconuts and palm products being the main cash crops. Phosphate sources are now exhausted and the mining left severe environmental damage causing most Banabans to resettle. The country is heavily dependent on overseas aid.

Quick facts:
Area : 726 sq km (280 sq miles)
Population : 75,690
Capital : Tarawa
Government : Republic
Religions : RC, Protestantism
Currency : Australian dollar

Korea, Democratic People's Republic of (formerly North Korea) occupies just over half of the Korean peninsula in east Asia. The Yala and Tumen rivers form its northern border with CHINA and the RUSSIAN FEDERATION. Its southern border with SOUTH KOREA is just north of the 38th parallel. It is a mountainous country, three quarters of which is forested highland or scrubland, with Mount Paektu at 2744 m (9003 ft) being its highest peak. The climate is warm temperate, although winters can be cold in the north. Most rain falls during the summer. Nearly 90% of its arable land is farmed by cooperatives which employ over 40% of the labour force and rice is the main crop grown. North Korea is quite well endowed with fuel and minerals such as magnesite, zinc, copper, lead, tungsten, gold and silver. Deposits of coal and hydro-electric power generate electricity, and substantial deposits of iron ore are found near P'yongyang and Musan. 60% of the labour force is employed in industry, the most important of which are metallurgical, building, cement and chemicals. Fishing is carried on with the main catches being tuna, anchovy and seaweeds.

Quick facts:
Area : 120,538 sq km (46,540 sq miles)
Population : 23,472,000
Capital : P'yongyang
Other major cities : Chongjin, Kaesong, Nampo, Sinuiju, Wonsan
Form of government : Socialist Republic
Religions : Chondoism, Buddhism
Currency : Won

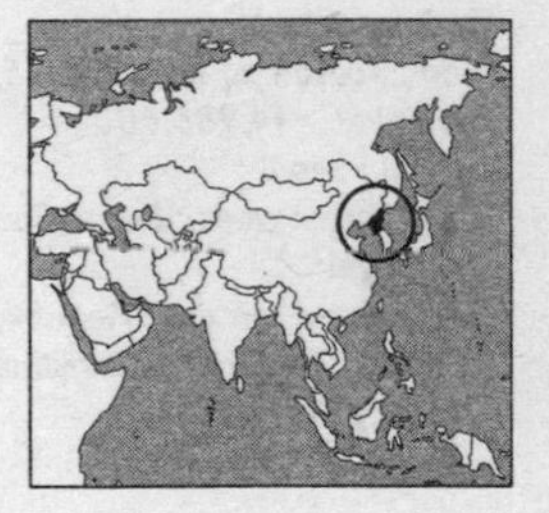

Korea, Republic of (formerly South Korea) occupies the southern half of the Korean peninsula and stretches about 400 km (249 miles), from the Korea Strait to the demilitarized zone bordering DEMOCRATIC PEOPLE'S REPUBLIC OF KOREA. It is predominantly mountainous with the highest ranges running north to south along the east coast. The west is lowland which is extremely densely populated. The extreme south has a humid warm temperate climate while farther north it is more continental. Most rain falls in summer. Cultivated land represents only 23% of the country's total area and the main crops are rice, onions, potatoes, barley and maize. An increasing amount of fruit such as melons, apples and peaches are now produced. The country has few natural resources but does produce coal, graphite and iron ire. It has a flourishing manufacturing industry and is the world's leading supplier of ships and footwear. Other important industries are electronic equipment, electrical goods, steel, petrochemicals, motor vehicles and toys. Its people enjoy a reasonably high standard of living brought about by hard work and determination.

Quick facts:
Area : 98,484 sq km (38,025 sq miles)
Population : 44,986,600
Capital : Seoul
Other major cities : Pusan, Taegu, Inch'on, Kwangju
Form of government : Republic
Religions : Buddhism, Christianity
Currency : Won

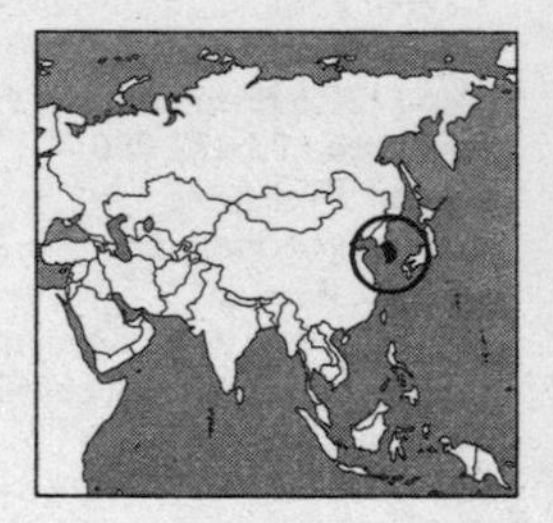

Kuwait is a tiny Arab state on The Gulf, comprising the city of Kuwait at the southern entrance of Kuwait Bay, a small undulating desert wedged between IRAQ and SAUDI ARABIA and nine small offshore islands. It has a dry desert climate, cool in winter but very hot and humid in summer. There is little agriculture due to lack of water; major crops produced are melons, tomatoes, onions and dates. The country's water comes from the desalination of seawater. Shrimp fishing is becoming an important industry. Large reserves of petroleum and natural gas are the mainstay of the economy although this wealth is limited. It has about 950 oil wells, however 600 were fired during the Iraqi occupation in 1991 and are unlikely to resume production for several years. Apart from oil, industry includes boat building, plastics, petrochemicals, gases, cement and building materials. Although there are no railways, there are over 2000 miles of roads and an international airport near the capital.

Quick facts:
Area : 18,049 sq km (6969 sq miles)
Population : 1,805,400
Capital : Kuwait city (Al Kuwayt)
Government : Constitutional Monarchy
Religion : Sunni Islam, Shia Islam
Currency : Kuwaiti dinar

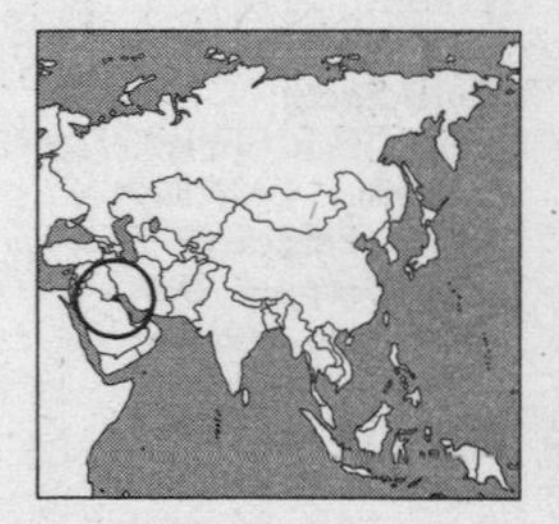

Kyrgyzstan, a central Asian republic of the former USSR, independent since 1991. It is located on the border with north-west CHINA. Much of the country is occupied by the Tian Shan Mountains which rise to spectacular peaks. The highest is Pik Pobedy 7439 m (24,406 ft), lying on the border with China. In the north-east of the country is Issyk-Kul', a large lake heated by volcanic action, so it never freezes. Most of the country is semi-arid or desert, but climate is greatly influenced by altitude. Soils are badly leached except in the valleys, where some grains are grown. Grazing of sheep, horses and cattle is extensive. Industries include non-ferrous metallurgy, machine building, coal mining, tobacco, food processing, textiles, gold mining and hydroelectricity. Silkworms are also raised and opium poppies are grown. There was considerable industrialization while under Soviet rule and there are large mineral deposits of gold, coal and uranium while deposits of natural gas and oil are in the Fergana Valley.

Quick facts:
Area : 198,501 sq km (76,642 sq miles)
Population : 4,436,800
Capital : Bishkek, (formerly Frunze)
Other major city : Osh
Government : Republic
Religion : Sunni Islam
Currency : Som

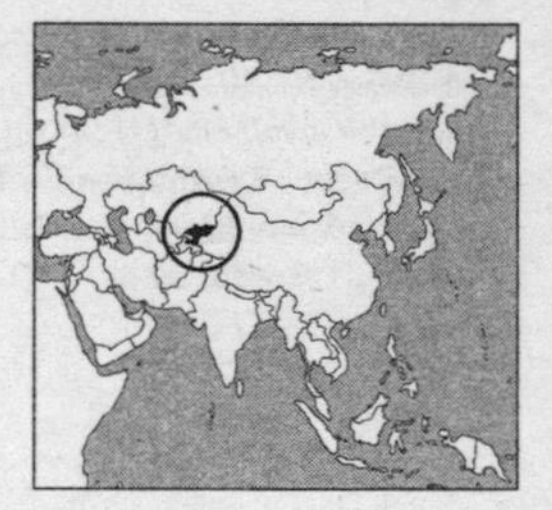

Laos is a landlocked country in South-East Asia which is ruggedly mountainous, apart from the Mekong river plains along its border with THAILAND. The Annam mountains, which reach 2500 m (8203 ft), form a natural border with VIETNAM. It has a tropical monsoon climate with high temperatures throughout the year and heavy rains in summer. Laos is one of the poorest countries in the world and its development has been retarded by war, drought and floods. It is primarily an agricultural country with the principal crop being rice, grown on small peasant plots. Corn, potatoes and cassava are also grown. There is some export of timber, coffee, tin and electricity. All manufactured goods must be imported and are mainly food, machinery, petroleum products and electrical equipment. The capital and largest city, Vientiane, is the country's main trade outlet via Thailand. Laos' main means of transportation are by the Mekong river and air transport.

Quick facts:
Area : 236,800 sq km (9!,428 sq miles)
Population : 4,793,000
Capital : Vientiane
Other major cities: Louangphrabang, Paksé, Savannakhét
Form of government : People's Republic
Religion : Buddhism
Currency : New kip

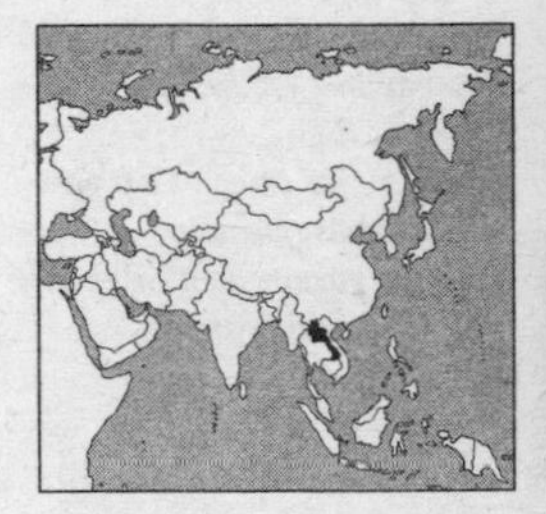

Latvia is a Baltic state that regained its independence in 1991 with the break-up of the former Soviet Union. It is located in north-east Europe on the Baltic Sea and is sandwiched between ESTONIA and LITHUANIA. It has cool summers, wet summers and long, cold winters. Latvians traditionally lived by forestry, fishing and livestock rearing. The chief agricultural occupations are cattle and dairy farming and the main crops grown are oats, barley, rye, potatoes and flax. Latvia's population is now over 70% urban and agriculture is no longer the mainstay of the economy. Cities such as Riga, the capital, Daugavpils, Ventspils and Liepaja now produce high quality textiles, machinery, electrical appliances, paper, chemicals, furniture and foodstuffs. Latvia has extensive deposits of peat which is used to manufacture briquettes. It also has deposits of gypsum and in the coastal areas amber is frequently found.

Quick facts:
Area : 63,700 sq km (24,595 sq miles)
Population : 2,639,750
Capital : Riga
Other major cities : Liepaja Daugavpils, Jurmala
Form of government : Republic
Religion : Lutheranism
Currency : Lat

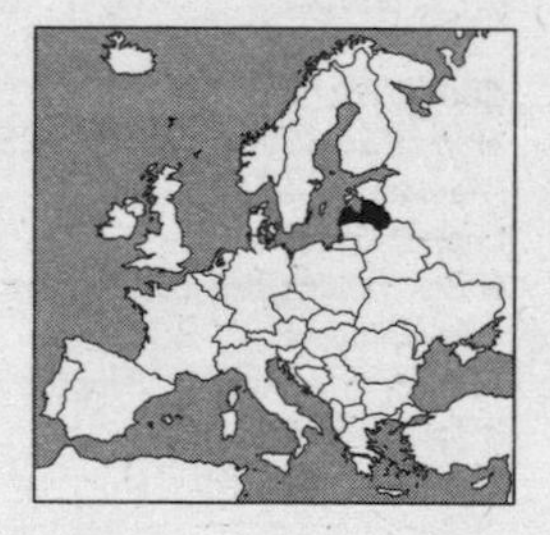

Lebanon is a mountainous country in the eastern Mediterranean. A narrow coastal plain runs parallel to its 240-km (149-mile) Mediterranean coast and gradually rises to the spectacular Lebanon Mountains, which are snow covered in winter. The Anti Lebanon Mountains form the border with SYRIA, and between the two ranges lies the Beqa'a Valley. The climate is Mediterranean with short warm winters and long hot and rainless summers. Rainfall can be torrential in winter and snow falls on high ground. Lebanon is an agricultural country, the main regions of production being the Beqa'a Valley and the coastal plain although erosion is a common problem in the uplands. Main products include olives, grapes, bananas, citrus fruits, apples, cotton, tobacco and sugar beet. Industry is small scale and manufactures include cement, fertilizers and jewellery. There are oil refineries at Tripoli and Sidon. Lebanon's main economy is based on commercial services such as banking but since the civil war, invasion by Israel and factional fighting the economy has suffered greatly causing high inflation and unemployment.

Quick facts:
Area : 10,400 sq km (4015 sq miles)
Population : 3,382,900
Capital : Beirut (Beyrouth)
Other important cities : Tripoli, Sidon, Zahle
Form of government : Republic
Religions : Shia Islam, Sunni Islam, Christianity
Currency : Lebanese pound

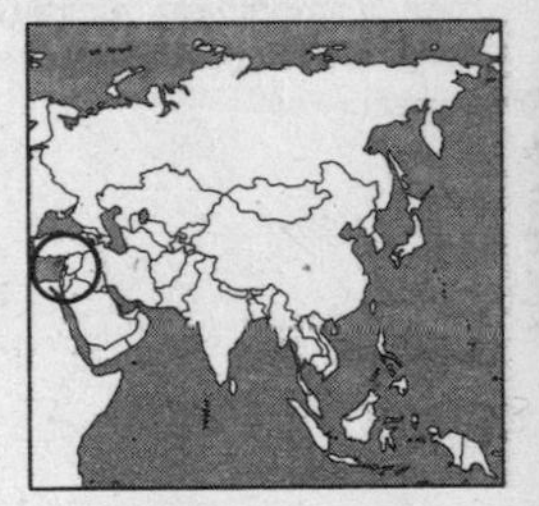

Lesotho is a small, landlocked kingdom entirely surrounded by the Republic of SOUTH AFRICA. Snow-capped mountains and treeless uplands, cut by spectacular gorges, cover two thirds of the country. The climate is pleasant with variable rainfall. Winters are generally dry with heavy frosts in lowland areas and frequent snow in the highlands. Due to the mountainous terrain, only one eighth of the land can be cultivated and the main crop is maize. Yields are low because of soil erosion on the steep slopes and over-grazing by herds of sheep and cattle. Wool and mohair are exported but most foreign exchange comes from money sent home by Lesotho workers in South Africa. Tourism is beginning to flourish, the main attraction to South Africans being the casinos in the capital Maseru, as gambling is prohibited in their own country.

Quick facts:
Area : 30,355 sq km (11,720 sq miles)
Population : 1,971,600
Capital : Maseru
Form of government : Constitutional monarchy
Religions : RC, other Christianity
Currency : Loti

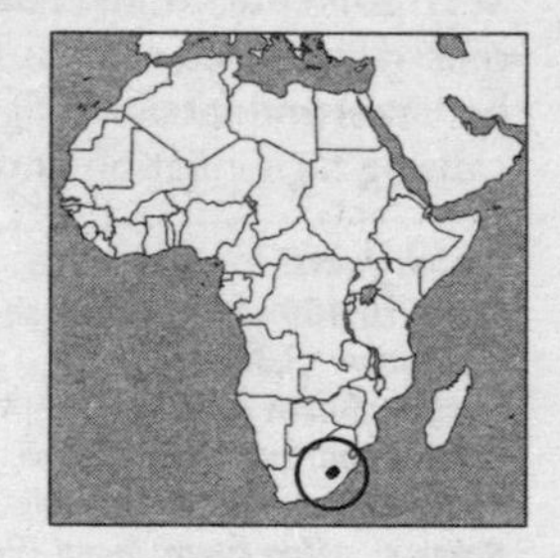

Liberia is located in West Africa and has a 560 km (348 mile) coast stretching from SIERRA LEONE to CÔTE D'IVOIRE. It is the only African country never to be ruled by a foreign power. It has a treacherous coast with rocky cliffs and lagoons enclosed by sand bars. Inland the land rises to a densely forested plateau dissected by deep, narrow valleys. Farther inland still, there are beautiful waterfalls and the Nimba Mountains rise to over 1700 m (5577 ft). Agriculture employs three quarters of the labour force and produces cassava and rice as subsistence crops and rubber, coffee and cocoa for export. Forest and animal reserves are magnificent and the beaches and lagoons are beautiful. The Nimba Mountains are rich in iron ore, which accounts for 70% of export earnings and wood, rubber, diamonds and coffee are also exported. Liberia has a very large tanker fleet, most of which have foreign owners. In the early 1990s the economy suffered greatly due to the civil war with food shortages and foreign investment drying up.

Quick facts:
Area : 111,369 sq km (43,000 sq miles)
Population : 2,938,700
Capital : Monrovia
Other major cities : Buchanan, Harper, Harbel
Form of government : Republic
Religion : Animism, Sunni Islam, Christianity
Currency : Liberian dollar

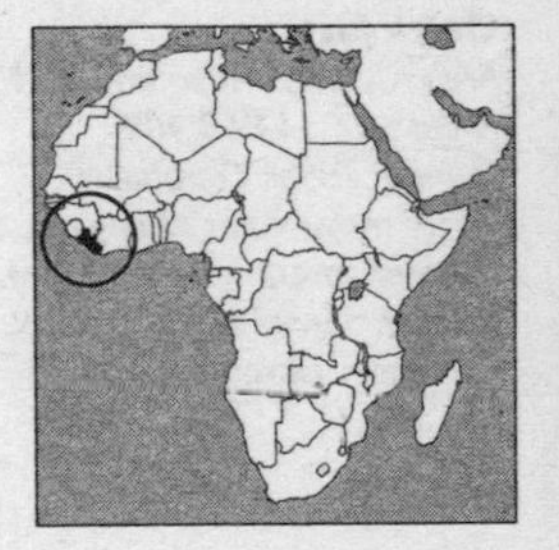

Libya is a large, north African country which stretches from the south coast of the Mediterranean to, and in some parts beyond, the Tropic of Cancer. The Sahara Desert covers much of the country extending right to the Mediterranean coast at the Gulf of Sirte. The only green areas are the scrublands found in the north-west and the forested hills near Benghazi. The coastal area has mild wet winters and hot dry summers but the interior has had some of the highest recorded temperatures of anywhere in the world. Around 18% of the people work on the land, the main agricultural region being in the north-west near Tripoli but this is dependent on rainfall. The main crops produced are wheat, tomatoes, fruits and barley. Many sheep, goats and cattle are reared and there is an export trade in skins, hides and hairs. Libya is one of the world's largest producers of oil and natural gas and also produces potash and marine salt. Other industries include food processing, textiles, cement and handicrafts. The majority of consumer products are imported.

Quick facts:
Area : 1,759,540 sq km (679,358 sq miles)
Population : 4,868,900
Capital : Tripoli (Tarabulus)
Other major cities : Benghazi, Misurata
Form of government : Socialist People's Republic
Religion : Sunni Islam
Currency : Libyan dinar

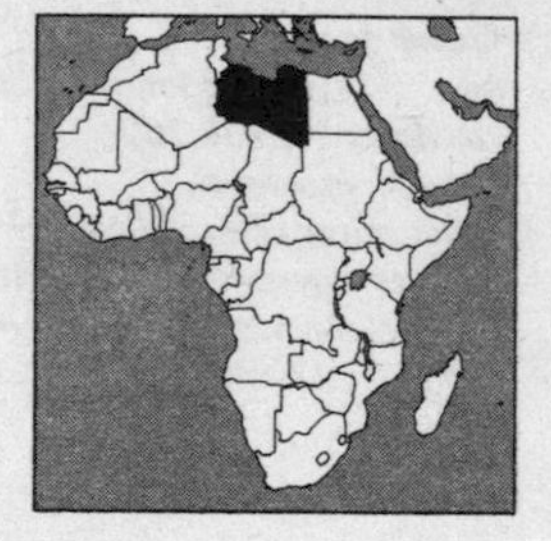

Liechtenstein the principality of Liechtenstein is a tiny central European state situated on the east bank of the River Rhine, bounded by AUSTRIA to the east and SWITZERLAND to the west. In the east of the principality the Alps rise to 2599 m (8527 ft) at Grauspitze. The climate is mild alpine. Approximately one third of the country is covered with forests and there are deer, fox, chamois and badger. Once an agricultural country, Liechtenstein has rapidly moved into industry in the last 30 years, with a variety of light industries such as textiles, high quality metal goods, precision instruments, ceramics and pharmaceuticals. It is a popular location for the headquarters of foreign companies, in order that they can benefit from the favourable tax laws. Tourism also thrives, beautiful scenery and good skiing being the main attractions. Other income is derived from banking and the sale of postage stamps.

Quick facts:
Area : 160 sq km (62 sq miles)
Population : 29,400
Capital : Vaduz
Form of government : Constitutional Monarchy (Principality)
Religion : RC
Currency : Swiss franc

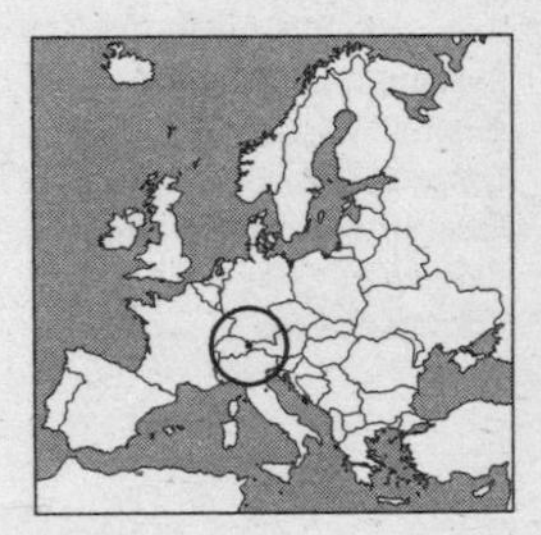

Lithuania lies to the north-west of the RUSSIAN FEDERATION and BELARUS and is bounded to the north by LATVIA and west by POLAND. It is the largest of the three former Soviet Baltic Republics. Before 1940 Lithuania was a mainly agricultural country but has since been considerably industrialized with shipbuilding, food processing and electrical machinery production being the most significant. Most of the land is lowland covered by forest and swamp, and the main products are rye, barley, sugar beet, flax, meat, milk and potatoes. About 20% of the population is engaged in agriculture, principally dairy farming and livestock production. Oil production has started from a small field at Kretinga in the west of the country, 16 km (10 miles) north of Klaipeda. Amber is found along the Baltic coast and used by Lithuanian craftsmen for making jewellery.

Quick facts:
Area : 65,200 sq km (25,174 sq miles)
Population : 3,724,000
Capital : Vilnius
Other major cities : Kaunas, Klaipeda, Siauliai
Form of government : Republic
Religion : RC
Currency : Litas

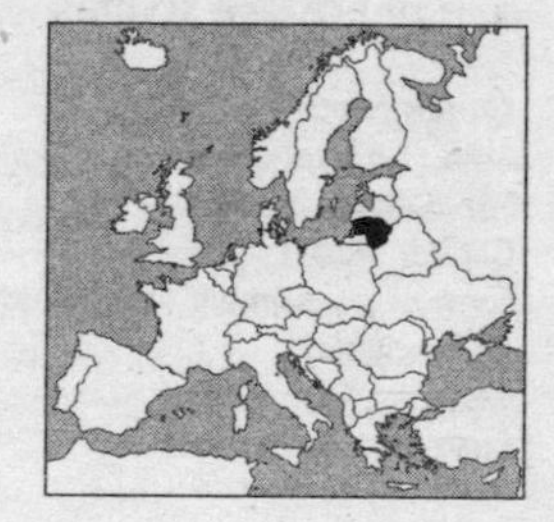

Luxembourg the Grand Duchy of Luxembourg is a small independent country bounded by BELGIUM on the west, FRANCE on the south and GERMANY on the east. In the north of the Duchy a wooded plateau, the Oesling, rises to 550 m/1804 ft and in the south a lowland area of valleys and ridges is known as the Gutland. Northern winters are cold and raw with snow covering the ground for almost a month, but in the south winters are mild and summers cool. In the south the land is fertile and crops grown include maize, roots, tubers and potatoes with livestock also being raised. It is in the south, also, that beds of iron ore are found and these form the basis of the country's iron and steel industry. The country is very industrialized with the financial sector playing an increasingly important part in the country's economy, as is tourism. In the east Luxembourg is bordered by the Moselle river in whose valley wines are produced.

Quick facts:
Area : 2586 sq km (998 sq miles)
Population : 392,950
Capital : Luxembourg City
Other major cities : Esch-sur-Algette, Differdange, Dudelange
Form of government : Constitutional Monarchy (Duchy)
Religion : RC
Currency : Luxembourg franc

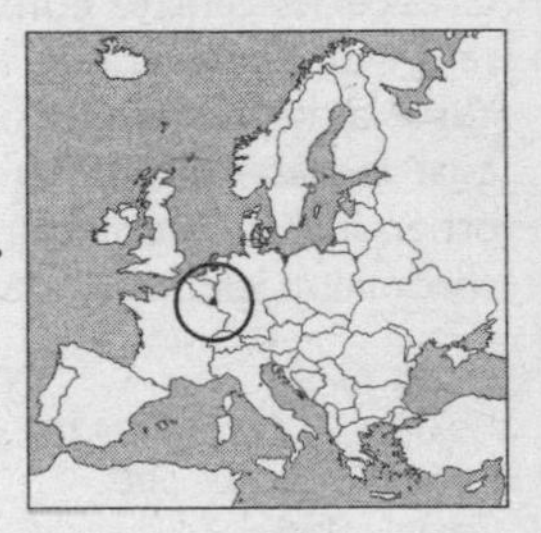

Macedonia, The Former Yugoslav Republic of, under the name of Macedonia, declared its independence from Yugoslavia in November, 1991. However GREECE, angered at the use of 'Macedonia' – also the name of the neighbouring Greek province – imposed a trade embargo and convinced the UN not to recognize the nation's independence. In 1993, Macedonia was admitted to the UN after changing its official name to The Former Yugoslav Republic of Macedonia. In 1995 an agreement was reached with Greece whereby both countries would respect the territory, sovereignty and independence of the other, with Macedonia agreeing to adopt a new flag. A landlocked country, Macedonia shares its borders with ALBANIA, BULGARIA, Greece and YUGOSLAVIA. Its terrain is mountainous, covered with deep valleys and has several large lakes. The Vardar River divides the country, is the country's longest river and flows into Greece. Its climate consists of hot, dry summers and cold winters with considerable snow. It is the poorest of the six former Yugoslav republics but sustains itself through agriculture and the coal industries although manufactured goods, machinery and other fuel is imported. Some of its natural resources include chromium, lead, zinc, nickel, iron ore and timber.

Quick facts:
Area : 25,713 sq km (9928 sq miles)
Population : 2,213, 000
Capital : Skopje
Other major cities : Kumanovo, Tetova, Prilep
Form of government : Republic
Religion : Eastern Orthodox, Muslim
Currency : Dinar

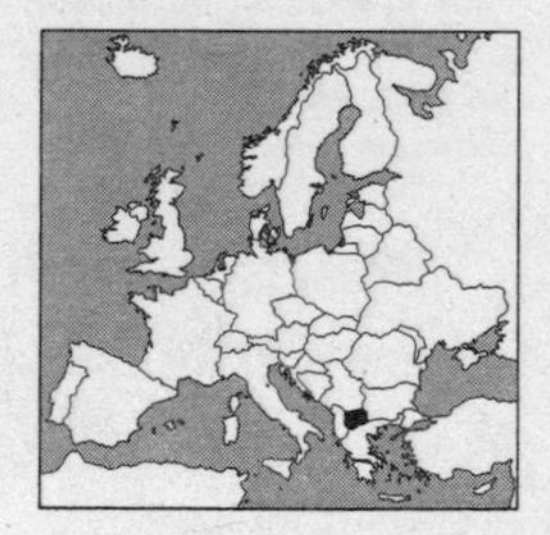

Madagascar is an island state situated off the south-east coast of Africa, separated from the mainland by the Mozambique Channel. Madagascar is the fourth largest island in the world and the centre of it is made up of high savanna-covered plateaux. In the east, forested mountains fall steeply to the coast and in the south-west, the land falls gradually through dry grassland and scrub. The staple food crop is rice and although only 5% of the land is cultivated, 80% of the population grow enough to feed themselves. Cassava, potatoes, maize, beans and bananas are also grown but some 58% of the land is pasture and there are more cattle than people. The main export earners are coffee, vanilla, cloves and sugar cane. There is mining for chromite, graphite, mica and salt and an oil refinery at Toamasina on the east coast. Upon independence in 1960, Madagascar became known as the Malagasy Republic, but was changed back by referendum in 1975.

Quick facts:
Area : 587,041 sq km (226,657 sq miles)
Population : 14,877,350 Capital : Antananarivo
Other major cities : Fianarantsoa, Mahajanga, Toamasina, Toliara
Form of government : Republic
Religions : Animism, RC, Protestantism
Currency : Malagasy franc

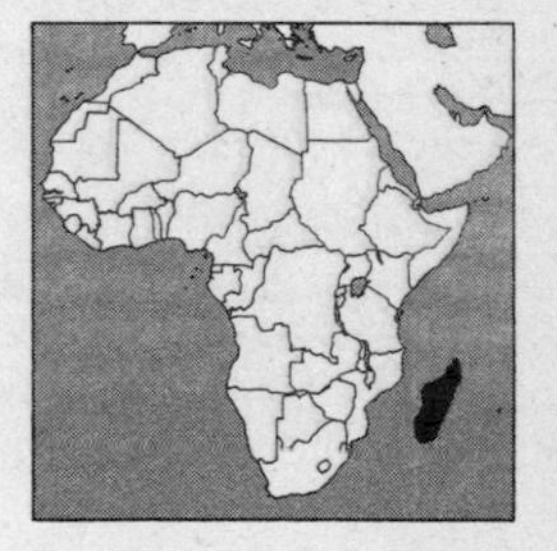

Malawi lies along the southern and western shores of the third largest lake in Africa, Lake Malawi. To the south of the lake the Shire river flows through a valley, overlooked by wooded, towering mountains. The tropical climate has a dry season from May to October and a wet season for the remaining months. Agriculture is the predominant occupation and many Malawians live on their own crops. Plantation farming is used for export crops. Exports include tea grown on the terraced hillsides in the south and tobacco on the central plateau plus peanuts and sugar, with maize also being an important crop. Malawi has bauxite and coal deposits but due to the inaccessibility of their locations, mining is limited. Hydroelectricity is now being used for the manufacturing industry but imports of manufactured goods remain high, and the country remains one of the poorest in the world. Malawi was formerly the British colony of Nyasaland, a name meaning 'Land of the Lake', which was given to it by the 19th century explorer, David Livingstone.

Quick facts:
Area : 118,484 sq km (45,747 sq miles)
Population : 10,883,000
Capital : Lilongwe
Other major cities : Blantyre, Mzuzu, Zomba
Form of government : Republic
Religions : Animism, RC, Presbyterianism
Currency : Kwacha

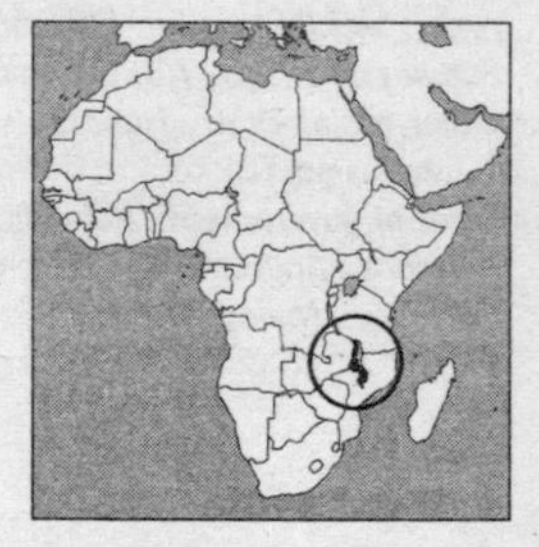

Malaysia the Federation of Malaysia lies in the South China Sea in south-east Asia, and comprises peninsular Malaysia on the Malay Peninsula and the states of Sabah and Sarawak on the island of Borneo. Malaysia is affected by the monsoon climate. The north-east monsoon brings rain to the east coast of peninsular Malaysia in winter, and the south-west monsoon brings rain to the west coast in summer. Throughout the country the climate is generally tropical and temperatures are uniformly hot throughout the year. Peninsular Malaysia has always had thriving rubber-growing and tin dredging industries and now oil palm growing is also important on the east coast. Sabah and Sarawak have grown rich by exploiting their natural resources, the forests. There is also some offshore oil and around the capital, Kuala Lumpur, new industries such as electronics are expanding. In recent years tourism has become an important industry and there are plans for a new international airport and a large dam for hydroelectric production.

Quick facts:
Area : 330,434 sq km (127,580 sq miles)
Population : 20,163,800
Capital : Kuala Lumpur
Other major cities : Ipoh, George Town, Johor Baharu
Form of government : Federal Constitutional Monarchy
Religion : Islam
Currency : Ringgit or Malaysian dollar

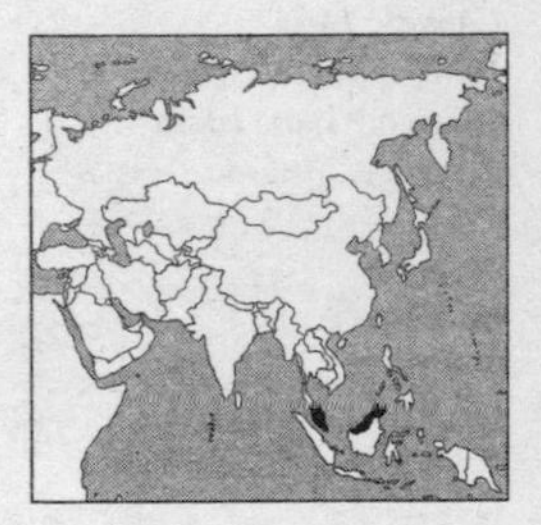

Maldives the Republic of Maldives lies 640 km (398 miles) south-west of SRI LANKA in the Indian Ocean and comprises 1200 low-lying coral islands grouped into 12 atolls. Roughly 202 of the islands are inhabited, and the highest point is only 1.5 m (5 ft) above sea level. Independence was gained in 1965 with a republic being formed three years later. The climate is hot and humid and affected by monsoons from May to August. The islands are covered with coconut palms, and some millet, cassava, yams and tropical fruit are grown. However, rice, the staple diet of its islanders, is imported. The most important natural resource is marine life and fishing is an important occupation. The chief export is now canned or frozen tuna. Tourism is now developing fast and has taken over fishing as the major foreign currency earner.

Quick facts:
Area : 298 sq km (115 sq miles)
Population : 251,650
Capital : Malé
Form of govt : Republic
Religion : Sunni Islam
Currency : Rufiyaa

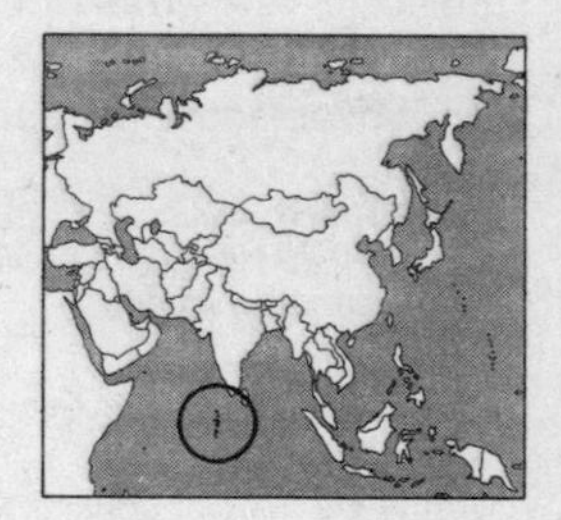

Mali is a landlocked state in West Africa. The country mainly comprises vast and monotonous plains and plateaux. It rises to 1155 m (3790 ft) in the Adrar des Iforas range in the north-east. The Sahara in the north of the country is encroaching southwards. Mali is one of the poorest countries in the world. In the south there is some rain and plains are covered by grassy savanna and a few scattered trees. The river Niger runs through the south of the country and small steamboats use it for shipping between Koulikoro and Gao. Fish are plentiful in the river and its water is used to irrigate the land. Only a fifth of the land can be cultivated. Rice, cassava and millet are grown for domestic consumption and cotton for export. Droughts in the 1970s and mid-80s resulted in thousands of cattle dying, crop failure with famine and disease killing many of the population. The country's main exports include cotton, gold, foodstuffs, livestock and mangoes. Iron ore and bauxite have been discovered but have yet to be exploited.

Quick facts:
Area : 1,240,192 sq km (478,838 sq miles)
Population : 10,726,600
Capital : Bamako
Other major cities : Gao, Kayes, Segou, Mopti, Sikasso
Form of government : Republic
Religions : Sunni Islam, Animism
Currency : CFA Franc

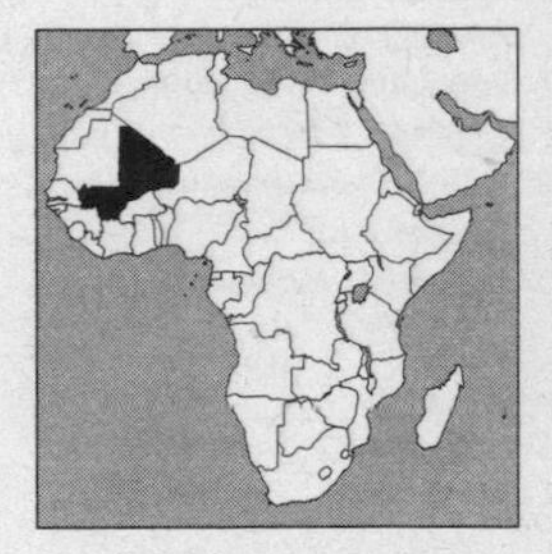

Malta, a small republic in the middle of the Mediterranean, lies just south of the island of Sicily. It comprises three islands, Malta, Gozo and Comino, which are made up of low limestone plateaux with little surface water. The climate is Mediterranean with hot, dry sunny summers and little rain. Lack of water has led to the production of desalination plants which produce up to 70% of the country's needs. Winters are cooler and wetter. Malta is virtually self-sufficient in agricultural products and exports potatoes, vegetables, wine and cut flowers. The British military base on Malta was once the mainstay of the economy but after the British withdrew in the late 1970s, the naval dockyard was converted for commercial shipbuilding and repairs, which is now one of the most important industries. Tourism has also boomed and the island has become popular for retirement in the sunshine with low taxes. Malta has a long history of civilization with remains found from Stone and Bronze Age peoples.

Quick facts:
Area : 316 sq km (122 sq miles)
Population : 367,000
Capital : Valletta
Form of government : Republic
Religion : RC
Currency : Maltese pound

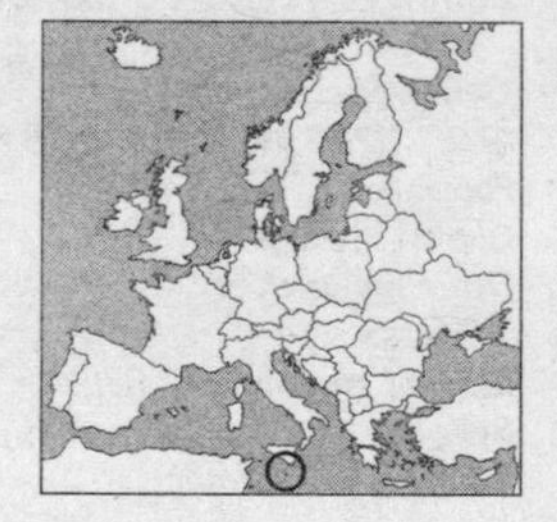

Marshall Islands formerly part of the US administered UN territory, this self-governing republic, independent since 1991, comprises a scattering of some 1250 coral atolls and 34 main islands, arranged in two parallel chains, Ratak and Ralik, located in eastern Micronesia in the western Pacific Ocean, and lying to the north-west of KIRIBATI. The climate is tropical maritime, with little variation in temperature, and rainfall that is heaviest from July to October. The republic remains in free association with the USA and the economy is almost totally dependent on US-related payments for use of the islands as bases. The Bikini Atoll was used as a nuclear testing area in 1946. The main occupations are fishing and agriculture with the chief export being copra. Attempts are being made to diversify the economy before US aid finishes in 2001.

Quick facts:
Area : 181 sq km/70 sq miles
Population : 49,320,300
Capital : Dalag-Uliga-Darrit (on Majuro atoll)
Form of govt : Republic in free association with the USA
Religion : Protestant
Currency : US dollar

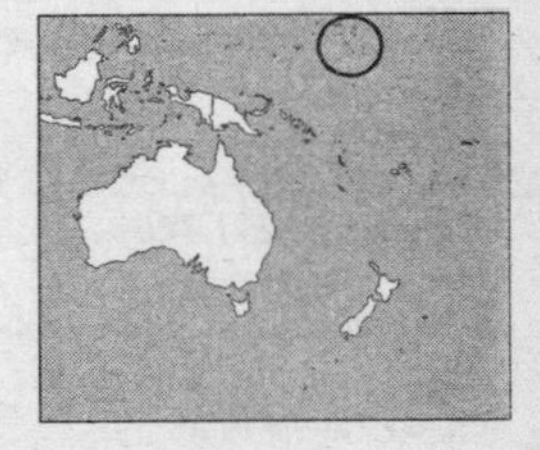

Mauritania, a country nearly twice the size of France, is located on the west coast of Africa. About 47% of the country is desert, the Sahara covering much of the north. The only settlements found in this area are around oases, where a little millet, dates and vegetables can be grown. The main agricultural regions are in the Senegal river valley in the south. The rest of the country is made up of the drought-stricken Sahel grasslands. The majority of the people are traditionally nomadic herdsmen, but severe droughts since the late 1960s and early 1970s have killed about 70% of the nation's animals, and the population has settled along the Senegal river. As a result, vast shanty towns have sprung up around all the towns. Production of iron ore and other deposits provide the country's main exports, and development of these and the fishing industry on the coast form the only hope for a brighter future since the country's economy is very reliant on foreign aid.

Quick facts:
Area : 1,025,520 sq km (395,953 sq miles)
Population : 2,291,700
Capital : Nouakchott
Other major cities : Kaédi, Nouadhibou, Rosso
Form of government : Republic
Religion : Sunni Islam
Currency : Ouguiya

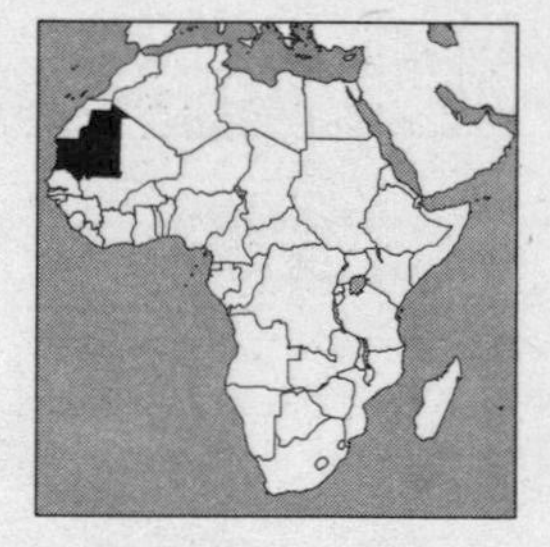

Mauritius is a beautiful island with tropical beaches which lies about 20° south in the Indian Ocean, 800 km (497 miles) east of MADAGASCAR and gained independence in 1968. The islands of Rodrigues and Agalega are also part of Mauritius. Mauritius is a volcanic island with many craters surrounded by lava flows. The central plateau rises to over 800 m (2625 ft), then drops sharply to the south and west coasts. The climate is hot and humid, south-westerly winds bring heavy rain in the uplands and there is the possibility of cyclones during December to April. The island has well-watered fertile soil, ideal for the sugar plantations that cover 45% of the island. Although the export of molasses and sugar still dominate the economy, diversification is being encouraged. Other crops such as tea, tobacco, peanuts and vegetables are grown. The clothing and electronic equipment industries are becoming increasingly important and tourism is now the third largest source of foreign exchange.

Quick facts:
Area : 2040 sq km (788 sq miles)
Population : 1,112,640
Capital : Port Louis
Form of government : Republic
Religions : Hinduism, RC, Sunni Islam
Currency : Mauritian rupee

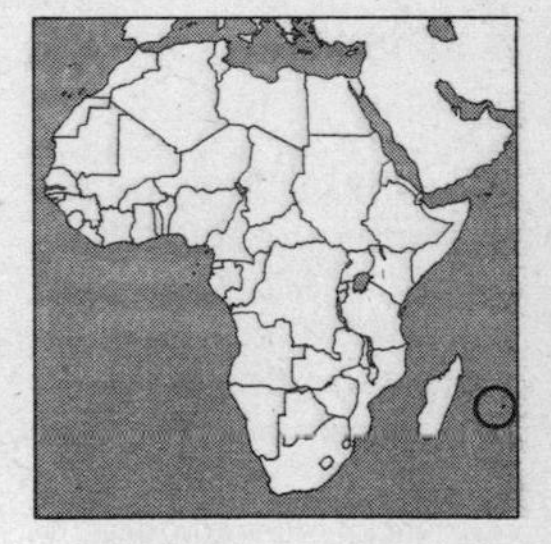

Mexico, the most southerly country in North America, has its longest border with the USA. to the north, a long coast on the Pacific Ocean and a smaller coast in the west of the Gulf of Mexico. It is a land of volcanic mountain ranges and high plateaux. The highest peak is Citlaltepetl, 5699 m (18,697 ft), which is permanently snow-capped. Coastal lowlands are found in the west and east. Its wide range of latitude and relief produce a variety of climates. In the north there are arid and semi-arid conditions while in the south there is a humid tropical climate. 30% of the labour force is involved in agriculture growing maize, wheat, kidney beans and rice for subsistence and coffee, cotton, fruit and vegetables for export although some irrigation is needed. Mexico has substantial and varied mineral deposits such as silver, coal, phosphates, gold uranium as well as large reserves of oil and natural gas. Forests cover around a quarter of the country with trees such as ebony, mahogany and walnut. Developing industries are petrochemicals, textiles, motor vehicles and food processing.

Quick facts:
Area : 1,958,201 sq km (756,061 sq miles)
Population : 93,469,800
Capital : México City
Other major cities : Guadalajara, León, Monterrey, Puebla, Tijuana
Form of government : Federal Republic
Religion : RC
Currency : Mexican peso

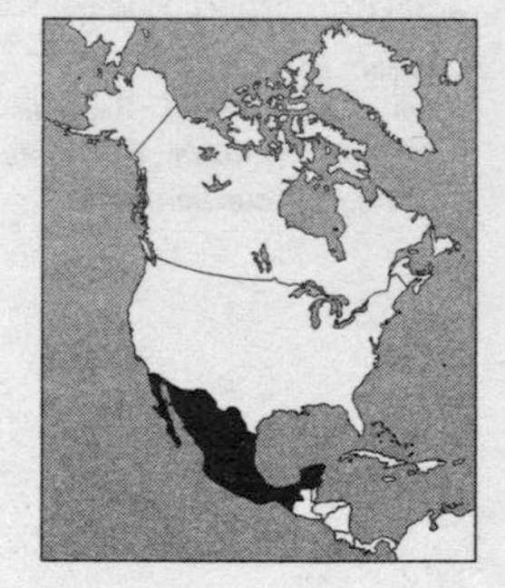

Micronesia, Federated States of formerly part of the US administered UN Trust Territory of the Pacific, known as the Caroline Islands, this self-governing republic became independent in 1991. It comprises an archipelago of over 600 islands, including Pohnpei (Ponape), Truk (Churk) Islands, Yap Islands and Kosrae, mostly uninhabited, they are located in the western Pacific Ocean 1600 km (1000 miles) north of PAPUA NEW GUINEA. The climate is tropical maritime, with high temperatures and rainfall all year round, but a pronounced precipitation peak between July and October. Micronesia is still closely linked to the USA, with a heavy reliance on aid. Attempts are being made to diversify the economy whose exports are mainly fishing and copra. There are significant phosphate deposits but the island's isolation restricts development.

Quick facts:
Area : 701 sq km (271 sq miles)
Population : 125,350
Capital : Kolonia (on Pohnpei), but a new capital is under construction to the southwest
Form of government :Republic
Religion : Christianity
Currency : US dollar

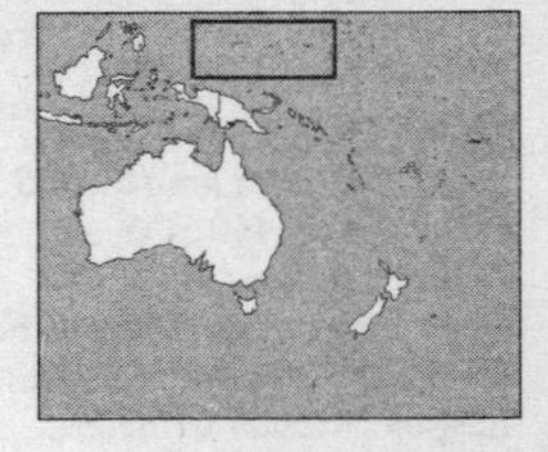

Moldova (Moldavia) was a Soviet socialist republic from 1940 until 1991 when it became independent of the former USSR. It is bounded to the west by ROMANIA and to the north, east and south by UKRAINE. The republic consists of a hilly plain that rises to 429 m (1408 ft) in the centre. Its main rivers are the Prut in the west and the Dniester in the north and east. Moldova's soils are fertile, and crops grown include wheat, corn, barley, tobacco, sugar beet, soybeans and sunflowers. There are also extensive fruit orchards, vineyards and walnut groves. Wildlife is abundant such as roe deer, weasels, martens and badgers. Bee-keeping and silkworm breeding are widespread throughout the country. Food processing is the main industry, particularly sugar refining and wine making. Other industries include metal working, engineering and the manufacture of electrical equipment. After independence the economy declined, inflation soared and assistance was gained from the IMF and others.

Quick facts:
Area : 33,700 sq km (13,000 sq miles)
Population : 4,460,500
Capital : Kishinev
Other major cities : Tiraspol, Bendery, Beltsy
Form of government : Republic
Religion : Russian Orthodox
Currency : Leu

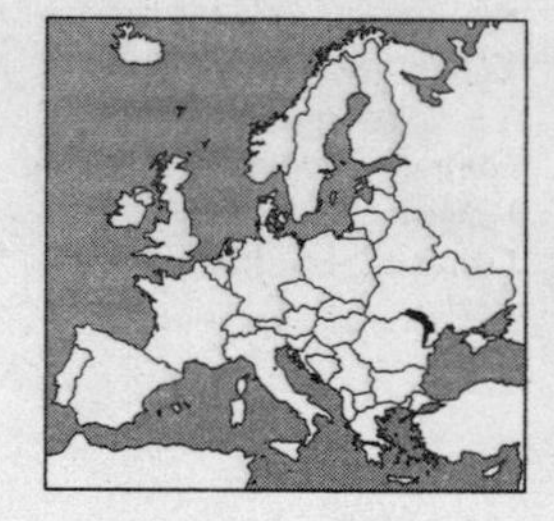

Monaco is a tiny principality on the Mediterranean surrounded landwards by the Alpes Maritimes department of FRANCE. It comprises a rocky peninsula and a narrow stretch of coast. It has mild moist winters and hot dry summers. The ancient fortified town of Monaco-Ville is situated on a rocky promontory and houses the royal palace and the cathedral. The Monte Carlo district has its world-famous casino and La Condamine has thriving businesses, shops, banks and attractive residential areas. Fontvieille is an area reclaimed from the sea where marinas and light industry are now located. Light industry includes chemicals, plastics, electronics, engineering and paper but it is tourism that is the main revenue earner. The sale of stamps, tobacco, insurance and banking industries also contribute to the economy. Well-known annual events such as the Monte Carlo Rally and Monaco Grand Prix are held in the principality.

Quick facts:
Area : 1.95 sq km/(0.75 sq miles)
Population : 31,300
Capital : Monaco-Ville
Form of government : Constitutional Monarchy
Religion : RC
Currency : French Franc

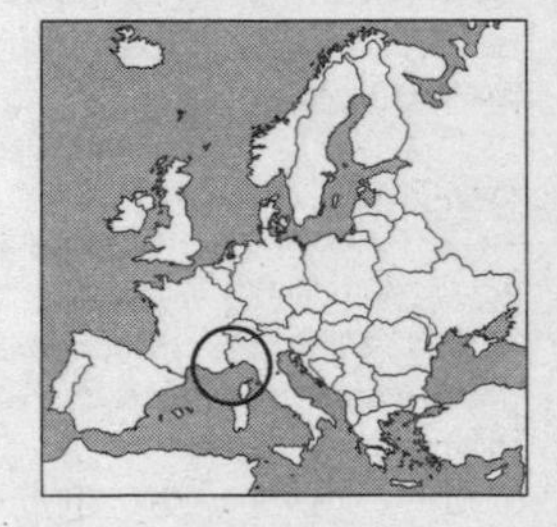

Mongolia is a landlocked country in north-east Asia which is bounded to the north by the RUSSIAN FEDERATION and by CHINA to the south, west and east. Most of Mongolia is mountainous and over 1500 m (4922 ft) above sea level. In the north-west are the Hangayn Mountains and the Altai, rising to 4362 m (14,312 ft). In the south there are grass-covered steppes and desert wastes of the Gobi. The climate is very extreme and dry. For six months the temperatures are below freezing and the summers are mild. Mongolia has had a nomadic pastoral economy for centuries and cereals, including fodder crops, are grown on a large scale on state farms. Its main imports include consumer goods, machinery and transport equipment. Industry is small-scale and dominated by food processing. Although not fully exploited, Mongolia has varied mineral resources such as iron, copper, coal, uranium, silver and gold. The collapse of trade with the former Soviet Union has created severe economic problems and Mongolia is increasingly looking to Japan and China for trade and economic assistance.

Quick facts:
Area : 1,566,500 sq km (604,826 sq miles)
Population : 2,313,400
Capital : Ulan Bator (Ulaanbaatar)
Other major cities : Darhan, Erdenet
Form of govt : Republic
Religion : Buddhist, Shamanist, Muslim
Currency : Tughrik

Morocco, in north-west Africa, is strategically placed at the western entrance to the Mediterranean Sea. It is a land of great contrasts with high rugged mountains, the arid Sahara and the green Atlantic and Mediterranean coasts. The country is split from south-west to north-east by the Atlas mountains. The north has a pleasant Mediterranean climate with hot dry summers and mild moist winters. Farther south winters are warmer and summers even hotter. Snow often falls in winter on the Atlas mountains. Morocco is mainly a farming country, wheat, barley and maize are the main food crops and it is one of the world's chief exporters of citrus fruit although agriculture accounts for less than 20% of the land use. Morocco's main wealth comes from phosphates, reserves of which are the largest in the world while coal, lead, iron and manganese ores are also produced. The economy is very mixed. Morocco is self-sufficient in textiles, it has car assembly plants, soap and cement factories and a large sea fishing industry. Tourism is a major source of revenue as are remittances sent home by Moroccans who work abroad.

Quick facts:
Area : 446,550 sq km (172,413 sq miles)
Population : 27,139,900
Capital : Rabat
Other major cities : Casablanca, Fez, Marrakech, Tangier
Form of government : Constitutional Monarchy
Religion : Sunni Islam
Currency : Dirham

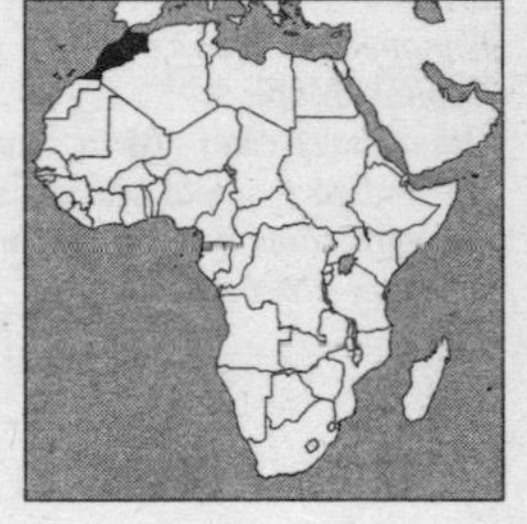

Mozambique is a republic located in south-east Africa and is one of the world's poorest. A coastal plain covers most of the southern and central territory, giving way to the western highlands and north to a plateau including the Nyasa Highlands. The Zambezi river separates the high plateaux in the north from the lowlands in the south. The country has a humid tropical climate with highest temperatures and rainfall in the north. Normally conditions are reasonably good for agriculture but a drought in the early 1980s, followed a few years later by severe flooding, resulted in famine and more than 100,000 deaths. A lot of industry was abandoned when the Portuguese left the country and, due to lack of expertise, was not taken over by the local people. The economy is now on the upturn although the drought and subsequent costs of the civil war such as rehoming the many displaced persons have severely hampered matters. This also has led to a black market which now accounts for a sizeable part of the economy. Forestry is mainly unexploited while fishing for lobster and shrimp are an important source of export revenue.

Quick facts:
Area : 801,590 sq km (309,494 sq miles)
Population : 17,283,000
Capital : Maputo
Other major cities : Beira, Nampula
Form of government : Republic
Religions : Animism, RC, Sunni Islam
Currency : Metical

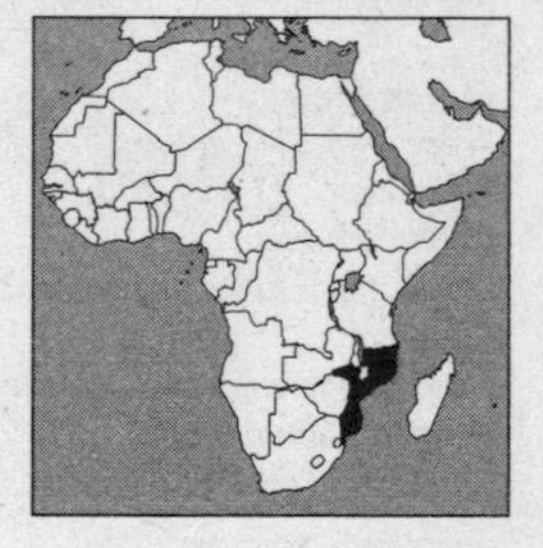

Myanmar the Union of Myanmar (formerly Burma) is the second largest country in South-East Asia. The heartland of the country is the valley of the Irrawaddy. The north and west of the country are mountainous and in the east the Shan Plateau runs along the border with THAILAND. The climate is equatorial at the coast, changing to tropical monsoon over most of the interior. The Irrawaddy river flows into the Andaman Sea, forming a huge delta area which is ideal land for rice cultivation. Rice is the country's staple food and accounts for half the country's export earnings. Tropical fruits such as bananas, mangoes, citrus and guavas grow well in the fertile coastal regions. Myanmar is rich in timber and mineral resources such as natural gas, petroleum, jade and natural rubies, but because of poor communications, lack of development and unrest among the ethnic groups, the resources have not been fully exploited although this has contributed to the preservation of the country's natural environment.

Quick facts:
Area : 676,552 sq km (261,218 sq miles)
Population : 44,863,000
Capital : Yangon (formerly Rangoon)
Other major cities : Mandalay, Moulmein, Pegu
Form of government : Republic
Religion : Buddhism
Currency : Kyat

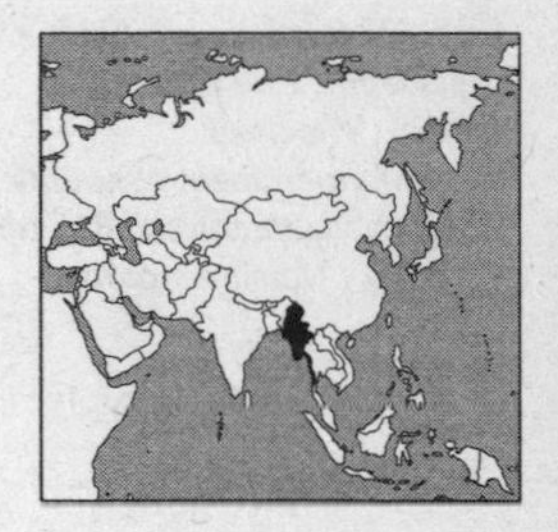

Namibia is situated on the Atlantic coast of south-west Africa. There are three main regions in the country. Running down the entire Atlantic coastline is the Namib Desert, east of which is the Central Plateau of mountains, rugged outcrops, sandy valleys and poor grasslands. East again and north is the Kalahari Desert. Namibia has a poor rainfall, the highest falling at Windhoek, the capital. Even here it only amounts to 200–250 mm (8–10 inches) per year. It is essentially a stock-rearing country with sheep, cattle and goats raised with subsistence agriculture mainly in the north. Diamonds are mined just north of the River Orange, as are other minerals such as silver, lead, uranium and copper. Namibia's output of diamonds amounts to almost a third of the world's total. One of Africa's richest fishing grounds lies off the coast of Namibia, and mackerel, anchovies and pilchards are an important export although production has dropped in recent years due to overfishing.

Quick facts:
Area : 824,292 sq km (318,259 sq miles)
Population : 1,649,000
Capital : Windhoek
Form of government : Republic
Religions : Lutheranism, RC, other Christianity
Currency : Namibian dollar

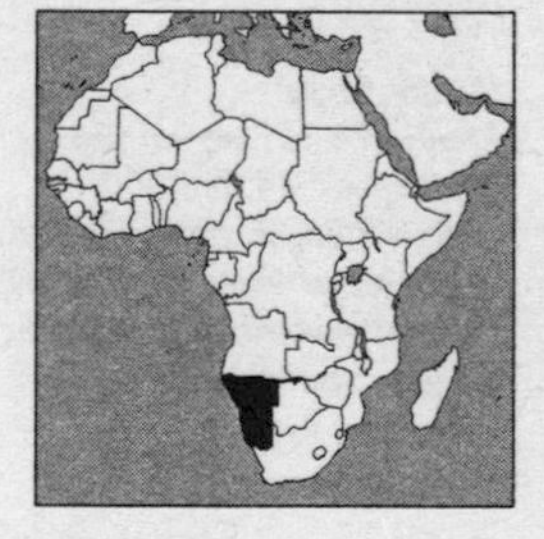

Nauru is the world's smallest republic. It is an island situated just 40 km (25 miles) south of the Equator and is halfway between AUSTRALIA and HAWAII. It is an oval-shaped coral island only 20 km (12 miles) in diameter and is surrounded by a reef. The centre of the island comprises a plateau which rises to 60 m (197 ft) above sea level. The majority of the population live along a narrow coastal belt of fertile land. The climate is tropical with a high and irregular rainfall. The country is rich, due entirely to the deposits of high quality phosphate rock in the central plateau. This is sold for fertilizer to AUSTRALIA, NEW ZEALAND, JAPAN and South KOREA. Phosphate deposits are likely to be exhausted around 2000 but the government is investing overseas and attempting to diversify to ensure the economic future of the country. Since around 80% of the land will be uninhabitable once the mines are exhausted, considerable rehabilitation will be required.

Quick facts:
Area : 21 sq km (8 sq miles)
Population : 11,680
Capital : Yaren
Form of government : Republic
Religions : Protestantism, RC
Currency : Australian dollar

Nepal is a long narrow rectangular country, landlocked between CHINA and INDIA on the flanks of the eastern Himalayas. Its northern border runs along the mountain tops. In this border area is Everest at 8848 m (29,028 ft), the highest mountain in the world, and Nepal also has the six other highest mountains within its borders. The climate is subtropical in the south, and all regions are affected by the monsoon. Nepal is one of the world's poorest and least developed countries, with most of the population trying to survive as peasant farmers. Some mineral deposits such as copper, iron ore, mica and ochre exist but, because of the country's inaccessible terrain, have not been completely charted. However with Indian and Chinese aid roads have been built from the north and south to Kathmandu. The construction of hydroelectric power schemes is underway although at a high cost. Nepal's main exports are carpets, foodstuffs, clothing and leather goods with principal sources of foreign revenue being tourism and Gurkha soldiers' foreign earnings.

Quick facts:

Area : 140,800 sq km (54,362 sq miles)
Population : 20,831,200 Capital : Kathmandu
Other major cities : Bhaktapur, Biratnagar, Lalitpur
Form of government : Constitutional Monarchy
Religion : Hinduism, Buddhism
Currency : Nepalese rupee

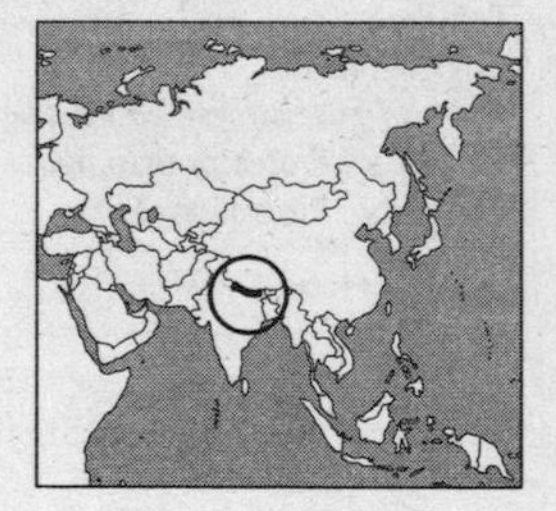

Netherlands, The situated in north-west Europe, the Netherlands is bounded to the north and west by the North Sea. Around one half of the Netherlands is below sea level and the Dutch have tackled some huge reclamation schemes to add some land area to the country. One such scheme is the IJsselmeer, where four large areas (polders) reclaimed have added an extra 1650 sq km (637 sq miles) for cultivation and an overspill town for Amsterdam. The Netherlands has mild winters and cool summers. Natural vegetation is now confined mainly to grasses and heathers with small areas of beech, ash, pine and oak forests being carefully maintained. Migratory birds visit the new habitats created by land reclamation. Agriculture and horticulture are highly mechanized, and the most notable feature is the sea of glass under which salad vegetables, fruit and flowers are grown. Manufacturing industries include chemicals, machinery, petroleum, refining, metallurgy and electrical engineering. The main port of the Netherlands, Rotterdam, is the largest in the world.

Quick facts:
Area : 37,330 sq km (15,770 sq miles)
Population : 15,495,600
Capital : Amsterdam
Seat of government : The Hague (Den Haag, 's-Gravenhage)
Other major cities : Eindhoven, Rotterdam
Form of government : Constitutional Monarchy
Religions : RC, Dutch reformed, Calvinism
Currency : Guilder

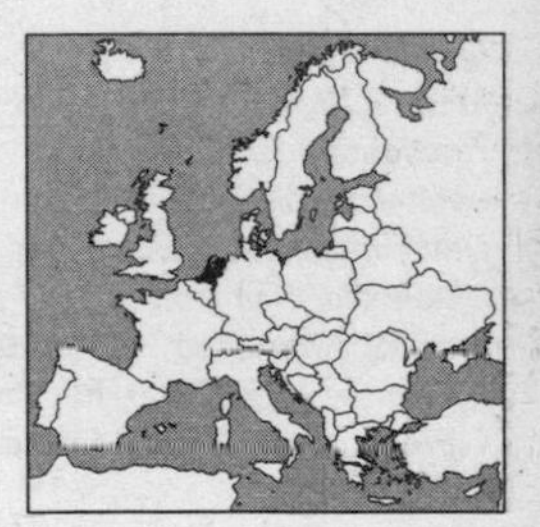

New Zealand lies south-east of AUSTRALIA in the South Pacific. It comprises two large islands, North Island and South Island, Stewart Island and the Chatham Islands with the vast majority of the population living on North Island. New Zealand enjoys very mild winters with regular rainfall and no extremes of heat or cold. North Island is hilly with isolated mountains, active volcanoes, hot mineral springs and geysers. Earthquakes occur and in 1987 considerable damage was caused by one at Edgecumbe. On South Island the Southern Alps run north to south, and the highest point is Mount Cook at 3753 m (12,313 ft). The Canterbury Plains lie to the east of the mountains. Two-thirds of New Zealand is suitable for agriculture and grazing, meat, wool and dairy goods being the main products. Forestry supports the pulp and paper industry and a considerable source of hydroelectric power produces cheap electricity for the manufacturing industry which now accounts for 30% of New Zealand's exports. Mining is also an important industry with petroleum, natural gas, limestone, gold and iron ore being exploited.

Quick facts:

Area : 270,986 sq km (104,629 sq miles)
Population : 3,551,900
Capital : Wellington
Other major cities : Auckland, Christchurch, Dunedin, Hamilton
Form of government : Constitutional Monarchy
Religions : Anglicanism, RC, Presbyterianism
Currency : New Zealand dollar

Nicaragua lies between the Pacific Ocean and the Caribbean Sea, on the isthmus of Central America, and is sandwiched between HONDURAS to the north and COSTA RICA to the south. The east coast contains forested lowland and is the wettest part of the island. Behind this is a range of volcanic mountains and the west coast is a belt of savanna lowland running parallel to the Pacific coast. The western region, which contains the two huge lakes, Nicaragua and Managua, is where most of the population live. The whole country is subject to devastating earthquakes. Nicaragua is primarily an agricultural country and 65% of the labour force work on the land. The main export crops are coffee, bananas, cotton, meat and gold. There are mineral deposits of gold, copper and silver with gold being of prime importance but the country's economy is dependent on foreign aid.

Quick facts:
Area : 130,000 sq km (50,193 sq miles)
Population : 4,492,550
Capital : Managua
Form of government : Republic
Religion : RC
Currency : Córdoba

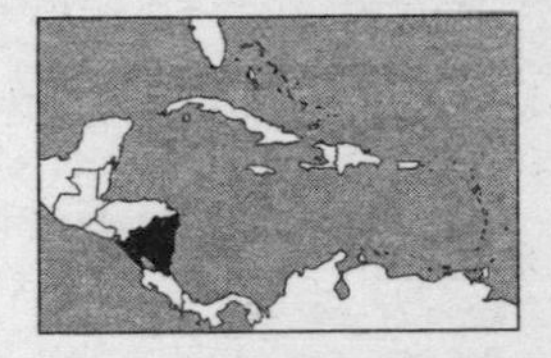

Niger is a landlocked republic in west Africa, just south of the Tropic of Cancer. Over half of the country is covered by the encroaching Sahara Desert in the north, and the south lies in the drought-stricken Sahel. In the extreme south-west corner, the river Niger flows through the country, and in the extreme south-east lies Lake Chad, but the rest of the country is very short of water. The people in the south-west fish and farm their own food, growing rice and vegetables on land flooded by the river. Farther from the river, crops have failed as a result of successive droughts since 1968. Niger is an agricultural country, mainly of subsistence farmers, with the raising of livestock being the major activity. It has recovered from the disastrous droughts and exports cotton and cowpeas, although uranium mined in the Aïr Mountains is Niger's main export.

Quick facts:
Area : 1,267,000 sq km (489,189 sq miles)
Population : 9,137,800
Capital : Niamey
Other major cities : Agadez, Maradi, Tahoua, Zinder
Form of govt : Republic
Religion : Sunni Islam
Currency : CFA Franc

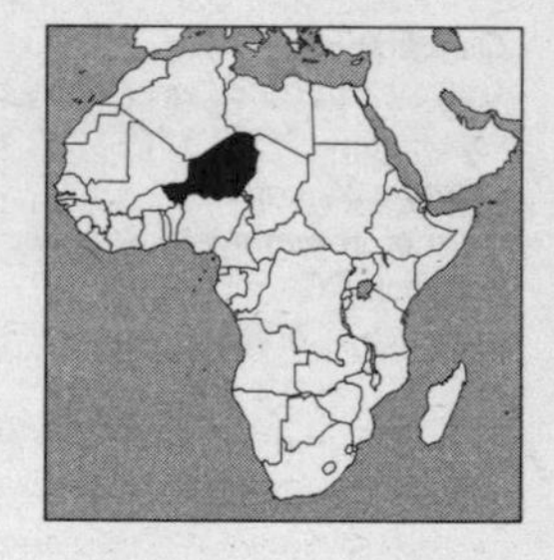

Nigeria is a large and populous country in west Africa, and from the Gulf of Guinea it extends north to the border with Niger. It has a variable landscape, from the swampy coastal areas and tropical forest belts of the interior, to the mountains and savanna of the north. The two main rivers are the Niger and the Benue, and just north of their confluence lies the Jos Plateau. The climate is hot and humid and rainfall, heavy at the coast, gradually decreases inland. The dry far north is affected by the Harmattan, a hot dry wind blowing from the Sahara. About three-quarters of the land is suitable for agriculture and a wide variety of crops is raised by the subsistence farmers, mainly on small, family-owned farms. The main agricultural products are cocoa, rubber, groundnuts and cotton with only cocoa being of any export significance. The country depends on revenue from its crude petroleum exports which have a low sulphur content and therefore produce less air pollution – this fact makes it attractive to American and European countries.

Quick facts:
Area : 923,768 sq km (356,667 sq miles)
Population : 123,159,800
Capital : Abuja (New Federal Capital)
Lagos (Capital until 1992)
Other major cities : Aba, Ede, Enugu, Ibadan, Kano, Ogbomosho
Form of government : Federal republic
Religions : Sunni Islam, Christianity
Currency : Naira

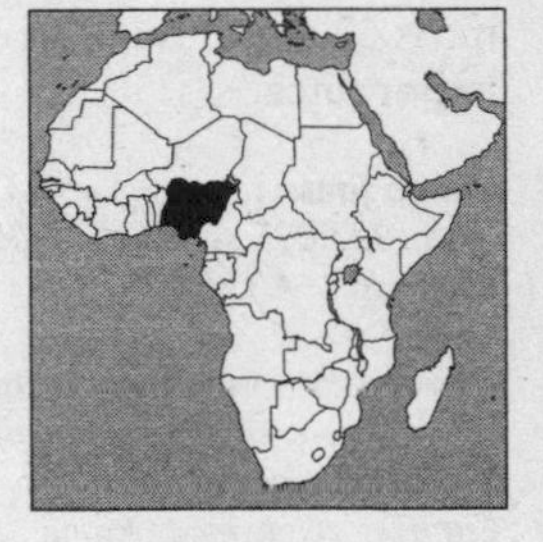

Norway occupies the western half of the Scandinavian peninsula in northern Europe, and is surrounded to the north, west and south by water. It shares most of its eastern border with SWEDEN and almost one third of the country is north of the Arctic Circle. It is a country of spectacular scenery of fjords, cliffs, rugged uplands and forested valleys. Two-thirds of the country is over 600 m (1969 ft), it has some of the deepest fjords in the world and has a huge number of glacial lakes. The climate is temperate as a result of the warming effect of the Gulf Stream. Summers are mild and although the winters are long and cold, the waters off the west coast remain ice-free. The country's longest river is the Glomma. Some southern lakes are affected by acid rain which concerns the country's environmentalists. Agriculture is chiefly concerned with dairying and fodder crops. Fishing is an important industry and the large reserves of forest, which cover just over a quarter of the country, provide timber for export. Industry is now dominated by petrochemicals based on the reserves of Norwegian oil in the North Sea. There are almost 60 airports in the country and transport by water is still of importance.

Quick facts:
Area : 323,895 sq km (125,056 sq miles)
Population : 4,356,400
Capital : Oslo
Other major cities : Bergen, Trondheim, Stavanger
Form of government : Constitutional Monarchy
Religion : Lutheranism
Currency : Norwegian krone

Oman situated in the south-east of the Arabian peninsula, Oman is a small country in two parts. It comprises a small mountainous area, overlooking the Strait of Hormuz, which controls the entrance to The Gulf, and the main part of the country, consisting of barren hills rising sharply behind a narrow coastal plain. Inland the hills extend into the unexplored Rub' al Khali (The Empty Quarter) in SAUDI ARABIA. Oman has a desert climate with exceptionally hot and humid conditions from April to October and as a result of the extremely arid environment, less than 1% of the country is cultivated, the main produce being dates and limes which are exported. The economy is almost entirely dependent on oil, providing 90% of its exports although there are deposits of asbestos, copper and marble and a smelter at Sohar. Over 15% of the resident population is made up by foreign workers. There are no political parties in Oman and the judicial system is centred on the law of Islam.

Quick facts:
Area : 212,457 sq km (82,030 sq miles)
Population : 2,105,600
Capital : Muscat (Musqat)
Other major city : Matrah
Form of government : Monarchy (sultanate)
Religion : Ibadi Islam, Sunni Islam
Currency : Rial Omani

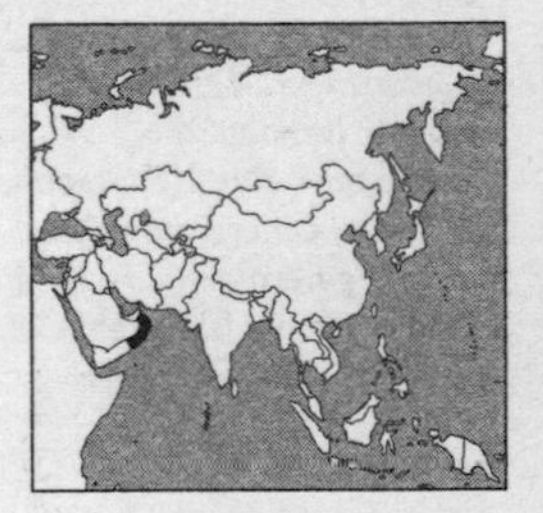

Pakistan lies just north of the Tropic of Cancer and has as its southern border the Arabian Sea. The valley of the Indus river splits the country into a highland region in the west, and a lowland region in the east. A weak form of tropical monsoon climate occurs over most of the country and conditions in the north and west are arid. Temperatures are high everywhere in summer but winters are cold in the mountains. Most agriculture is subsistence, with wheat and rice as the main crops. Cotton and rice are the main cash crops, but the cultivated area is restricted because of waterlogging and saline soils. Pakistan's wide range of mineral resources has not been extensively developed and industry concentrates on food processing, textiles, consumer goods with handicrafts including carpets and pottery. A lack of modern transport due to its mountainous terrain hinders the country's economic progress.

Quick facts:
Area : 796,095 sq km (307,372 sq miles)
Population : 139,862,400
Capital : Islamabad
Other major cities : Faisalabad, Hyderabad, Karachi, Lahore, Rawalpindi
Form of government : Federal Islamic Republic
Religion : Sunni Islam, Shia Islam
Currency : Pakistan rupee

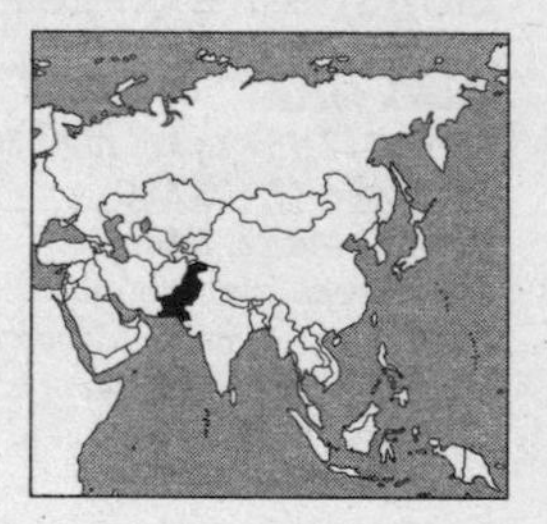

Palau is a republic consisting of a group of approximately 350 islands, lying in the western Pacific, 7° north of the Equator and about 900 km (625 miles) equidistant from New Guinea to the south and the PHILIPPINES to the west. A barrier reef to the west forms a large lagoon dotted with islands. Coral formations and marine life here are amongst the richest in the world. Formerly known as Belau, the republic has an agreement of free association with the USA. The main language is English. Subsistence fishing and agriculture are the mainstays of the economy but there is also some tourism. In addition, natural resources include minerals (particularly gold and seabed deposits) and forests.

Quick facts:
Area : 458 sq km (177 sq miles)
Population : 16,950
Capital : Koror (but a new capital being built)
Form of government : Free Associated Republic
Religion : RC and Modekngei
Currency : US dollar

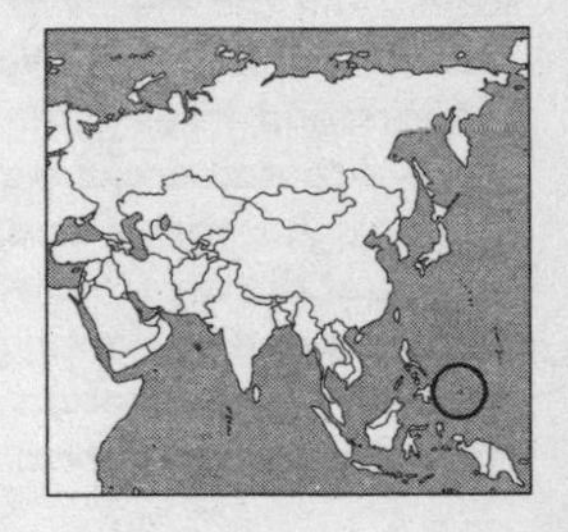

Palestine an ancient historic region on the eastern shore of the Mediterranean Sea, also known as 'The Holy Land' because of its symbolic importance for Christians, Jews and Muslims. It was part of the Ottoman Empire from the early part of the 16th century until 1917, when Palestine was captured by the British. The Balfour Declaration of 1917 increased Jewish hopes that they may be enabled to establish a Jewish state. This was realised in 1948 with the UN creation of the state of Israel. This created hostility among Israel's Arab neighbours and Palestinians indigenous to the area, many of whom left. Since this time the territory has been disputed, leading to a series of wars between the Arabs and Israelis and more recently to conflict between Israeli forces and the Palestine Liberation Organization. The disputed territories are the West Bank, the Gaza Strip, the Golan Heights, and Jerusalem. In 1994 limited autonomy of some of these disputed areas was granted to the appointed Palestinian National Authority, and Israeli military forces began a withdrawal of the area. However, the whole peace process has been compromised by continuing the violent conflict that has erupted since the assassination of the Israeli Prime Minister, Yitzak Rabin, by Jewish extremists in 1995.

Quick facts:
Area : Gaza - 360 sq km (146 sq mi);
Jericho - 70 sq km (27 sq mi);
West Bank - 5860 sq km (2,269 sq mi)
Population : Gaza - 924,200;
Jericho - 20,600;
West Bank - 2,050,000
Form of government : Republic, with limited powers
Religion : Sunni Islam, Shia Islam, Eastern Catholics
Currency : None (Israeli and Jordanian currency used)

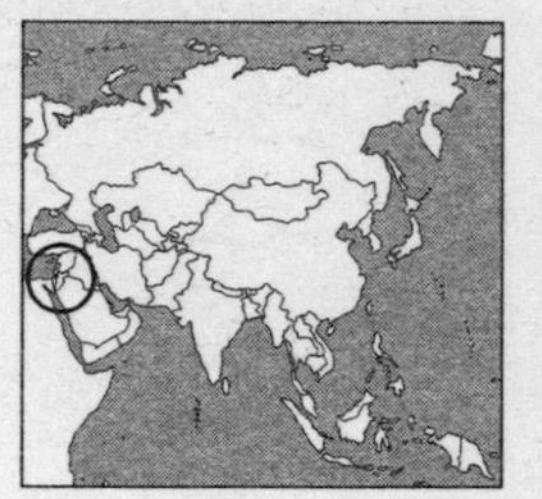

Panama is located at the narrowest point in Central America. Only 58 km (36 miles) separates the Caribbean Sea from the Pacific Ocean at Panama, and the Panama Canal which divides the country is the main routeway from the Caribbean and Atlantic to the Pacific. The climate is tropical with high temperatures throughout the year and only a short dry season from January to April. The country is heavily forested and very little is cultivated. Rice is the staple food. The economy is heavily dependent on the Canal and income from it is a major foreign currency earner. Panama is due to acquire full control of it by 2000. The country has extensive timber resources, and mahogany is an important export. Other exports include petroleum products, coffee, shrimps and raw sugar. In 1989 the country was briefly invaded by US military forces in order to depose the corrupt dictator, General Noriega.

Quick facts:
Area : 77,082 sq km (29,761 sq miles)
Population : 2,629,000
Capital : Panama City
Other major cities : San Miguelito, Colón, David
Form of government : Republic
Religion : RC
Currency : Balboa

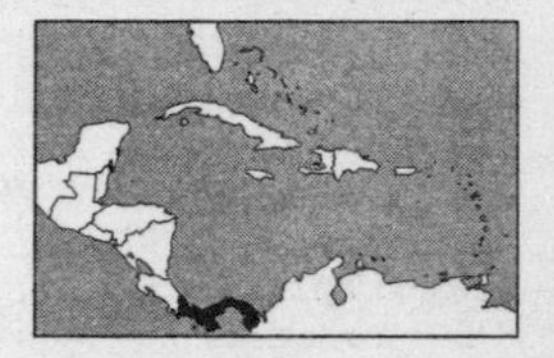

Papua New Guinea in the south-west Pacific, comprises the eastern half of the island of New Guinea, together with hundreds of islands of which New Britain, Bougainville and New Ireland are the largest. There are active volcanoes on some of the islands and mainland and almost 100,000 people were evacuated in 1994 when two erupted on New Britain. The country has a mountainous interior surrounded by broad swampy plains. The climate is tropical with high temperatures and heavy rainfall. Subsistence farming is the main economic activity although some coffee, cocoa and copra are grown for cash. Timber is cut for export and fishing and fish processing industries are developing. The country's wildlife is plentiful and varied while the coastal waters support an abundance of sea life. Minerals such as copper, gold, silver and oil form the mainstay of the economy. The country still receives valuable aid from AUSTRALIA, which governed it before independence was gained in 1975, although there are continuing signs of unrest.

Quick facts:
Area : 462,840 sq km (178,703 sq miles)
Population : 4,213,900
Capital : Port Moresby
Other major cities : Lae, Madang
Form of government : Republic
Religion : Protestantism, RC
Currency : Kina

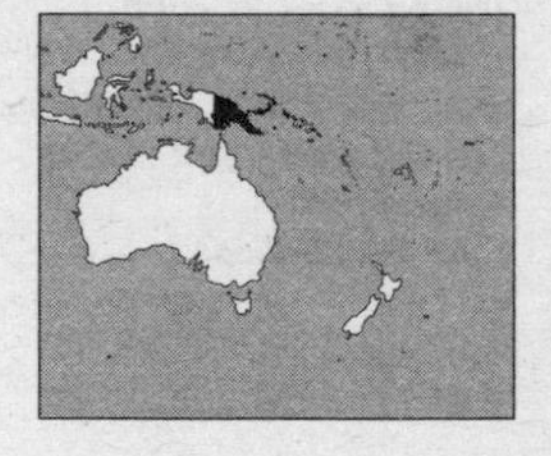

Paraguay, located in central South America, is a country without a coastline and is bordered by BOLIVIA, BRAZIL and ARGENTINA. The climate is tropical with abundant rain and a short dry season. The River Paraguay splits the country into the Chaco, a flat semi-arid plain on the west, and a partly forested undulating plateau on the east. Almost 95% of the population live east of the river, where crops grown on the fertile plains include cassava, sugar cane, maize, cotton and soya beans. Immediately west of the river, on the low Chaco, are huge cattle ranches which provide meat for export. Other livestock raised includes sheep, horses and pigs. Although there are deposits of minerals such as iron, petroleum and manganese these are not exploited commercially. However, the timber industry is important with tannin and petitgrain oil also being produced. The world's largest hydroelectric dam has been built at Itaipú and cheap power from this has stimulated industry. Industry includes food processing, vegetable oil refining, textiles and cement.

Quick facts:
Area : 406,752 sq km (157,047 sq miles)
Population : 5,163,300
Capital : Asunción
Other major cities : Ciudad del Este, Concepción, Coronel Oviedo, Encarnación
Form of government : Republic
Religion : RC
Currency : Guaraní

Peru is located just south of the Equator, on the Pacific coast of South America. The country has three distinct regions from west to east: the coast, the high sierra of the Andes, and the tropical jungle. The climate on the narrow coastal belt is mainly desert, while the Andes are wet, and east of the mountains is equatorial with tropical forests. Most large-scale agriculture is in the oases and fertile, irrigated river valleys that cut across the coastal desert. Sugar and cotton are the main exports. Sheep, llamas, vicuñas and alpacas are kept for wool. The fishing industry was once the largest in the world but recently the shoals have become depleted although anchovies are the bulk of the catch and used to make fish meal. Minerals such as iron ore, silver, copper and lead as well as natural gas and petroleum are extracted in large quantities and are an important part of the economy. The economy in the late 1980s was damaged due to the declining value of exports, inflation, drought and guerrilla warfare which made the government introduce an austerity programme in 1990.

Quick facts:
Area : 1,285,216 sq km (496,235 sq miles)
Population : 25,039,800
Capital : Lima
Other major cities : Arequipa, Callao, Chiclayo, Cuzco, Trujillo
Form of government : Republic
Religion : RC
Currency : Nuevo sol

Philippines comprise a group of islands in the western Pacific which are scattered over a great area. There are four main groups, Luzon and Mindoro to the north, the Visayan Islands in the centre, Mindanao and the Sulu Archipelago in the south, and Palawan in the south-west. Manila, the capital, is on Luzon. Most of the island group is mountainous and earthquakes are common. The climate is humid with high temperatures and high rainfall. Typhoons are frequent. Rice, cassava, sweet potatoes and maize are the main subsistence crops and coconuts, sugar cane, pineapples and bananas are grown for export. Agriculture employs around 42% of the workforce. Mining is an important industry and its main products include gold, silver, nickel, copper and salt. Fishing is of major importance too while there are sponge fisheries by some of the islands. Other prime industries include textiles, food processing, chemicals and electrical engineering.

Quick facts:
Area : 300,439 sq km (116,000 sq miles)
Population : 64,591,300
Capital : Manila
Other major cities : Cebu, Davao, Quezon City, Zamboanga
Form of government : Republic
Religions : Sunni Islam, RC, Animism
Currency : Philippine peso

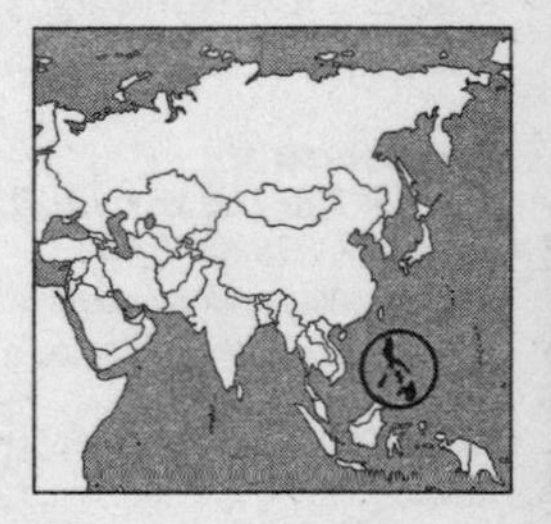

Poland is situated on the North European Plain. It borders GERMANY to the west, the CZECH REPUBLIC and SLOVAKIA to the south and BELARUS and UKRAINE to the east. Poland consists mainly of lowlands and the climate is continental, marked by long severe winters and short warm summers. Over one-quarter of the labour force is involved in predominantly small-scale agriculture. The main crops are potatoes, wheat, barley, sugar beet and fodder crops. The industrial sector of the economy is large scale. Poland has large deposits of coal and reserves of natural gas, copper and silver and is a main producer of sulphur. Vast forests stretching inland from the coast supply the paper and furniture industries. Other industries include food processing, engineering, shipbuilding, textiles and chemicals. The country has serious environmental problems due to factors such as untreated sewage, industrial discharges, air pollution and soil contamination although some progress has been made to rectify matters. Tourism is increasing with the Baltic resorts, mountains and cultural and historic sites being of prime importance.

Quick facts:
Area : 312,677 sq km (120,725 sq miles)
Population : 38,687,200
Capital : Warsaw (Warszawa)
Other major cities : Gdansk, Kraków, Lódz, Poznan, Wroclaw
Form of government : Republic
Religion : RC
Currency : Zloty

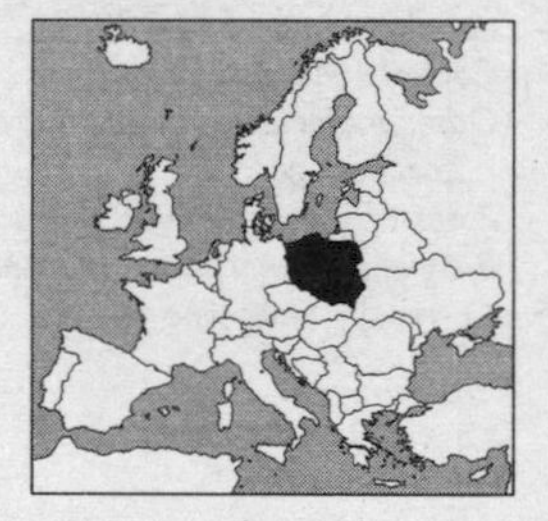

Portugal, in the south-west corner of Europe, makes up about 15% of the Iberian peninsula and is the least developed in western Europe. The most mountainous areas of Portugal lie to the north of the river Tagus. In the north-east are the steep sided mountains of Tras-os-Montes and to south of this the Douro valley, running from the Spanish border to Oporto, on the Atlantic coast. South of the Tagus river is the Alentajo, with its wheat fields and cork plantations, which continues to the hinterland of the Algarve with its beautiful groves of almond, fig and olive trees. Agriculture employs one quarter of the labour force, and crops include wheat, maize, grapes and tomatoes. Portugal's most important natural resources are its minerals, largely developed after World War II, and include coal, iron ore, tin and copper. Port and Madeira wine are renowned and the country is a main exporter of olive oil. Manufacturing industry includes textiles, clothing, footwear, food processing and cork products. Tourism, particularly in the south, is the main foreign currency earner.

Quick facts:
Area : 92,389 sq km (35,671 sq miles)
Population : 10,630,000
Capital : Lisbon (Lisboa)
Other major cities : Braga, Coimbra, Faro, Oporto, Setúbal
Form of government : Republic
Religion : RC
Currency : Escudo

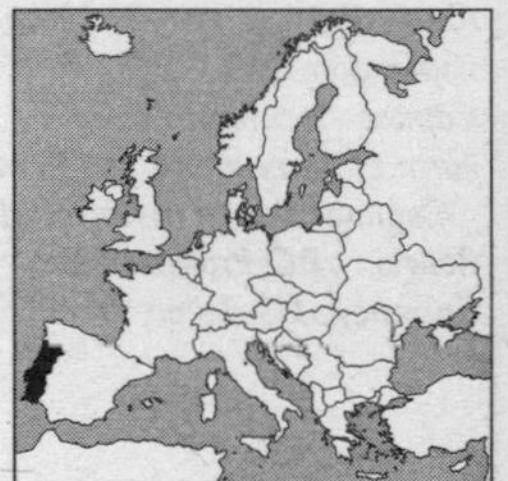

Puerto Rico is the most easterly of the Greater Antilles and lies in the Caribbean between the Dominican Republic and the US Virgin Islands. It is a self-governing commonwealth in association with the USA and includes the main island, Puerto Rico, the two small islands of Vieques and Culebra and a fringe of smaller uninhabited islands. The climate is tropical, modified slightly by cooling sea breezes. The main mountains on Puerto Rico are the Cordillera Central, which reach 1338 m (4390 ft) at the peak of Cerro de Punta. Dairy farming is the most important agricultural activity but the whole agricultural sector has been overtaken by industry in recent years. Tax relief and cheap labour encourages American businesses to be based in Puerto Rico. Products include textiles, clothing, electrical and electronic goods, plastics, pharmaceuticals and petrochemicals. Tourism is another developing industry and there is potential for oil exploration both on and offshore. San Juan is one of the largest and best natural harbours in the Caribbean.

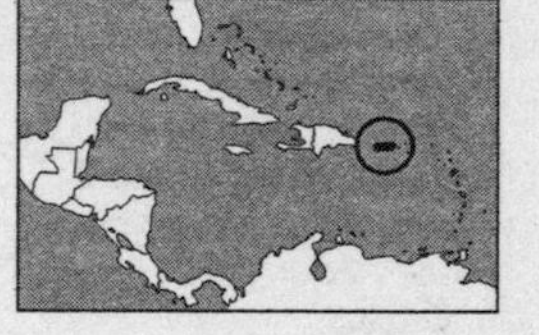

Quick facts:
Area : 8959 sq km (3459 sq miles)
Population : 3,819,600
Capital : San Juan
Form of government : Self-governing Commonwealth (associated with the USA)
Religion : RC, Protestantism
Currency : US dollar

Qatar is a little emirate which lies halfway along the coast of The Gulf. It consists of a low barren peninsula and a few small islands. The climate is hot and uncomfortably humid in summer and the winters are mild with rain in the north. Most fresh water comes from natural springs and wells or from desalination plants. Some vegetables and fruit are grown but the herding of sheep, goats and some cattle is the main agricultural activity. The country is famous for its high quality camels. The discovery and exploitation of oil has resulted in a high standard of living for the people of Qatar with some of the revenue being used to build hospitals, a road system and provide free education and medical care. The Dukhan oil field has an expected life of 40 years and the reserves of natural gas are enormous. In order to diversify the economy, new industries such as iron and steel, cement, fertilizers, and petrochemical plants have been developed.

Quick facts:
Area : 11,430 sq km (4410 sq miles)
Population : 563,400
Capital : Doha (Ad Dawhah)
Form of government : Monarchy
Religions : Wahhabi Sunni Islam
Currency : Qatar riyal

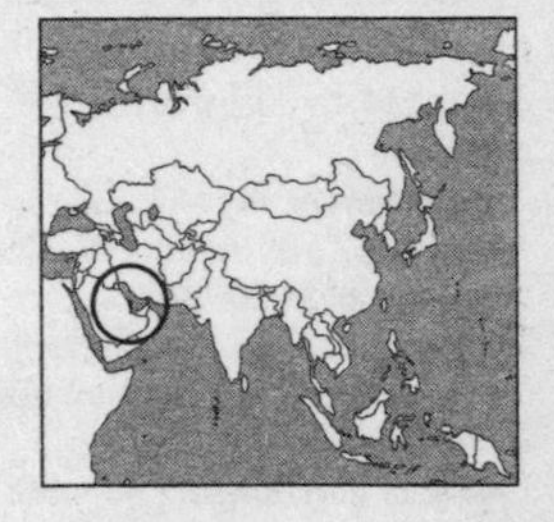

Romania apart from a small extension towards the Black Sea, Romania is almost a circular country. It is located in south-east Europe and bordered by UKRAINE, HUNGARY, SERBIA and BULGARIA. The Carpathian Mountains run through the north, east and centre of Romania and these are enclosed by a ring of rich agricultural plains which are flat in the south and west but hilly in the east. The core of Romania is Transylvania within the Carpathian arc. Romania's main river is the Danube which forms a delta in its lower course. The country has cold snowy winters and hot summers. Agriculture in Romania has been neglected in favour of industry but major crops include maize, sugar beet, wheat, potatoes and grapes for wine. There are now severe food shortages with high unemployment and a low standard of living. Industry is state owned and includes mining, metallurgy, mechanical engineering and chemicals. Forests support timber and furniture making industries in the Carpathians. After the overthrow of the Communist régime in 1989, a new constitution was approved by referendum.

Quick facts:
Area : 237,500 sq km (91,699 sq miles)
Population 23,203,000
Capital : Bucharest (Bucuresti)
Other major cities : Brasov, Constanta, Galati, Iasi, Timisoara
Form of government : Republic
Religions : Romanian Orthodox, RC
Currency : Leu

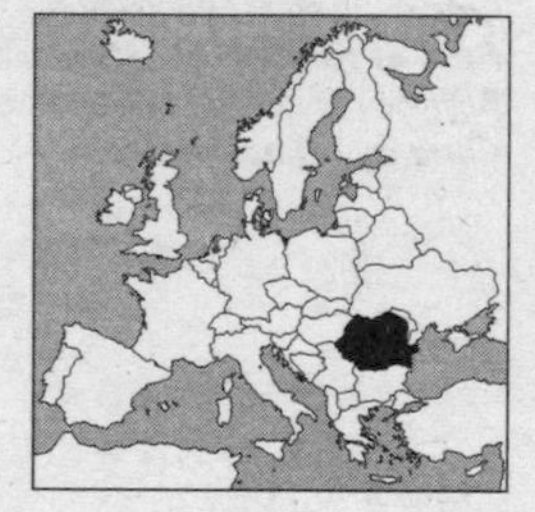

Russian Federation, The, which is the largest country in the world (with over one ninth of the world's land area), extends from Eastern Europe through the Ural Mountains east to the Pacific Ocean. The Caucasus Range forms its boundary with GEORGIA and AZERBAIJAN, and it is here that the highest peak in Europe, Mt Elbrus, is located. In the east, Siberia is drained toward the Arctic Ocean by the great rivers Ob', Yenisey, Lena and their tributaries. Just to the south of the Central Siberian Plateau lies Lake Baikal, the world's deepest freshwater lake, 1637 m (5370 ft). The Ural Mountains form the boundary between Asia and Europe and are where a variety of mineral resources are found. The environment ranges from vast frozen wastes in the north to subtropical deserts in the south. Agriculture is organized into either state or collective farms, which mainly produce sugar beet, cotton, potatoes and vegetables. The country has extensive reserves of coal, oil, gas, iron ore and manganese. Major industries include iron and steel, cement, transport equipment, engineering, armaments, electronic equipment and chemicals. The Russian Federation declared itself independent in 1991. The future is fraught with political and economic uncertainty with major reforms endeavouring to being put into practice.

Quick facts:
Area : 17,075,200 sq km (6,592,800 sq miles)
Population : 149,340,600
Capital : Moscow (Moskva)
Other major cities : St Petersburg (formerly Leningrad), Nizhniy Novgorod, Novosibirsk, Samara
Form of government : Republic
Religions : Russian Orthodox, Sunni Islam, Shia Islam, RC
Currency : Rouble

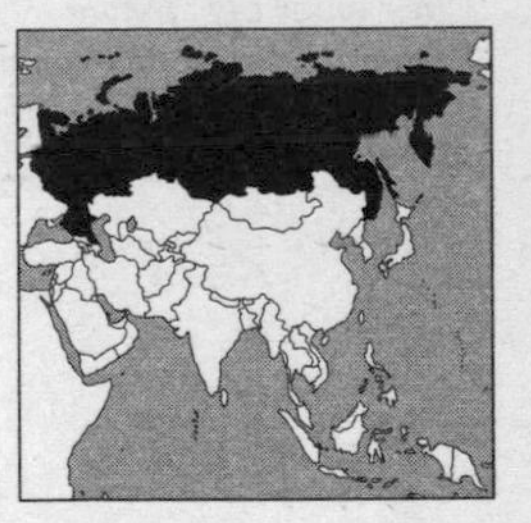

Rwanda is a small republic in the heart of central Africa which lies just 2° south of the Equator. It is a mountainous country with a central spine of highlands from which streams flow west to the Congo river and east to the Nile. Active volcanoes are found in the north where the land rises to about 4500 m (14,765 ft). The climate is highland tropical with temperatures decreasing with altitude. The soils are not fertile and subsistence agriculture dominates the economy. Staple food crops are sweet potatoes, cassava, dry beans, sorghum and potatoes. There are problems of soil erosion, over-grazing and droughts leading to famine, making the country very dependent on foreign aid. Unfortunately, Rwanda also has a very high incidence of AIDS. The main cash crops are arabic coffee, tea and pyrethrum. There are major reserves of natural gas under Lake Kivu in the west, but these are largely unexploited. The country is, however, faced with massive upheaval and disruption of economic life following the tragic tribal genocide wars in 1994 with ethnic division and rivalry between the Hutus and Tutsis continuing.

Quick facts:
Area : 26,338 sq km (10,169 sq miles)
Population : 8,144,900
Capital : Kigali
Other major city : Butare
Form of government : Republic
Religions : RC, Animism
Currency : Rwanda franc

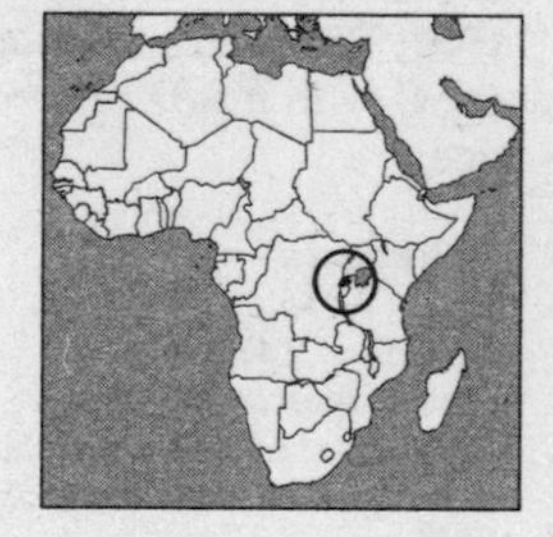

San Marino is a tiny landlocked state in central ITALY, lying in the eastern foothills of the Apennines and is one of the smallest republics in the world. Tradition has it that in AD 301, a Christian sought refuge from persecution on Mount Titano. The resulting community prospered and was recognized in 1291 by Pope Nicholas IV as being independent. San Marino has wooded mountains and pasture land clustered around Mount Titano's limestone peaks which rise to 739 m (2425 ft). San Marino has a mild Mediterranean climate. The majority of the population works on the land or in forestry. Wheat, barley, maize, olives and vines are grown, and the main exports are wood machinery, chemicals, wine, textiles, tiles, varnishes and ceramics while dairy produce is the main agricultural product. Some 3.5 million tourists visit the country each year, and much of the country's revenue comes from the sale of stamps, postcards, souvenirs and duty-free liquor. Italian currency is in general use but San Marino issues its own coins. In 1992 San Marino became a member of the United Nations.

Quick facts:
Area : 61 sq km (24 sq miles)
Population : 25,740
Capital : San Marino
Other major cities : Borgo Maggiore, Serravalle
Form of government : Republic
Religion : RC
Currency : Lira

São Tomé and Príncipe are volcanic islands which lie off the west coast of Africa. São Tomé is covered in extinct volcanic cones, reaching 2024 m (6641 ft) at the highest peak. The coastal areas are hot and humid. Príncipe is a craggy island lying to the north-east of São Tomé. The climate is tropical with heavy rainfall from October to May. 70% of the workforce work on the land, mainly in state-owned cocoa plantations which were nationalized in 1975 after independence. The other main agricultural products are coconuts, melons, copra, bananas and melons. Since crops grown are primarily for export, about 90% of food has to be imported. Small manufacturing industries include food processing and timber products. The islands were colonized by the Portuguese in the 15th century where they settled convicts and other exiles, developed a slave trade and grew sugar cane.

Quick facts:
Area : 964 sq km (372 sq miles)
Population : 133,219
Capital : São Tomé
Form of government : Republic
Religion : RC
Currency : Dobra

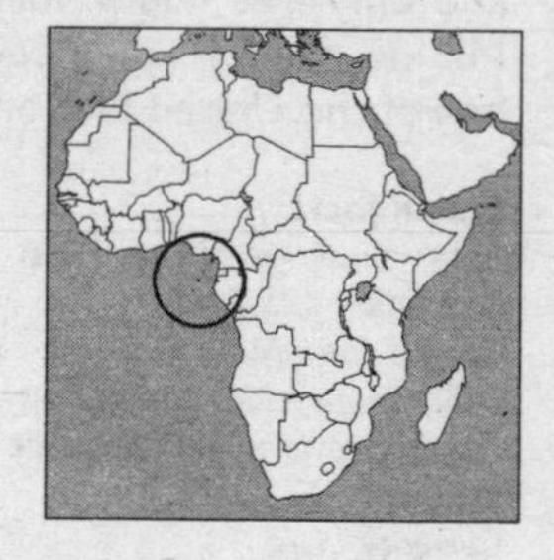

Saudi Arabia occupies over 70% of the Arabian Peninsula. Over 95% of the country is desert and the largest expanse of sand in the world, Rub'al-Khali (The Empty Quarter), is found in the south-east of the country. In the west, a narrow, humid coastal plain along the Red Sea is backed by steep mountains. The climate is hot with very little rain and some areas have no precipitation for years. The government has spent a considerable amount on reclamation of the desert for agriculture, and the main products are dates, tomatoes, watermelons and wheat which are grown in the fertile land around the oases. Saudi Arabia exports wheat and shrimps and is self-sufficient in some dairy products. The country's prosperity, however, is based almost entirely on the exploitation of its vast reserves of oil and natural gas. Industries include petroleum refining, petrochemicals and fertilizers. As a result of the Gulf War in 1990–91, 460 km (285 miles) of the Saudi coastline has been polluted by oil threatening desalination plants and damaging the wildlife of saltmarshes, mangrove forest, and mudflats.

Quick facts:
Area : 2,149,690 sq km (829,995 sq miles)
Population : 18,318,900
Capital : Riyadh
Other major cities : Ad Dammam, Al Jubayl, Jeddah, Mecca, Medina
Form of government : Monarchy
Religions : Sunni Islam, Shia Islam
Currency : Riyal

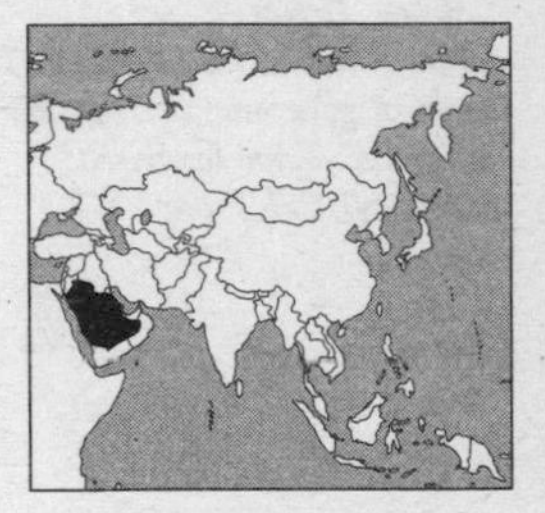

Senegal is a former French colony in West Africa which extends from the most western point in Africa, CAPE VERDE, to the border with MALI. Senegal is mostly low-lying and covered by savanna. The Fouta Djallon mountains in the south rise to 1515 m (4971 ft). The climate is tropical with a dry season from October to June. The most densely populated region is in the southwest. Almost 80% of the labour force work in agriculture, growing peanuts and cotton for export and millet, sugar cane, maize, rice and sorghum as subsistence crops. Increased production of crops such as rice and tomatoes is encouraged in order to achieve self-sufficiency in food. The country's economy is largely dependent on peanuts but there is a growing manufacturing sector including food processing, cement, chemicals and tinned tuna while tourism is also expanding. Senegal is dependent on foreign aid.

Quick facts:
Area : 196,722 sq km (75,954 sq miles)
Population : 8,377,400
Capital : Dakar
Other major cities : Kaolack, Thiès, St Louis
Form of government : Republic
Religions : Sunni Islam, RC
Currency : CFA Franc

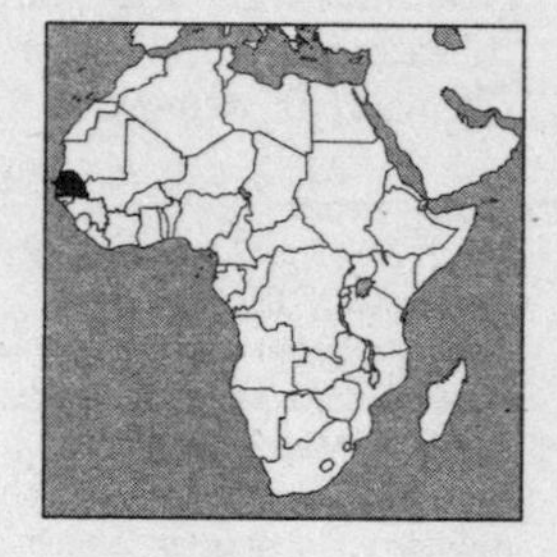

Seychelles are a group of volcanic islands which lie in the western Indian Ocean about 1200 km (746 miles) from the coast of East Africa. About 40 of the islands are mountainous and consist of granite while just over 50 are coral islands. The climate is tropical maritime with heavy rain. About 90% of the people live on the island of Mahé which is the site of the capital, Victoria. The staple food is coconut, imported rice and fish while some fruits are grown for home consumption. Tourism accounts for about 90% of the country's foreign exchange earnings and employs one-third of the labour force. Export trade is based on petroleum (after importation), copra, cinnamon bark and fish. The only mineral resource is guano. The Seychelles were a one party socialist state until 1991, when a new constitution was introduced. The first free elections were held in 1993.

Quick facts:
Area : 455 sq km (175 sq miles)
Population : 74,830
Capital : Victoria
Form of government : Republic
Religion : RC
Currency : Seychelles rupee

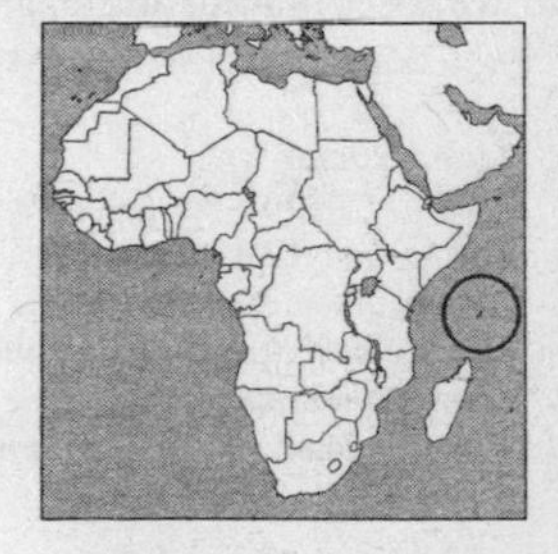

Sierra Leone, on the Atlantic coast of West Africa, is bounded by GUINEA to the north and east and by LIBERIA to the south-east. The coastal areas consist of wide swampy forested plains and these rise to a mountainous plateau in the east. The highest parts of the mountains are just under 2000 m (6562 ft). The climate is tropical with a dry season from November to June. The main food of Sierra Leoneans is rice and this is grown in the swamplands at the coast by the subsistence farmers. Other crops raised include sorghum, cassava, millet, sugar and peanuts. In the tropical forest areas, small plantations produce coffee, cocoa and palm oil. In the plateau much forest has been cleared for growing of groundnuts. Most of the country's revenue comes from agriculture and mining, principally of rutile, although bauxite is produced in significant quantities. Diamonds are also mined, although in much-reduced amounts and there are deposits of iron ore with some gold and platinum.

Quick facts:
Area : 71,740 sq km (27,699 sq miles)
Population : 4,689,900
Capital : Freetown
Other major cities : Bo, Kenema
Form of government : Republic
Religion : Animism, Sunni Islam, Christianity
Currency : Leone

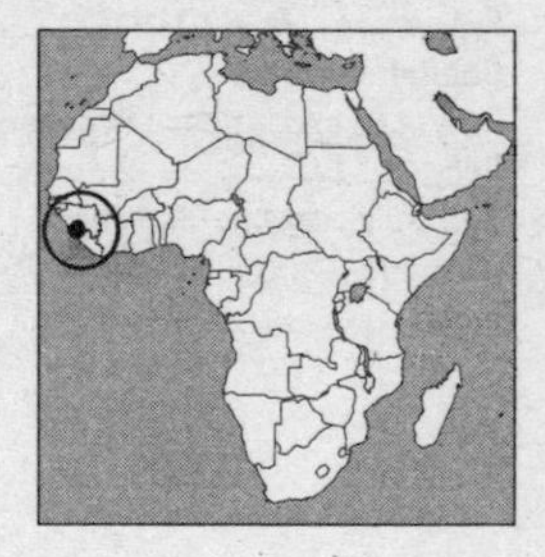

Singapore, one of the world's smallest yet most successful countries, comprises one main island and 59 islets which are located at the foot of the Malay peninsula in South-East Asia. The main island of Singapore is very low-lying, and the climate is hot and wet throughout the year. Only 1.6% of the land area is used for agriculture and most food is imported. The country has a flourishing manufacturing industry for which it relies heavily on imports. Products traded in Singapore include machinery and appliances, petroleum, food and beverages, chemicals, transport equipment, paper products and printing, and clothes. Shipbuilding is also an important industry. The Jurong Industrial Estate on the south of the island has approximately 2,300 companies and employs nearly 141,000 workers. International banking and tourism are important sources of foreign revenue. Singapore's airport is one of the largest in Asia.

Quick facts:
Area : 640 sq km (247 sq miles)
Population : 2,983,400
Capital : Singapore
Form of government : Parliamentary Democracy
Religions : Buddhism, Sunni Islam, Christianity and Hinduism
Currency : Singapore dollar

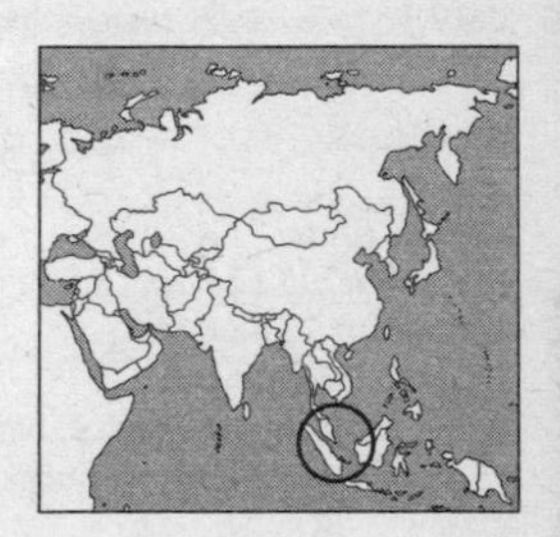

Slovakia (Slovak Republic) was constituted on 1 January, 1993 as a new independent nation, following the dissolution of the 74 year old federal republic of Czechoslovakia. Landlocked in central Europe, its neighbours are the CZECH REPUBLIC to the west, POLAND to the north, AUSTRIA and HUNGARY to the south, and a short border with UKRAINE in the east. The northern half of the republic is occupied by the Tatra Mountains which form the northern arm of the Carpathian Mountains. This region has vast forests and pastures used for intensive sheep grazing, and is rich in high-grade minerals such as copper, iron, zinc and lead. The southern part of Slovakia is a plain drained by the Danube and its tributaries. Farms, vineyards, orchards and pastures for stock form the basis of southern Slovakia's economy. Slovakia has many economic and environmental problems as a legacy of the inefficient industrialisation of the old régime. In the early 1990s unemployment increased and inflation was high, resulting in a lowering in the standard of living. Tourism is now increasing at the ski resorts and historic cities.

Quick facts:
Area : 49,032 sq km (18,931 sq miles)
Population : 5,431,800
Capital : Bratislava
Other major cities : Kosice, Nitra, Presov, Zilind
Form of government : Republic
Religion : RC
Currency : Slovak koruna

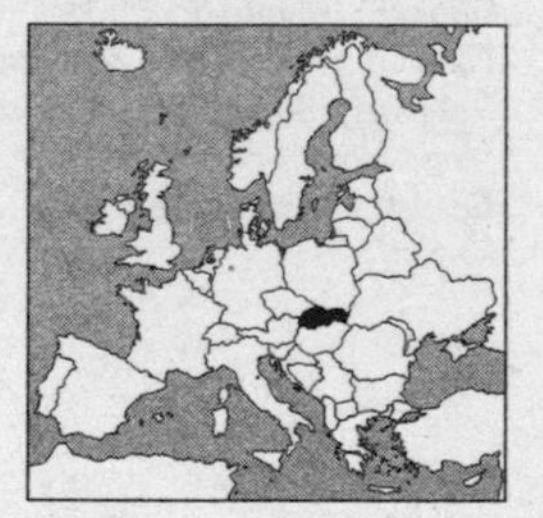

Slovenia is a republic which made a unilateral declaration of independence from former YUGOSLAVIA on 25 June, 1991. Sovereignty was not formally recognized by the European Community and the United Nations until early in 1992. It is bounded to the north by AUSTRIA, to the west by ITALY, to the east by HUNGARY, and to the south by CROATIA. Most of Slovenia is situated in the Karst Plateau and in the Julian Alps which has Mount Triglav as its highest point at 2863 m (9393 ft). Although farming and livestock raising are the chief occupations, Slovenia is very industrialized and urbanized. Iron, steel and aluminium are produced, and mineral resources include oil, coal, lead, uranium and mercury. There is also natural gas and petroleum. Tourism is an important industry. The Julian Alps are renowned for their scenery, and the Karst Plateau contains spectacular cave systems. The north-east of the republic is famous for its wine production. Slovenia has also been successful in establishing many new light industries and this has given the country a well-balanced economic base for the future with unemployment lessening and industrial output increasing.

Quick facts:
Area : 20,251 sq km (7817 sq miles)
Population : 2,132,900
Capital : Ljubljana
Other major cities : Maribor, Celje, Kranj
Form of government : Republic
Religion : RC
Currency : Tolar

Solomon Islands lie in an area between 5° and 12° south of the Equator to the east of PAPUA NEW GUINEA, in the Pacific Ocean. The nation consists of six large islands and innumerable smaller ones. The larger islands are mountainous and covered in forests with rivers prone to flooding. Guadalcanal is the main island and the site of the capital, Honiara. The climate is hot and wet and typhoons are frequent. The main food crops grown are coconut, cassava, sweet potatoes, plantains, yams, rice, taros and bananas. Other products include copra, processed fish, timber and trochus shells. Mineral resources such as phosphate rock and bauxite are found in large amounts and some alluvial gold is produced. Other industries include palm-oil milling, saw milling, food, tobacco and soft drinks. Due to over-logging in the early 1990s it was proposed that a ban be introduced. There are high rates of unemployment and illiteracy among the people.

Quick facts:
Area : 28,896 sq km (11,157 sq mi)
Population : 378,500
Capital : Honiara
Form of government : Constitutional Monarchy
Religions : Anglicanism, RC, other Christianity
Currency : Solomon Island dollar

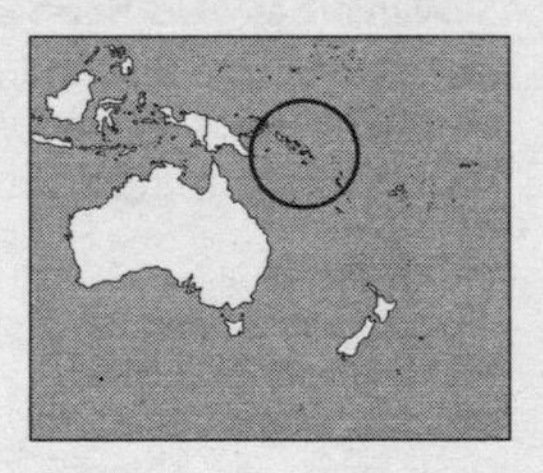

Somalia is shaped like a large number seven and lies on the horn of Africa's east coast. It is bounded north by the Gulf of Aden, south and east by the Indian Ocean, and its neighbours include DJIBOUTI, ETHIOPIA, and KENYA. The country is arid and most of it is low plateaux with scrub vegetation. Its two main rivers, the Juba and Shebelle, are used to irrigate crops. Most of the population lives in the mountains and river valleys and there are a few towns on the coast. The country has little in the way of natural resources but there are deposits of copper, petroleum, iron, manganese and marble although not commercially exploited. Main exports are live animals, meat, hides and skins. A few large-scale banana plantations are found by the rivers. Years of drought have left Somalia heavily dependent on foreign aid, and many of the younger population are emigrating to oil-rich Arab states. Due to the continuing civil war, the country's economy collapsed and there has been devastating famine with international relief being desperately required.

Quick facts:
Area : 637,657 sq km (246,199 sq miles)
Population : 9,986,400
Capital : Mogadishu
Other major cities : Hargeisa, Baidoa, Burao, Kismaayo, Marka
Form of government : Republic
Religion : Sunni Islam
Currency : Somali shilling

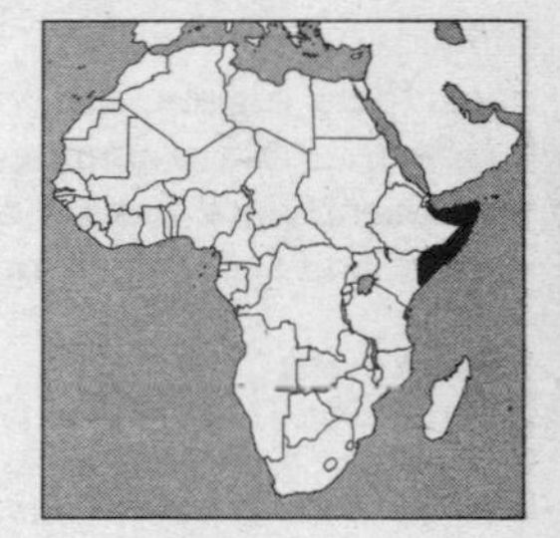

South Africa is a republic that lies at the southern tip of the African continent and has a huge coastline on both the Atlantic and Indian Oceans. The country occupies a huge saucer-shaped plateau, surrounding a belt of land that drops in steps to the sea. The rim of the saucer rises in the east to 3482 m (11,424 ft) in the Drakensberg. In general the climate is healthy, with plenty of sunshine and relatively low rainfall, but varies with latitude, distance from the sea and altitude. Of the total land area 58% is used as natural pasture although soil erosion is a problem. The main crops grown are maize, sorghum, wheat, groundnuts, sugar cane and a drought-resistant variety of cotton. It is South Africa's mineral wealth that overshadows all its other natural resources. These include gold, coal, copper, iron ore, manganese, diamonds and chrome ore. A system of apartheid existed in South Africa from 1948 until the early 1990s during which time it was subjected to international economic and political sanctions. In 1990 F. W. de Klerk, then president, lifted the ban on the outlawed African National Congress and released its leader, Nelson Mandela, from prison. This heralded the dismantling of the apartheid regime, and in the first multi-racial elections, held in 1994, the ANC triumphed, with Mandela voted in as the country's president. Since this time South Africa has once again become an active and recognized member of the international community.

Quick facts:

Area : 1,221,037 sq km (471,442 sq miles)
Population : 43,887,700
Capital : Pretoria (Administrative), Cape Town (Legislative)
Other major cities : Durban, Johannesburg, Port Elizabeth, Port Germiston, Soweto
Form of government : Republic
Religions : Dutch reformed, Independent African, other Christianity, Hinduism
Currency : Rand

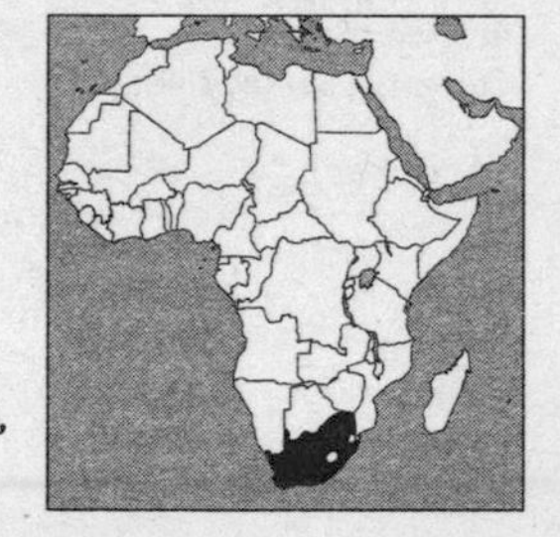

Spain is located in south-west Europe and occupies the greater part of the Iberian peninsula, which it shares with PORTUGAL. It is a mountainous country, sealed off from the rest of Europe by the Pyrénées, which rise to over 3400 m (11,155 ft). Much of the country is a vast plateau, the Meseta Central, cut across by valleys and gorges. Its longest shoreline is the one that borders the Mediterranean Sea. Most of the country has a form of Mediterranean climate with mild moist winters and hot dry summers. Spain's major rivers such as the Douro, Tagus and Guadiana flow to the Atlantic Ocean while the Guadalquivir is the deepest. Although not generally navigable, they are of use for hydroelectric power. Spain's principal agricultural products are cereals, vegetables and potatoes, and large areas are under vines for the wine industry. The soil is good with almost one third cultivable. Livestock production is important, particularly sheep and goats. Industry represents 72% of the country's export value, and production includes textiles, paper, cement, steel and chemicals. Tourism is a major revenue earner, especially from the resorts on the east coast.

Quick facts:
Area : 504,782 sq km (194,896 sq miles)
Population : 39,540,400
Capital : Madrid
Other major cities : Barcelona, Bilbao, Malaga, Seville, Valencia, Zaragosa
Form of government : Constitutional Monarchy
Religion : RC
Currency : Peseta

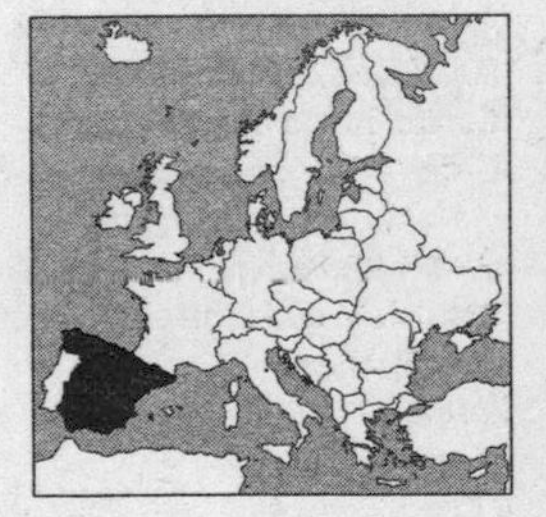

Sri Lanka is a teardrop-shaped island in the Indian Ocean, lying south of the Indian peninsula from which it is separated by the Palk Strait. The climate is equatorial with a low annual temperature range but it is affected by both the north-east and south-west monsoons. Rainfall is heaviest in the south-west while the north and east are relatively dry. Agriculture engages 47% of the work force and the main crops are rice, tea, rubber and coconuts although sugar, rice and wheat have to be imported. Amongst the chief minerals mined and exported are precious and semiprecious stones. Graphite is also important. The main industries are food, beverages and tobacco, textiles, clothing and leather goods, chemicals and plastics. Attempts are being made to increase the revenue from tourism. Politically, Sri Lanka has been afflicted by ethnic divisions between the Sinhalese and Tamils. In the 1980s attempts by the Tamil extremists to establish an independent homeland bought the north-east of the country to the brink of civil war and the situation remains extremely volatile.

Quick facts:
Area : 65,610 sq km (25,332 sq miles)
Population : 18,343,900
Capital : Colombo
Other major cities : Dehiwela-Mt. Lavinia, Moratuwa, Jaffna, Kandy
Form of government : Republic
Religions : Buddhism, Hinduism, Christianity, Sunni Islam
Currency : Sri Lankan rupee

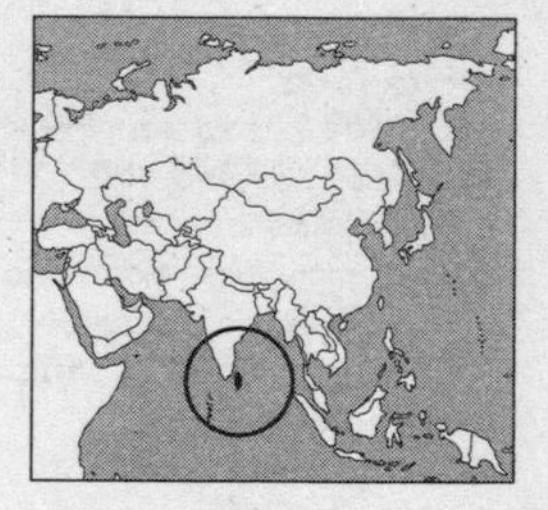

St Christopher (St Kitts) and Nevis, Federation of, the islands of St Christopher (popularly known as St Kitts) and Nevis lie in the Leeward group in the eastern Caribbean. In 1983 it became a sovereign democratic federal state with Elizabeth II as head of state. St Kitts consists of three extinct volcanoes linked by a sandy isthmus to other volcanic remains in the south. The highest point on St. Kitts is Mount Liamuiga, 1315 m (4314 ft) and the islands have a tropical climate. Around most of the island sugar cane is grown on fertile soil covering the gentle slopes. Sugar is the chief export crop but market gardening and livestock are being expanded on the steeper slopes above the cane fields. Some vegetables, coconuts, fruits and cereals are grown. Industry includes sugar processing, brewing, distilling and bottling. St Kitts has a major tourist development at Frigate Bay. Nevis, 3 km (2 miles) south, is an extinct volcano. Farming is declining and tourism is now the main source of income.

Quick facts:
Area : 262 sq km (101 sq miles)
Population : 44,830
Capital : Basseterre
Other major city : Charlestown
Form of government : Constitutional Monarchy
Religions : Anglicanism, Methodism
Currency : East Caribbean dollar

St Lucia is one of the Windward Islands in the eastern Caribbean. It lies to the south of MARTINIQUE and to the north of ST. VINCENT. It was controlled alternately by the French and the British for some 200 years before becoming fully independent in 1979. St Lucia is an island of extinct volcanoes and the highest peak is 950 m (3117 ft). In the west are the peaks of Pitons which rise directly from the sea to over 750 m (2461 ft). The climate is tropical with a rainy season from May to August. The economy depends on the production of bananas and, to a lesser extent, coconuts and mangoes. Production, however, is often affected by hurricanes, drought and disease. There is some manufacturing industry which produces clothing, cardboard boxes, plastics, electrical parts and drinks and the country has two airports. Tourism is increasing in importance and Castries, the capital, is a popular calling point for cruise liners.

Quick facts:
Area : 622 sq km (240 sq miles)
Population : 149,860
Capital : Castries
Form of Government : Constitutional Monarchy
Religion : RC
Currency : East Caribbean dollar

St Vincent and the Grenadines St Vincent is an island of the Lesser Antilles, situated in the eastern Caribbean between St Lucia and Grenada. It is separated from Grenada by a chain of some 600 small islands known as the Grenadines, the northern islands of which form the other part of the country. The largest of these islands are Bequia, Mustique, Canouan, Mayreau and Union. The climate is tropical, with very heavy rain in the mountains. St Vincent Island is mountainous and a chain of volcanoes runs up the middle of the island. The volcano, Soufrière (1234 m/4049 ft), is active and it last erupted in 1979. Farming is the main occupation on the island. Bananas for the UK are the main export, and it is the world's leading producer of arrowroot starch. There is little manufacturing and the government is trying to promote tourism. However, unemployment is high and tropical storms are always a threat to crops.

Quick facts:
Area : 388 sq km (150 sq miles)
Population : 118,300
Capital : Kingstown
Form of government : Constitutional Monarchy
Religions : Anglicanism, Methodism, RC
Currency : East Caribbean dollar

Sudan is the largest country in Africa, lying just south of the Tropic of Cancer in north-east Africa. The country covers much of the upper Nile basin and in the north the river winds through the Nubian and Libyan deserts, forming a palm-fringed strip of habitable land. In 1994, the country was divided into 26 states, compared to the original nine. The climate is tropical and temperatures are high throughout the year. In winter, nights are very cold. Rainfall increases in amount from north to south, the northern areas being virtually desert. Sudan is an agricultural country, subsistence farming accounting for 80% of production and livestock is also raised. Cotton is farmed commercially and accounts for about two-thirds of Sudan's exports. Sudan is the world's greatest source of gum arabic used in medicines, perfumes, processed foods and inks. Other forest products are tannin, beeswax, senna and timber. Due to the combination of years of civil war and drought, Sudan has a large foreign debt estimated to be three times its gross national product.

Quick facts:
Area : 2,505,813 sq km (967,494 sq miles)
Population : 29,975,800
Capital : Khartoum (El Khartum)
Other major cities : Omdurman, Khartoum North, Port Sudan
Form of government : Republic
Religions : Sunni Islam, Animism, Christianity
Currency : Sudanese pound

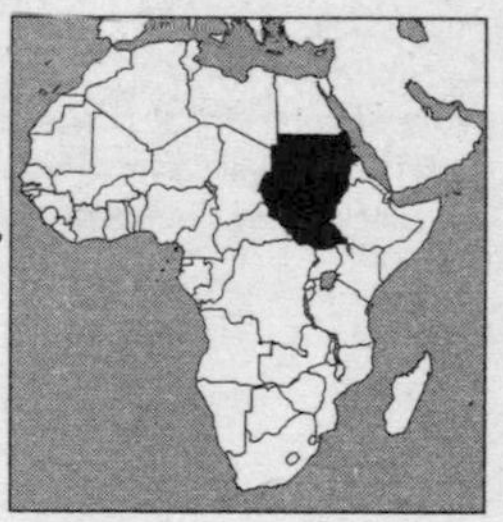

Suriname is a republic in north-east South America, bordered to the west by GUYANA, to the east by GUIANA, and to the south by BRAZIL. The country, formerly a Dutch colony, declared independence in 1975. Suriname comprises a swampy coastal plain, a forested central plateau, and southern mountains. The climate is tropical with heavy rainfall concentrated mainly from December to April. Temperatures at Paramaribo average 26–27°C all year round. Rice, cocoa, fruits, coffee and sugar cane are farmed on the coastal plains but the mining of bauxite is the economy's mainstay and accounts for 80% of exports. There is an increasing amount of fishing along the coast, the main catch being shrimp. Suriname has resources of oil and timber but these are so far under-exploited. The country is politically very unstable and in need of financial aid to develop these resources.

Quick facts:
Area : 163,265 sq km (63,037 sq miles)
Population : 458,200
Capital : Paramaribo
Form of government : Republic
Religions : Hinduism, RC, Sunni Islam
Currency : Suriname guilder

Swaziland is a landlocked hilly enclave almost entirely within the borders of the Republic of SOUTH AFRICA. The mountains in the west of the country rise to almost 2000 m (6562 ft), then descend in steps of savanna toward hilly country in the east. The climate is subtropical moderated by altitude. The land between 400 m (1312 ft) and 850 m (2789 ft) is planted with orange groves and pineapple fields, while on the lower land sugar cane flourishes in irrigated areas. Other important crops are citrus fruits, cotton and pineapples. Forestry is an important industry, production centring mainly on pine since it matures extremely quickly due to Swaziland's climate. Coal is mined and also asbestos although in lessening amounts due to its associated health risks. Manufacturing includes fertilisers, textiles, leather and tableware. Tourism is a growing industry, with the country's game preserves, mountain scenery, spas and casinos proving popular destinations for visitors.

Quick facts:
Area : 17,360 sq km (6716 sq miles)
Population : 857,700
Capital : Mbabane
Other major cities : Big Bend, Manzini, Mhlume, Lobamba
Form of government : Monarchy
Religion : Christianity, Animism
Currency : Lilangeni

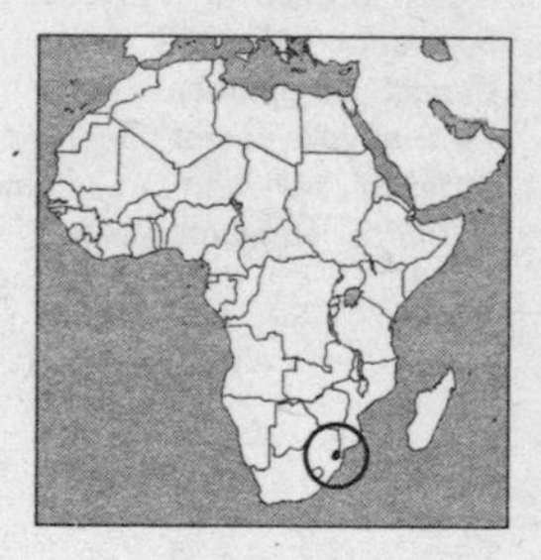

Sweden is a large country in northern Europe which makes up half of the Scandinavian peninsula. It stretches from the Baltic Sea north, to well within the Arctic Circle. The south is generally flat with many lakes, the north mountainous, and along the coast there are over 20,000 islands and islets. Summers are warm but short while winters are long and cold. In the north snow may lie for four to seven months. Dairy farming is the predominant agricultural activity and also the production of livestock including cattle, pigs and sheep. Only 7% of Sweden is cultivated, with the emphasis on fodder crops, potatoes, rape seed, grain and sugar beet. About 57% of the country is covered in forest, and the sawmill, wood pulp and paper industries are all of great importance. Sweden is one of the world's leading producers of iron ore, most of which is extracted from within the Arctic Circle. Other main industries are engineering and electrical goods, motor vehicles and furniture making. In a referendum during 1994, Swedish voters approved of membership to the European Union and became a member on 1st January, 1995.

Quick facts:
Area : 449,964 sq km (173,731 sq miles)
Population : 8,793,400
Capital : Stockholm
Other major cities : Göteborg, Malmö, Uppsala, Orebro, Linköping
Form of government : Constitutional Monarchy
Religion : Lutheranism
Currency : Krona

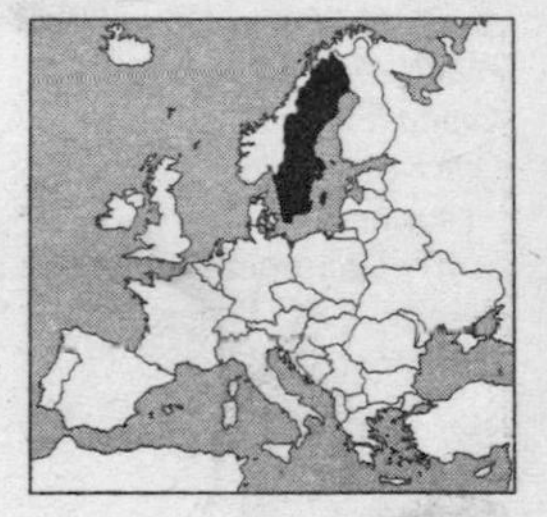

Switzerland is a landlocked country in central Europe, sharing its borders with FRANCE, ITALY, AUSTRIA, LIECHTENSTEIN and GERMANY. The Alps occupy over 70% of the country's area, forming two main east-west chains divided by the rivers Rhine and Rhône. The climate is either continental or mountain type. Summers are generally warm and winters cold, and both are affected by altitude. Northern Switzerland is the industrial part of the country and where its most important cities are located. Basle is famous for its pharmaceuticals and Zürich for electrical engineering and machinery. Although the country has to import much of its raw materials, these have become high-value exports such as clocks, watches and other precision engineering products. It is also in this region that the famous cheeses and chocolates are produced. Hydroelectricity accounts for approximately 60% of its power supplies with most of the remainder coming from nuclear power plants. Switzerland has huge earnings from international finance and tourism.

Quick facts:
Area : 41,288 sq km (15,943 sq miles)
Population : 7,230,600
Capital : Berne
Other major cities : Zürich, Basle, Geneva, Lausanne
Form of government : Federal republic
Religions : RC, Protestantism
Currency : Swiss franc

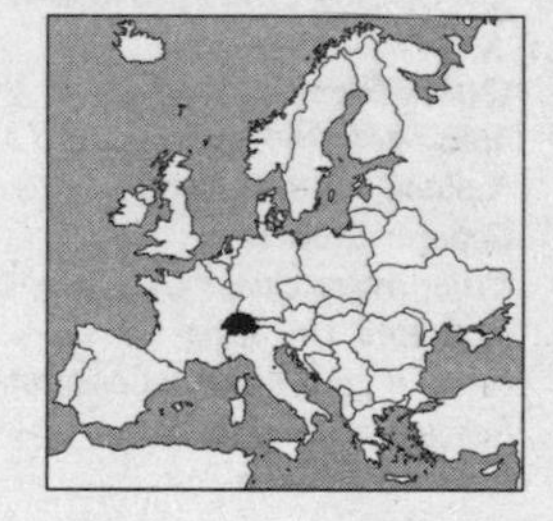

Syria is a country in south-west Asia which borders on the Mediterranean Sea in the west. Much of the country is mountainous behind the narrow fertile coastal plain. The eastern region is desert or semi-desert, a stony inhospitable land. The coast has a Mediterranean climate with hot dry summers and mild wet winters. About 50% of the workforce get their living from agriculture; sheep, goats and cattle are raised and cotton, barley, wheat, tobacco, grapes, olives and vegetables are grown although some land is unused due to lack of irrigation. Reserves of oil are small compared to neighbouring IRAQ but it has enough to make the country self-sufficient and provide three-quarters of the nation's export earnings. Industries such as textiles, leather, chemicals and cement have developed rapidly in the last 20 years with the country's craftsmen producing fine rugs and silk brocades. Foreign revenue is gained from tourism and also from countries who pipe oil through Syria. The country is dependent on the main Arab oil-producing countries for aid.

Quick facts:
Area : 185,180 sq km (71,498 sq miles)
Population : 14,739,900
Capital : Damascus (Dimashq)
Other major cities : Halab, Hims, Latakia, Hamal
Form of government : Republic
Religion : Sunni Islam
Currency : Syrian pound

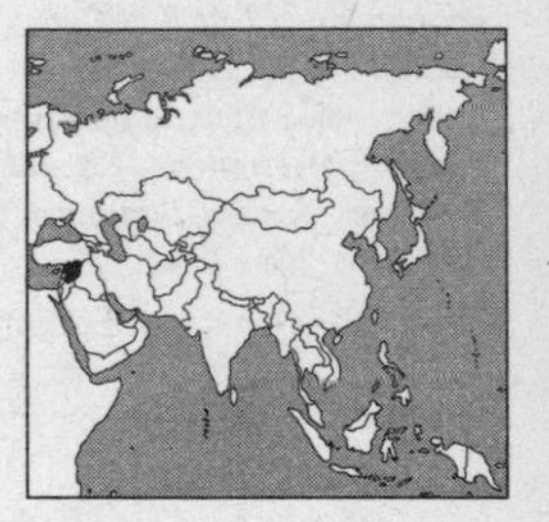

Taiwan is an island which straddles the Tropic of Cancer in East Asia. It lies about 160 km (99 miles) off the south-east coast of mainland CHINA. It is predominantly mountainous in the interior, the tallest peak rising to 3997 m (13,114 ft) at Yu Shan. Taiwan's independence, resulting from the island's seizure by nationalists in 1949, is not fully accepted internationally and China lays claim to the territory. The climate is warm and humid for most of the year and winters are mild with summers rainy. The soils are fertile, and a wide range of crops, including tea, rice, sugar cane and bananas, is grown. Natural resources include gas, marble, limestone and small coal deposits. Taiwan is a major international trading nation with some of the most successful export-processing zones in the world, accommodating domestic and overseas companies. Exports include machinery, electronics, textiles, footwear, toys and sporting goods.

Quick facts:
Area : 35,980 sq km (13,892 sq miles)
Population : 21,465,900
Capital : Taipei (T'ai-pei)
Other major cities : Kaohsiung, Taichung, Tainan
Form of government : Republic
Religions : Taoism, Buddhism, Christianity
Currency : New Taiwan dollar

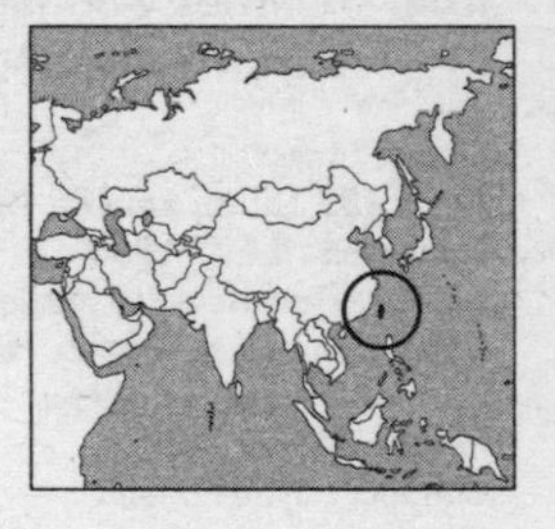

Tajikistan, a republic of southern central former USSR, declared itself independent in 1991. It is situated near the Afghani and Chinese borders. The south is occupied by the Pamir mountain range, whose snow-capped peaks dominate the country. More than half the country lies over 3000 m (9843 ft). Most of the country is desert or semi-desert, and pastoral farming of cattle, sheep, horses and goats is important. Some yaks are kept in the higher regions. The lowland areas in the Fergana and Amudar'ya valleys are irrigated so that cotton, mulberry trees, fruit, wheat and vegetables can be grown. The Amudar'ya river is also used to produce hydro-electricity for industries such as cotton and silk processing. The republic is rich in deposits of coal, lead, zinc, oil and uranium, which were being exploited. There has been a continuing civil war in which tens of thousands of people have been killed or made homeless with the United Nations initiating peace talks.

Quick facts:
Area : 143,100 sq km (55,250 sq miles)
Population : 6,098,800
Capital : Dushanbe
Other major city : Khujand
Form of Government : Republic
Religion : Shia Islam
Currency : Tajik rouble

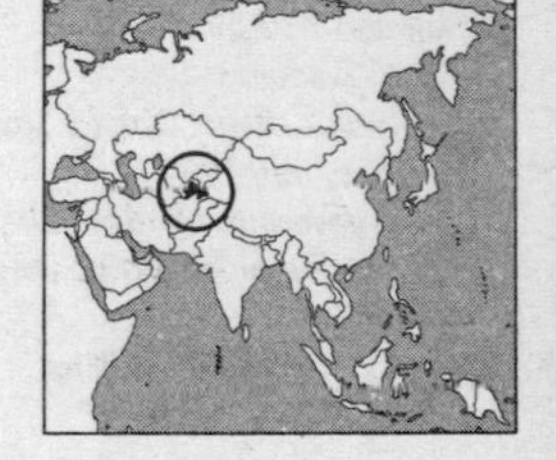

Tanzania lies on the east coast of central Africa and comprises a large mainland area and the islands of Pemba and Zanzibar. The mainland consists mostly of plateaux broken by mountainous areas and the east African section of the Great Rift Valley. The climate is very varied and is controlled largely by altitude and distance from the sea. The coast is hot and humid, the central plateau drier, and the mountains semi-temperate. 80% of Tanzanians make a living from the land, producing corn, cassava, millet, rice, plantains and sorghum for home consumption. Cash crops include cotton, tobacco, tea, sisal, cashews and coffee. The two islands produce the bulk of the world's needs of cloves. Diamond mining is an important industry and there are also sizeable deposits of iron ore, coal and tin. Fishing is an important activity with the bulk of the catch (over 85%) caught in inland waters.

Quick facts:
Area : 945,087 sq km (364,898 sq miles)
Population : 30,498,100
Capital : Dodoma
Other major cities : Dar es Salaam, Zanzibar, Mwanza, Tanga
Form of government : Republic
Religions : Sunni Islam, RC, Anglicanism, Hinduism
Currency : Tanzanian shilling

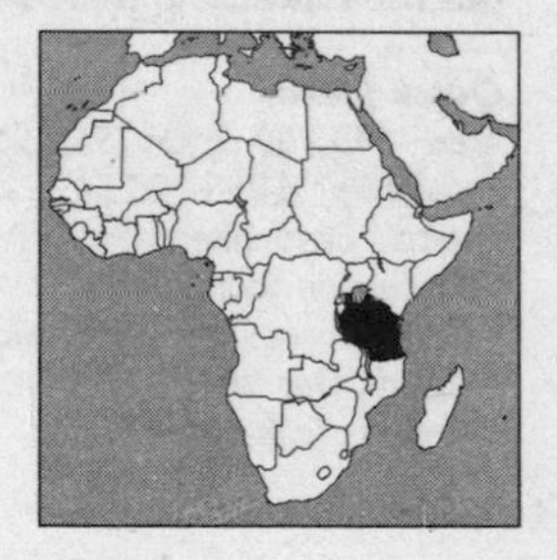

Thailand, a country about the same size as FRANCE located in South-East Asia, is a tropical country of mountains and jungles, rain forests and green plains. Central Thailand is a densely populated, fertile plain and the mountainous Isthmus of Kra joins southern Thailand to MALAYSIA. Thailand has a subtropical climate with heavy monsoon rains from June to October, a cool season from October to March, and a hot season from March to June. It is rich in many natural resources such as mineral deposits of gold, coal, lead and precious stones with rich soils, extensive areas of tropical forests and natural gas offshore. The central plain of Thailand contains vast expanses of paddy fields which grow enough rice to rank Thailand as one of the world's leading producers. The narrow southern peninsula is very wet, and it is here that rubber is produced. Other crops grown are cassava, maize, pineapples and sugar cane. Fishing is an increasingly important industry with prawns being sold for export.

Quick facts:
Area : 513,115 sq km (198,114 sq miles)
Population : 58,427,600
Capital : Bangkok (Krung Thep)
Other major cities : Chiang Mai, Nakhon Si Thammarat, Ratchasima, Songkhla
Form of government : Constitutional Monarchy
Religions : Buddhism, Sunni Islam
Currency : Baht

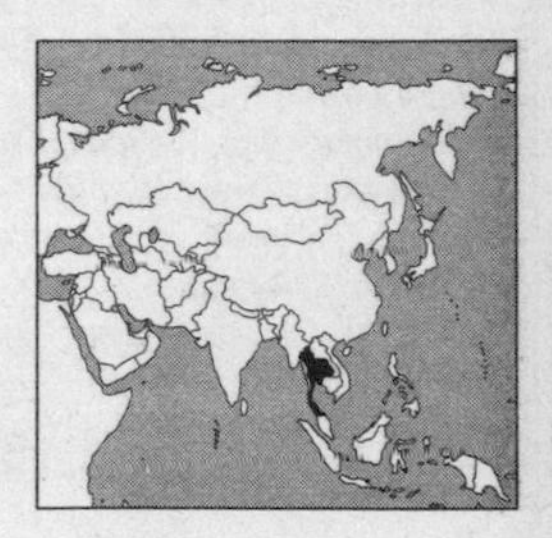

Togo is a tiny country with a narrow coastal plain on the Gulf of Guinea in West Africa. Grassy plains in the north and south are separated by the Togo Highlands, which run from south-west to north-east and rise to nearly 1000 m (3281 ft). High plateaux, mainly in the more southerly ranges, are heavily forested with teak, mahogany and bamboo. Over 80% of the population is involved in subsistence agriculture with yams, cassava, sorghum and millet as the principal crops. Minerals, particularly phosphates, are now the main export earners along with raw cotton, coffee, cocoa, cement and palm kernels. Togo's main imports include food, machinery, construction equipment, textiles and electrical equipment. The official language is French with Ewe and Kabre (main African languages) also being used in the schools.

Quick facts:
Area : 56,785 sq km (21,925 sq miles)
Population : 4,139,800
Capital : Lomé
Other major cities : Sokodé, Kpalimé
Form of government : Republic
Religions : Animism, RC, Sunni Islam
Currency : CFA Franc

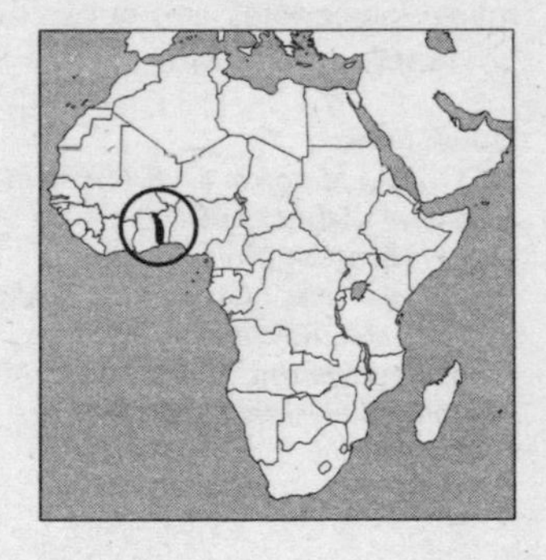

Tonga is situated about 20° south of the Equator and just west of the International Date Line in the Pacific Ocean. It comprises over 170 islands and only about 40 of them are inhabited. It comprises a low limestone chain of islands in the east and a higher volcanic chain in the west. The climate is warm with heavy rainfall and destructive cyclones are likely to occur every few years. The government owns all the land, and males can rent an allotment for growing food. Yams, cassava and taro are grown as subsistence crops, and fish from the sea supplement the diet while foods such as pumpkins, bananas, vanilla and coconuts are exported. The main industry is coconut processing. About 70% of the workforce is occupied in either fishing or agriculture while many Tongans are employed overseas. Tourism, foreign aid from countries such as the UK, AUSTRALIA and NEW ZEALAND and the income sent home from overseas workers all contribute to the country's economy.

Quick facts:
Area : 750 sq km (290 sq miles)
Population : 106,368
Capital : Nuku'alofa
Form of government : Constitutional Monarchy
Religions : Methodism, RC
Currency : Pa'anga

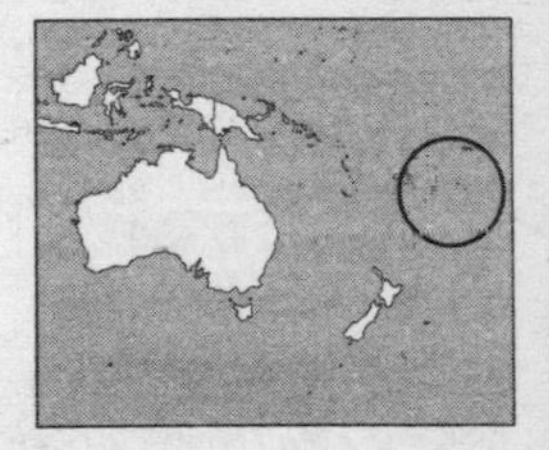

Trinidad and Tobago form the third largest British Commonwealth country in the West Indies and are situated off the Orinoco Delta in north-eastern VENEZUELA. The islands are the most southerly of the Lesser Antilles. Trinidad consists of a mountainous Northern Range in the north and undulating plains in the south. It has a huge, asphalt-producing lake, Pitch Lake, which is approx 42 ha (104 acres) in size. Tobago is actually a mountain that is about 550 m (1800 ft) above sea level at its peak. The climate is tropical with little variation in temperatures throughout the year and a rainy season from June to December. Trinidad is one of the oldest oil-producing countries in the world. Output is small but provides 90% of Trinidad's exports. Sugar cane, cocoa, citrus fruits, vegetables and rubber trees are some that are grown for export, but imports of food now account for 10% of total imports. Tobago depends mainly on tourism for revenue. A slump in the economy in the 1980s and early 1990s saw widespread unemployment but economic growth has improved in recent times.

Quick facts:
Area : 5130 sq km (1981 sq miles)
Population : 1,287,400
Capital : Port-of-Spain
Other major cities : San Fernando, Arima
Form of government : Republic
Religions : RC, Hinduism, Anglicanism, Sunni Islam
Currency : Trinidad and Tobago dollar

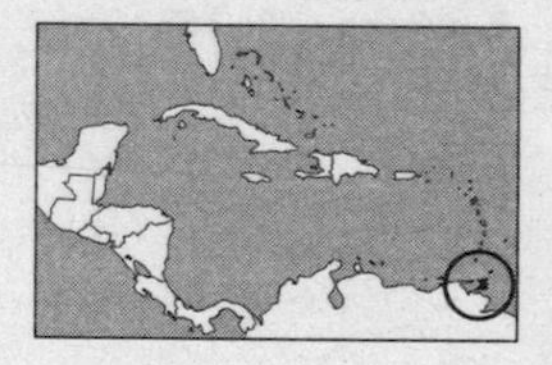

Tunisia is a North African country which lies on the south coast of the Mediterranean Sea. It's bounded by ALGERIA to the west and LIBYA to the south. Northern Tunisia consists of hills, plains and valleys. Inland mountains separate the coastal zone from the central plains before the land drops down to an area of salt pans and the Sahara Desert. The climate ranges from warm temperate in the north where there are vineyards and forests of pine, cork oak and junipers, to desert in the south. Agriculture produces wheat, barley, olives, grapes, tomatoes, dates, vegetables and citrus fruits and the fishing industry is of growing importance producing mainly pilchards, sardines and tuna. 26% of the workforce is engaged in these two occupations but overall there is a general lack of employment. The mainstay of Tunisia's modern economy, however, is oil from the Sahara, phosphates natural gas and tourism on the Mediterranean coast. Tourists are attracted by the good beaches and historic sites such as the ancient city of Carthage.

Quick facts:
Area : 163,610 sq km (63,170 sq miles)
Population : 8,928,100
Capital : Tunis
Other major cities : Sfax, Bizerte, Djerba, Sousse
Form of government : Republic
Religion : Sunni Islam
Currency : Dinar

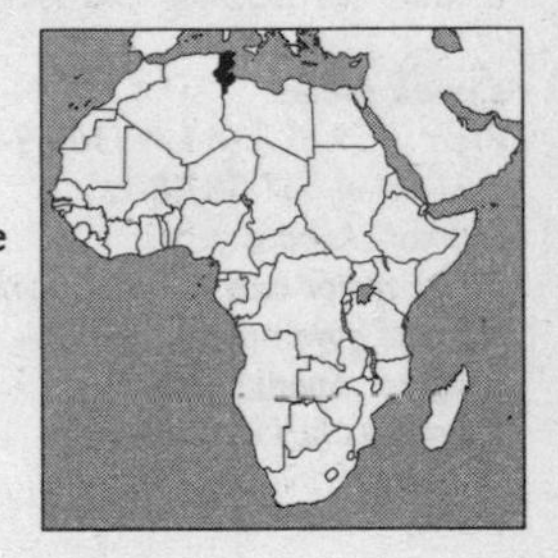

Turkey with land on the continents of Europe and Asia, Turkey forms a bridge between the two. It guards the sea passage between the Mediterranean and the Black Sea. Only 5% of its area, Thrace, is in Europe and the much larger area, known as Anatolia, is in Asia. European Turkey is fertile agricultural land with a Mediterranean climate. Asiatic Turkey is bordered to the north by the Pontine Mountains and to the south by the Taurus Mountains. The climate here ranges from Mediterranean to hot summers and bitterly cold winters in the central plains. Agriculture employs almost half the workforce with the major crops being wheat, sugar beet, barley, fruits, maize and oil seeds. The country's main exports were iron and steel, textiles, dried fruits, tobacco, leather, clothes and petroleum products. Manufacturing industry includes iron and steel, textiles, motor vehicles and Turkey's famous carpets. The main mineral resources are iron ore, coal, chromium, magnetite, zinc and lead. Hydroelectric power is supplied by the Tigris and Euphrates. Tourism is a fast-developing industry.

Quick facts:
Area : 779,452 sq km (300,946 sq miles)
Population : 61,887,800
Capital : Ankara
Other major cities : Istanbul, Izmir, Adana, Bursa
Form of government : Republic
Religion : Sunni Islam
Currency : Turkish lira

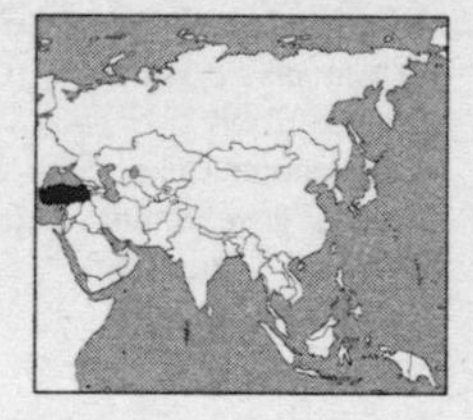

Turkmenistan, a central Asian republic of the former USSR, declared itself a republic in 1991. It lies to the east of the Caspian Sea and borders IRAN and AFGHANISTAN to the south. Much of the west and central areas of Turkmenistan are covered by the sandy Kara Kum Desert. The east is a plateau, which is bordered by the Amudar'ya river. The climate is extremely dry, and most of the population live in oasis settlements near the rivers and by the extensive network of canals. Agriculture is intensive around the settlements and consists of growing cotton, cereals, silk, fruit, and rearing Karakul sheep. This occupies around 45% of the workforce. There are rich mineral deposits, particularly natural gas, petroleum, sulphur, coal, salt and copper. There is some other manufacturing industry such as textile manufacturing, food processing and carpet weaving. Unlike most other former Soviet republics, there has not been a wholesale emigration of ethnic minorities.

Quick facts:
Area : 488,100 sq km (186,400 sq miles)
Population : 4,239,800
Capital : Ashgabat
Form of government : Republic
Religion : Sunni Islam
Currency : Manat

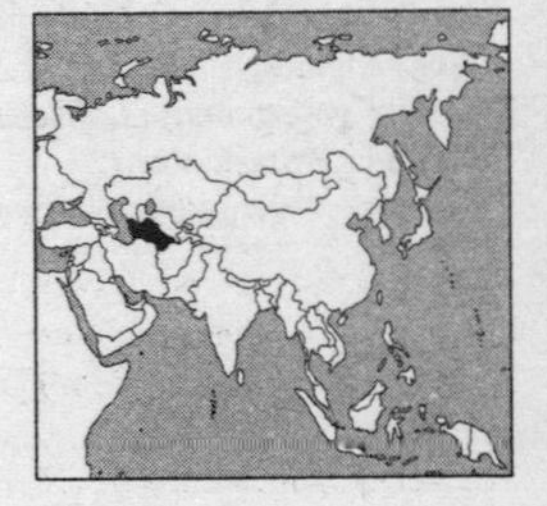

Tuvalu is located just north of Fiji, in the South Pacific, and consists of nine coral atolls. The group was formerly known as the Ellice Islands, and the main island and capital is Funafuti Atoll. Tuvalu became independent in 1978. The climate is tropical with temperatures averaging 30°C and an annual average rainfall ranges of 3050 mm (120 in.). Coconut palms are the main crop and fruit and vegetables are grown for local consumption. Sea fishing is extremely good and largely unexploited, although licences have been granted to Japan, Taiwan and South Korea to fish the local waters. Revenue comes from the sale of elaborate postage stamps to philatelists, foreign aid, copra the only export product, and income sent home from Tuvaluans who work abroad. English and Tuvaluan are both spoken by the Polynesian population and there is an airport situated on Funafuti Atoll.

Quick facts:
Area : 24 sq km (10 sq miles)
Population : 9,367 Capital : Funafuti (or Fongafale)
Form of government : Constitutional Monarchy
Religion : Protestantism
Currency : Tuvalu dollar/Australian dollar

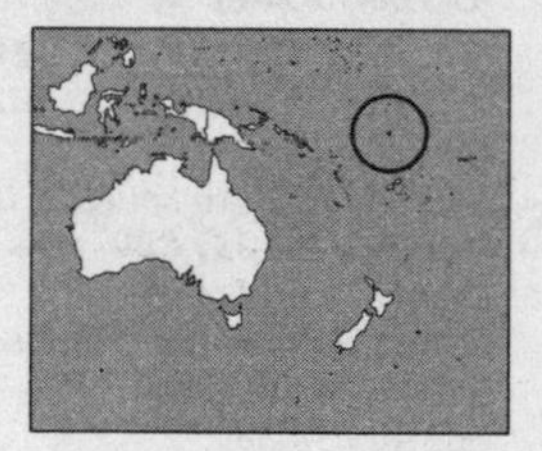

Uganda is a landlocked country in east central Africa. The Equator runs through the south of the country, and for the most part it is a richly fertile land, well-watered with a kindly climate. In the west are the Ruwenzori Mountains, which rise to over 5000 m (16,405 ft) and are snow-capped. The lowlands around Lake Victoria, once forested, have now mostly been cleared for cultivation. Agriculture employs over 80% of the labour force, and the main crops grown for subsistence are plantains, cassava and sweet potatoes. Coffee is the main cash crop and accounts for over 90% of the country's exports although cotton and tea are important. Attempts are being made to expand the tea plantations in the west, to develop a copper mine and to introduce new industries to Kampala, the capital. Forestry is of importance with the major export being mahogany, while the bulk of other wood is used as fuel. Virtually all of the country's power is produced by hydroelectricity, the plant on the Victoria Nile being of major importance.

Quick facts:
Area : 235,880 sq km (91,073 sq miles)
Population : 21,466,000
Capital : Kampala
Other major cities : Jinja, Masaka, Mbale
Form of government: Republic
Religions : RC, Protestantism, Animism, Sunni Islam
Currency : Uganda shilling

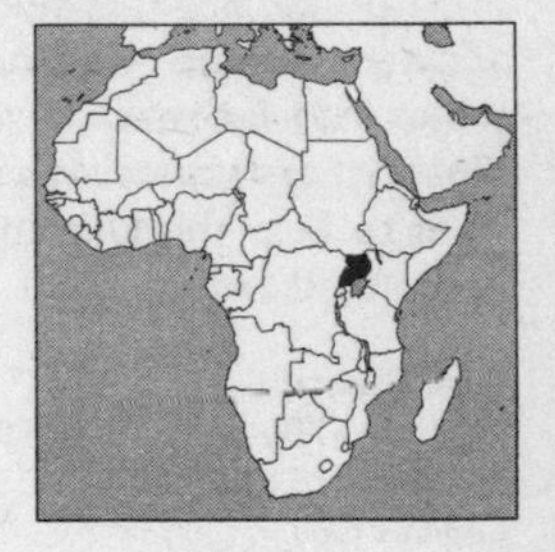

Ukraine, formerly a Soviet socialist republic, declared itself independent of the former USSR in 1991. Its neighbours to the west are POLAND, SLOVAKIA, HUNGARY and ROMANIA, and it is bounded to the south by the Black Sea. To the east lies the RUSSIAN FEDERATION and to the north the republic of BELARUS. Drained by the Dnepr, Dnestr, Southern Bug and Donets rivers, Ukraine consists largely of fertile steppes. The climate is continental, although this is greatly modified by the proximity of the Black Sea. The Ukrainian steppe is one of the chief wheat-producing regions of Europe. Other major crops include corn, sugar beet, flax, tobacco, soya, hops and potatoes with agriculture accounting for about a quarter of all employment. There are rich reserves of coal and raw materials for industry, but the country is still reliant on the other former Soviet republics for natural gas and oil. The central and eastern regions form one of the world's densest industrial concentrations. Manufacturing industries include ferrous metallurgy, heavy machinery, chemicals, food processing, gas and oil refining. In 1986 the catastrophic accident at the Chernobyl nuclear power station occurred which had far-reaching effects and widespread contamination. Financial assistance was agreed in 1996 with a number of countries to help the Ukraine close the station which is due to be completed before 2000.

Quick facts:
Area : 603,700 sq km (233,100 sq miles)
Population : 51,868,900
Capital : Kiev
Other major cities : Dnepropetrovsk, Donetsk, Kharkov, Odessa
Form of government : Republic
Religions : Russian Orthodox, RC
Currency : Rouble

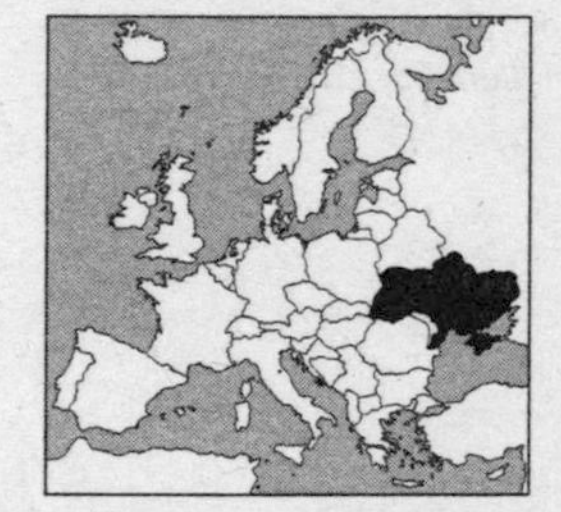

United Arab Emirates (UAE) the United Arab Emirates is a federation of seven oil-rich sheikdoms located in The Gulf. As well as its main coast on the Gulf, the country has a short coast on the Gulf of Oman. The land is mainly flat sandy desert except to the north on the peninsula where the Hajar Mountains rise to 2081 m (6828 ft). The summers are hot and humid with temperatures reaching 49°C, but from October to May the weather is warm and sunny with pleasant, cool evenings. The only fertile areas are the emirate of Ras al Khaymah, the coastal plain of Al Fujayrah and the oases. Abu Dhabi and Dubai are the main industrial centres and, using their wealth from the oil industry, they are now diversifying industry by building aluminium smelters, cement factories and steel-rolling mills. The level of adult illiteracy has improved enormously since the mid 1970s with compulsory education for 12 years from the age of six. Prior to development of the oil industry, traditional occupations were pearl diving, growing dates, fishing and camel breeding. Dubai is the richest state in the world.

Quick facts:
Area : 83,600 sq km (32,278 sq miles)
Population : 2,017,000
Capital : Abu Dhabi
Other major cities : Dubai, Sharjh, Ras al Khaymah
Form of government: Monarchy (emirates)
Religion : Sunni Islam
Currency : Dirham

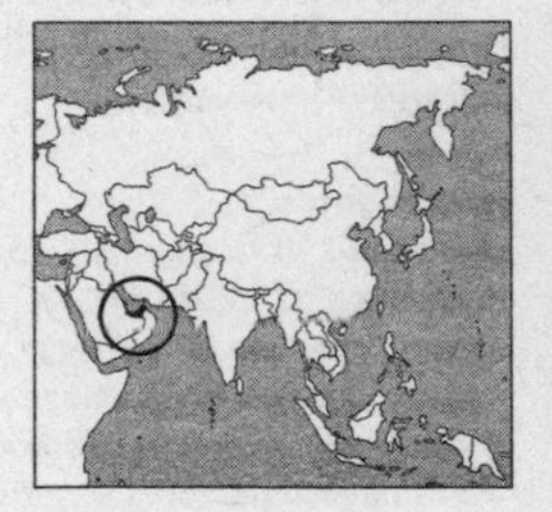

United Kingdom (UK) situated in north-west Europe, the United Kingdom of Great Britain and Northern Ireland comprises the island of Great Britain and the north-east of Ireland, plus many smaller islands, especially off the west coast of Scotland. The south and east of Britain is low-lying, and the Pennines form a backbone running through northern England. Scotland has the largest area of upland, and Wales is a highland block. Northern Ireland has a few hilly areas. The climate is cool temperate with mild conditions and an even annual rainfall. The principal crops are wheat, barley, sugar beet, fodder crops and potatoes. Livestock includes cattle, sheep, pigs and poultry. Fishing is important off the east coast. The UK is primarily a highly urbanised industrial and commercial country, although the recession has left high unemployment in some areas and led to the decline of some of the older industries, such as coal, textiles and heavy engineering. A growing industry is electronics, much of it defence-related. Due to the large population, around 60% of its foodstuffs is imported and also approximately 90% of timber. The UK pioneered the development of nuclear energy for electricity production and by the early 1990s about 16% was supplied by this method.

Quick facts:
Area : 244,111 sq km (94,252 sq miles)
Population : 58,206,000
Capital : London
Other major cities : Birmingham, Cardiff, Edinburgh, Glasgow, Liverpool, Manchester
Form of government : Constitutional Monarchy
Religion : Anglicanism, RC, Presbyterianism, Methodism
Currency : Pound sterling

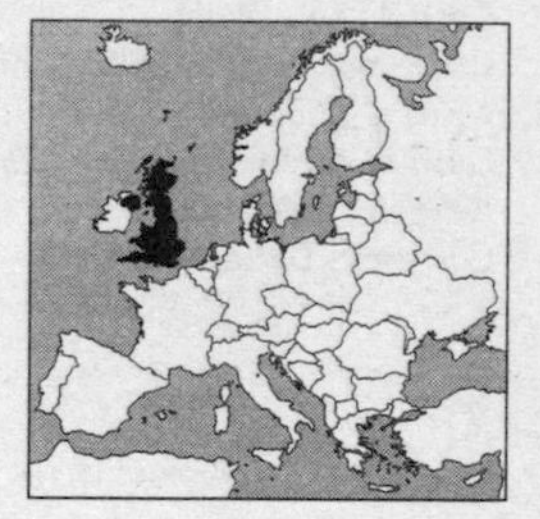

United States of America (USA) stretches across central north America, from the Atlantic Ocean in the east to the Pacific Ocean in the west, and from CANADA in the north to MEXICO and the Gulf of Mexico in the south. It consists of fifty states, including outlying Alaska, north-west of Canada, and Hawaii in the Pacific Ocean. The climate varies a great deal in such a large country. In Alaska there are polar conditions, and in the Gulf coast and in Florida conditions may be subtropical. The highest point is Mount McKinley at 6194 m. Natural resources include vast mineral reserves including oil and gas, coal, copper, lead, uranium gold, tungsten and timber. Although agricultural production is high, it employs only 1.5% of the population because primarily of its advanced technology. The USA is a world leader in oil production. The main industries are iron and steel, chemicals, motor vehicles, aircraft, telecommunications equipment, computers, electronics and textiles. The USA is the richest and most powerful nation in the world.

Quick facts:
Area : 9,809,431 sq km (3,787,421 sq miles)
Population : 266,480,000
Capital : Washington, D.C.
Other major cities : New York, Chicago, Detroit, Houston, Los Angeles, Philadelphia, San Diego, San Francisco
Form of government : Federal Republic
Religion : Protestantism, RC, Judaism, Eastern Orthodox
Currency : US dollar

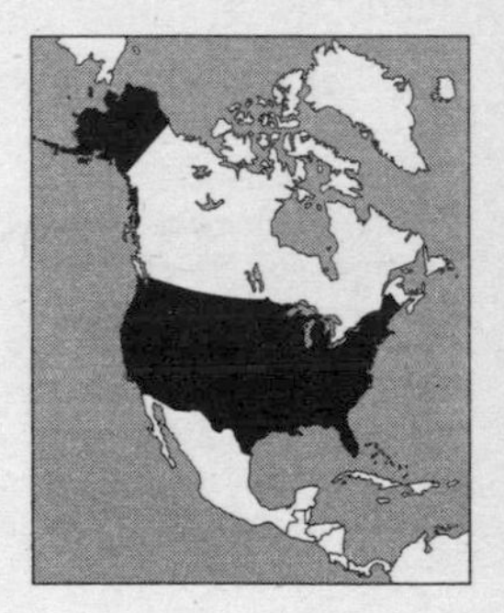

Uruguay is one of the smallest countries in South America. It lies on the east coast of the continent, to the south of BRAZIL, and is bordered to the west by the Uruguay river, Rio de la Plata to the south, and the Atlantic Ocean to the east. The country consists of low plains and plateaux. In the south-east, hills rise to 500 m (1641 ft). About 90% of the land is suitable for agriculture but only about 8% is cultivated, the remainder being used to graze vast herds of cattle and sheep which provide over 35% of Uruguay's exports in the form of wool, hides and meat. The cultivated land is made up of vineyards, rice fields and groves of olives and citrus fruits. The main crops grown are sugar beets and cane, rice, wheat, potatoes, corn and sorghum. The country has scarce mineral resources, but has built hydroelectric power stations at Palmar and Salto Grande. Important industries include textile manufacture, food processing, oil refining, steel, aluminium and electrical equipment. Uruguay has one of the highest rates of literacy in Latin America.

Quick facts:
Area : 177,414 sq km (68,500 sq miles)
Population : 3,186,300
Capital : Montevideo
Form of government : Republic
Religions : RC, Protestantism
Currency : Peso uruguayos

Uzbekistan, a central Asian republic of the former USSR, declared itself independent in 1991. It lies between KAZAKHSTAN and TURKMENISTAN and encompasses the southern half of the Aral Sea. The republic has many contrasting regions. The Tian Shan region is mountainous, the Fergana region is irrigated and fertile, the Kyzlkum Desert (one of the world's largest) is rich in oil and gas, the lower Amudar'ya river region is irrigated and has oasis settlements, and the Usturt Plateau is a stony desert. Uzbekistan is one of the world's leading cotton producers, and Karakul lambs are reared for wool and meat. Its main industrial products are agricultural machinery, textiles and chemicals. It also has significant reserves of natural gas. Economic growth has been checked by concerns about political instability and much of the economy remains based on the centralized state-owned model. There are serious pollution problems where the Aral Sea lies. This has greatly decreased in size from use as irrigation and is contaminated with toxins, salts and sands which poison the water supply of the surrounding population.

Quick facts:
Area : 447,400 sq km (172,748 sq miles)
Population : 21,938,400
Capital : Tashkent
Other major city : Samarkand, Namangan, Andizhan
Form of government : Republic
Religion : Sunni Islam
Currency : Soum

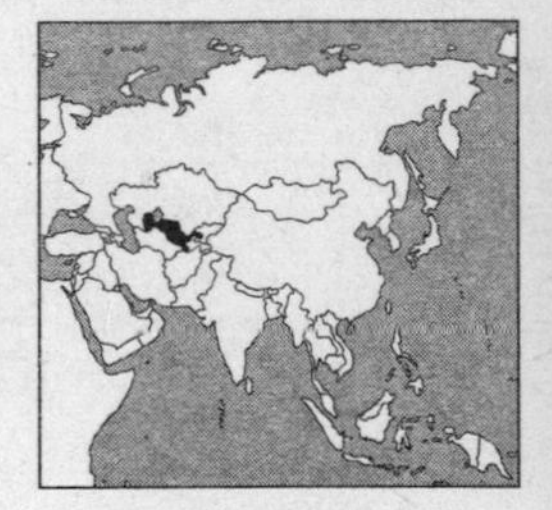

Vanuatu, formerly known as the New Hebrides (named by Captain Cook in 1774), is located in the western Pacific, south-east of the Solomon Islands and about 1750 km (1087 miles) east of AUSTRALIA. About 80 islands comprise the group. Some of the islands are mountainous and include active volcanoes. The largest islands are Espírtu Santo, Malekula and Efate, on which the capital Vila is sited. Vanuatu has a tropical climate which is moderated by the south-east trade winds from May to October. The majority of the labour force is engaged in subsistence farming raising taro, yams and bananas, and the main exports include copra, fish, cattle, cocoa and coffee. Tourism is becoming an important industry and Vanuatu has international airports. The islands gained independence on 30 July, 1980.

Quick facts:
Area : 12,189 sq km (4706 sq miles)
Population : 162,300
Capital : Vila
Form of government : Republic
Religion : Protestantism, Animism
Currency : Vatu

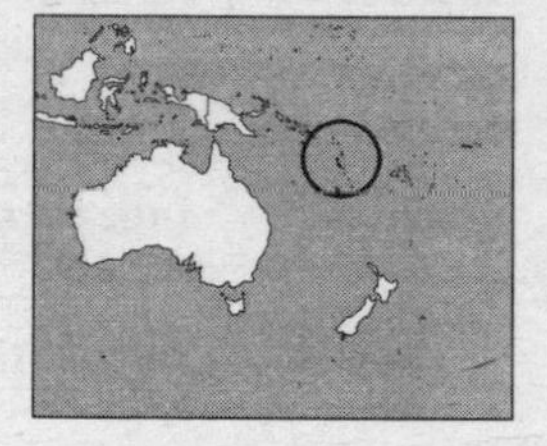

Vatican City State lies in the heart of Rome on a low hill on the west bank of the river Tiber. It is the world's smallest independent state and headquarters of the Roman Catholic Church and was established in 1929. It is a walled city made up of the Vatican Palace, the Papal Gardens, St Peter's Square and St Peter's Basilica and has six gates. The state has its own police, newspaper, telephone and telegraph services, coinage, stamps, radio station and railway station. The radio station, 'Radio Vaticana,' broadcasts a service in 34 languages from transmitters within the Vatican City. Its main tourist attractions are the frescoes of the Sistine Chapel, painted by Michelangelo Buonarroti (1475–1564). It also has outstanding museums with collections of antiquities and works by Italian masters and the Vatican Library's collection of ancient manuscripts is priceless. The Pope exercises sovereignty and has absolute legislative, executive and judicial powers.

Quick facts:
Area : 0.44 sq km (0.17 sq miles)
Population : 1000
Capital : Vatican City (Citta del Vaticano)
Form of government : Papal Commission
Religion : RC
Currency : Vatican City lira

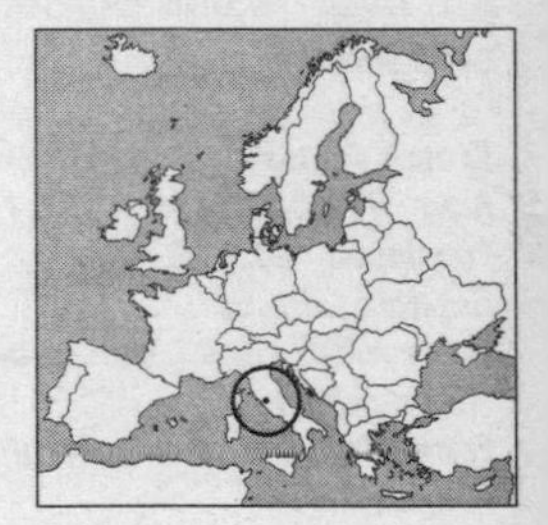

Venezuela forms the northernmost crest of South America. Its northern coast lies along the Caribbean Sea and it is bounded to the west by COLUMBIA and to the south-east and south by GUYANA and BRAZIL. In the north-west a spur of the Andes runs south-west to north-east. Venezuela has one of the highest waterfalls in the world, the Angel Falls. The river Orinoco cuts the country in two, and north of the river run the undulating plains known as the Llanos. South of the river are the Guiana Highlands. The climate ranges from warm temperate to tropical. Temperatures vary little throughout the year and rainfall is plentiful. In the Llanos area cattle are herded across the plains, and this region makes the country almost self-sufficient in meat. Sugar cane and coffee are grown for export but petroleum and gas account for around 80% of export earnings with aluminium, bauxite, chemicals and steel being some of the others. The oil fields lie in the north-west near Lake Maracaibo, where there are over 10,000 oil derricks. Venezuela has seven international airports.

Quick facts:
Area : 912,050 sq km (352,143 sq miles)
Population : 21,715,700
Capital : Caracas
Other major cities : Maracaibo, Valencia, Barquisimeto
Form of government : Federal Republic
Religion : RC
Currency : Bolívar

Vietnam is a long narrow country in south-east Asia which runs down the coast of the South China Sea. It has a narrow central area which links broader plains centred on the Red and Mekong rivers. The narrow zone, now known as Mien Trung, is hilly and makes communications between north and south difficult. The climate is humid with tropical conditions in the south and subtropical in the north. The far north can be very cold when polar air blows over Asia. Agriculture, fishing and forestry employ around 74% of the labour force. The main crop is rice but cassava, maize and sweet potatoes are also grown for domestic consumption. Soya beans, tea, coffee and rubber are grown for export. Major industries are food processing, textiles, cement, cotton and silk manufacture. Fishing is also an important export trade which is conducted mainly on the South China Sea, although there is some fish farming in flooded inland areas. Vietnam, however, remains underdeveloped and is still recovering from the ravages of many wars this century.

Quick facts:
Area : 331,689 sq km (128,065 sq miles)
Population : 74,387,900
Capital : Hanoi
Other major cities : Ho Chi Minh City, Haiphong, Hue, Dà Nang
Form of government : Socialist Republic
Religion : Buddhism, Taoism, RC
Currency : New dong

Western Sahara is a disputed territory of western Africa, with a coastline on the Atlantic Ocean. Consisting mainly of desert, it is rich in phosphates. It was a Spanish overseas province until 1976, when it was partitioned between Morocco and Mauritania. Since 1979, the entire territory has been claimed and administered by Morocco, against the wishes of an active separatist movement, the Frente Polisario. Moroccan sovereignty is not universally recognized, and the UN has attempted to oversee a referendum to decide the struggle, but without success so far. It is a poor country with many following a nomadic existence. The bulk of the food for the towns has to be imported. Phosphates comprise two-thirds of the meagre exports.

Quick facts:

Area : 266,770 sq km (103,000 sq mi)
Population : 222,600
Capital : El Aaiún (Laâyoune)
Form of government : Republic (de facto controlled by Morocco)
Religion : Sunni Islam
Currency : Moroccan Dirham

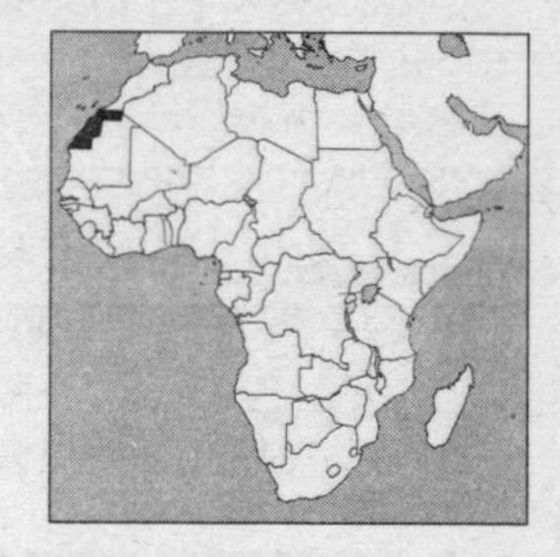

Western Samoa lies in the Polynesian sector of the Pacific Ocean, about 720 km (447 miles) north-east of FIJI. It consists of seven small islands and two larger volcanic islands, Savai'i and Upolu. Savai'i is largely covered with volcanic peaks and lava plateaux. Upolu is home to two-thirds of the population and the capital Apia. The climate is tropical with high temperatures and very heavy rainfall. The islands have been fought over by the Dutch, British, Germans and Americans, but they now have the lifestyle of traditional Polynesians. Subsistence agriculture is the main activity, and copra, cocoa and coconuts are the main exports. Many tourists visit the grave of the Scottish writer Robert Louis Stevenson (1850–94) who died here and whose home is now the official home of the king. There are some light manufacturing industries including clothing manufacture and a car components factory which is now the largest private employer and major export industry.

Quick facts:
Area : 2831 sq km (1093 sq miles)
Population : 203,680
Capital : Apia
Form of government : Constitutional Monarchy
Religion : Protestantism
Currency : Tala

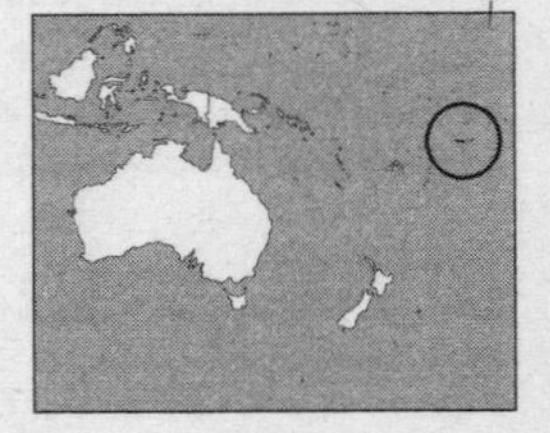

Yemen, Republic of is bounded by SAUDI ARABIA in the north, OMAN in the east, the Gulf of Aden in the south, and the Red Sea in the west. The country was formed after the unification of the previous Yemen Arab Republic and the People's Democratic Republic of Yemen (South Yemen) in 1989. However, at this point there was no active integration of the two countries and politically the country remained divided between north and south. In 1994 a civil war, which lasted three months, broke out between the former North and South Yemen which resulted in a high rate of inflation, damage to the infrastructure and devaluation of the currency. Most of the country comprises rugged mountains and trackless desert lands. The country is almost entirely dependent on agriculture even though a very small percentage is fertile. The main crops are coffee, cotton, wheat, vegetables, millet, sorghum and fruit. Fishing is an important industry with mackerel, tuna, lobster and cod caught and there are some canning factories along the coast. Other industry is on a very small scale. There are textile factories, and plastic, rubber and aluminium goods, paints and matches are produced. Modernization of industry is slow because of lack of funds.

Quick facts:
Area : 527,970 sq km (203,849 sq miles)
Population : 14,239,400
Capital : Sana'a, Commercial Capital : Aden
Other major cities : Al Hudaydah, Ta'izz, Sa'dah
Form of government : Republic
Religion : Zaidism, Shia Islam, Sunni Islam
Currency : Riyal

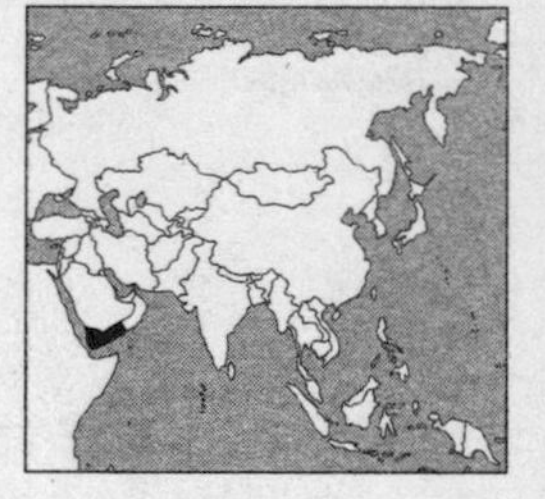

Yugoslavia, (FRY), the Federal Republic of which was created in 1918, became a single federal republic after World War II under the leadership of Marshal Tito (1892–1980). The six constituent republics were SERBIA, CROATIA, SLOVENIA, BOSNIA & HERZEGOVINA, MACEDONIA and Montenegro. Yugoslavia today refers only to Serbia and Montenegro, which operate as two equal republics under a federal authority. However, the situation remains particularly complex, with each republic operating its own legislature. The other republics, beginning with Slovenia and Croatia in 1991, have all declared their independence from Yugoslavia. The economy was devastated by the wars in Bosnia and Croatia, then by inflation to the degree that the financial infrastructure all but collapsed in late 1993 with soaring inflation and high unemployment. After the Dayton peace accord was signed in November, 1995, sanctions were suspended by the United Nations. The economy has only just begun to take the first steps to recovery. It is largely agricultural, and produce includes wheat, maize, grapes and citrus fruit. Its most important natural resources are minerals such as antimony and lead while coal, natural gas, oil, gold and copper are also found. Exports include chemicals, machinery, textiles and clothing.

Quick facts:
Area : 102,172 sq km (39,449 sq miles)
Population : 10,881,000
Capital : Belgrade (Beograd)
Other Major Cities : Nis, Titograd, Novi Sad, Podgorica, Pristina
Form of government : Federal Republic
Religions : Eastern Orthodox
Currency : New dinar

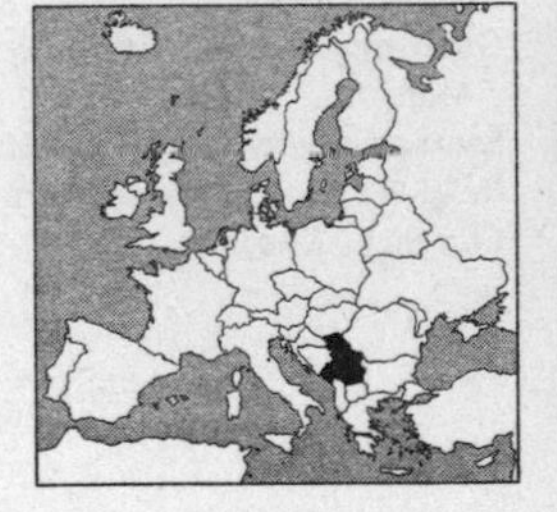

Zambia, situated in central Africa, is made up of high plateaux. Bordering it to the south is the Zambezi river, and in the south-west it borders on the Kalahari Desert. It has some other large rivers, including the Luangwa, and lakes, the largest of which is Lake Bangweulu. The climate is tropical, modified somewhat by altitude. The country has a wide range of wildlife, and there are large game parks on the Luangwa and Kafue rivers. Agriculture is underdeveloped and vulnerable to weather variations leading to some food shortages, as a consequence of which large quantities have to be imported. The principal subsistence crops grown are corn, sugar cane and cassava with cattle raised. and most foodstuffs have to be imported. Zambia's economy relies heavily on the mining of copper, lead, zinc and cobalt. The poor market prospects for copper, which will eventually be exhausted, make it imperative for Zambia to develop her vast agricultural potential. The majority of the country's power is provided by the Kariba Dam on the Zambezi River and there is potential for further hydroelectric development.

Quick facts:
Area : 752,614 sq km (290,584 sq miles)
Population : 9,500,000
Capital : Lusaka
Other major cities : Kitwe, Luanshya, Ndola, Mufulira
Form of government : Republic
Religion : Christianity, Animism
Currency : Kwacha

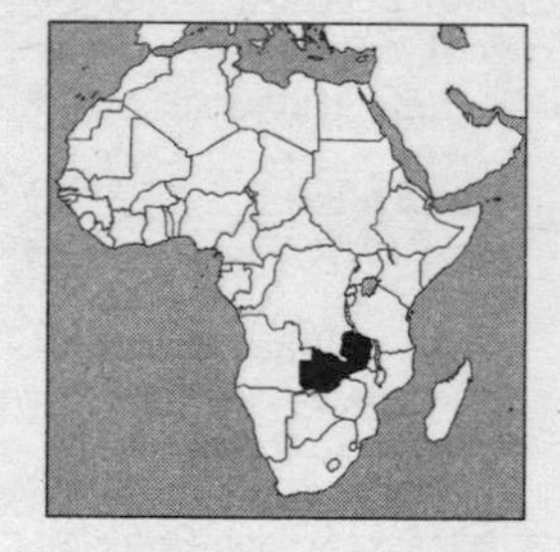

Zimbabwe is a landlocked country in southern Africa. It is a country with spectacular physical features and is teeming with wildlife. It is bordered in the north by the Zambezi river, which flows over the mile-wide Victoria Falls before entering Lake Kariba. In the south, the River Limpopo marks its border with SOUTH AFRICA. Most of the country is over 300 m (984 ft) above sea level, and a great plateau between 1200 m (3937 ft) and 1500 m (4922 ft) occupies the central area. Massive granite outcrops, called *kopjes*, also dot the landscape. The climate is tropical in the lowlands and subtropical in the higher land. About 75% of the labour force are employed in agriculture. Tobacco, sugar cane, cotton, wheat and maize are exported and form the basis of processing industries. Zimbabwe is rich in mineral resources such as coal, chromium, nickel, gold, platinum and precious metals and mining accounts for around 30% of foreign revenue while only employing under 5% of the workforce. Tourism is a major growth industry.

Quick facts:
Area : 390,760 sq km (150,872 sq miles)
Population : 11,484,400
Capital : Harare
Other major cities : Bulawayo, Mutare, Gweru, Kwekwe
Form of government : Republic
Religion : Animism, Anglicanism, RC
Currency : Zimbabwe dollar

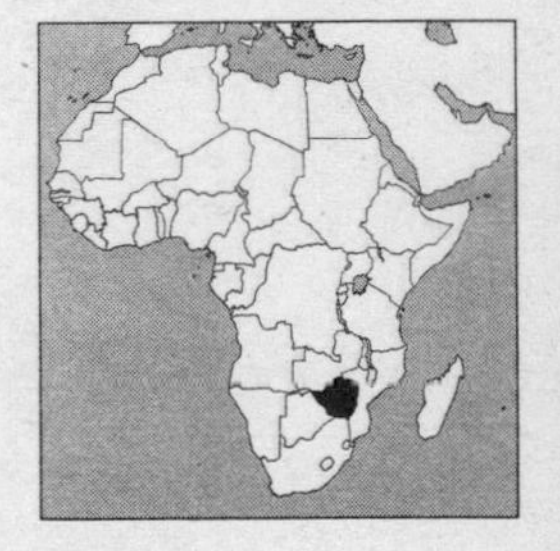

Earth's Statistics

Earth's Vital Statistics

Age:	Approx 4600 million years
Weight:	Approx 5.976 x 10^{21} tonnes
Diameter:	Pole to Pole through the centre of the Earth 12 713 km (7900 miles) Across the Equator through the centre of the Earth 12 756 km (7926 miles)
Circumference:	Around the Poles 40 008 km (24 861 miles) Around the Equator 40 091 km (24 912 miles)
Area:	Land 148 326 000 sq km (57 268 700 sq miles) 29% of surface Water 361 740 000 sq km (139 667 810 sq miles) 71% of surface
Volume:	1 084 000 million cubic km (260 160 million cubic miles)
Volume of the oceans:	1321 million cubic km (317 million cubic miles)
Average height of land:	840 m (2756 ft) above sea level
Average depth of ocean:	3808 m (12 493 ft) below sea level
Density:	5.52 times water
Mean temperature:	22°C (72°F)
Length of year:	365.25 days

Length of one rotation:	23 hours 56 minutes
Mean distance from Sun:	149 600 000 km (92 960 000 miles)
Mean velocity in orbit:	29.8 km (18.5 miles) per second
Escape velocity:	11.2 km (6.96 miles) per second
Atmosphere:	Main constituents: nitrogen (78.5%), oxygen (21%)
Crust:	Main constituents: oxygen (47%), silicon (28%), aluminium (8%), iron (5%).
Known satellites:	One (The moon)

Oceans

	Max. Depth		Area	
	metres	*feet*	*sq km*	*sq miles*
Pacific	11 033	36 197	165 384 000	63 860 000
Atlantic	8381	27 496	82,217 000	31 744 000
Indian	8047	26 401	73 481 000	28 371 000
Arctic	5450	17 880	14 056 000	5 427 000

Deserts

	sq km	*sq miles*
Sahara	9 065 000	3 500 000
Australian Desert	1 550 000	598 455
Arabian Desert	1 300 000	501 930
Gobi Desert	1 295 000	500 000
Kalahari	520 000	200 772

Largest Islands

Island (location)	*Population*	*Area sq km*	*sq miles*
Greenland (N. Atlantic)	54 600	2 175 600	839 740
New Guinea (S.W. Pacific)	4 528 682	808 510	312 085
Borneo (S.W. Pacific)	11 263 087	751 900	292 220
Madagascar (Indian Ocean)	11 238 000	594 180	229 355
Sumatra (Indian Ocean)	36 881 990	524 100	202 300
Baffin I. (Canadian Arctic)	8298	476 070	183 760
Honshu (N.W. Pacific)	98 352 000	230 455	88 955
Great Britain (N. Atlantic)	54 285 422	229 880	88 730
Victoria I. (Canadian Arctic)	1410	212 200	81 910
Ellesmere (Canadian Arctic)	54	212 690	82 100

Principal Mountains of the World

Name (location)	*Height m*	*ft*
Everest (Tibet-Nepal)	8848	29 028
Godwin-Austen or K2 (Kashmir-Sinkiang)	8611	28 250
Kangchenjunga (Nepal-India)	8587	28 170
Makalu (Nepal)	8463	27 766
Dhaulagiri (Nepal)	8167	26 795
Nanga Parbat (India)	8125	26 657
Annapurna (Nepal)	8091	26 545
Gosainthan (Tibet)	8012	26 286
Nanda Devi (India)	7816	25 643
Kamet (India)	7756	25 446

Name (location)	*Height* m	ft
Namcha Barwa (Tibet)	7756	25 446
Gurla Mandhata (Tibet)	7728	25 355
Kongur (China)	7720	25 325
Tirich Mir (Pakistan)	7691	25 230
Minya Kanka (China)	7556	24 790
Kula Kangri (Tibet)	7555	24 784
Muztagh Ata (China)	7546	24 757
Kommunizma (Tajikistan)	7495	24 590
Pobedy (Russian Fed.-China)	7439	24 406
Chomo Lhari (Bhutan-Tibet)	7313	23 992
Api (Nepal)	7132	23 399

Name (location)	*Height m*	*ft*
Lenina (Kyrgyzstan-Tajikistan)	7134	23 405
Acongagua (volcano) (Argentina)	6960	22 834
Ojos del Salado (Argentina)	6908	22 664
Tupungato (Argentina-Chile)	6801	22 310
Mercedario (Argentina)	6770	22 211
Huascarán (Peru)	6769	22 205
Llullailaco (Chile)	6723	22 057
Neradas de Cachi (Argentina)	6720	22 047
Kailas (Tibet)	6714	22 027
Incahuasi (Argentina)	6709	22 011
Tengri Khan (Kyrgyzstan)	6695	21 965

Name (location)	*Height* *m*	*ft*
Sajama (Bolivia)	6542	21,463
Illampu (Bolivia)	6485	21 276
Antofalla (volcanic) (Argentina)	6441	21 129
Illimani (Bolivia)	6402	21 004
Chimborazo (volcanic) (Ecuador)	6310	20 702
Cumbre de la Mejicana (Argentina)	6249	20 500
McKinley (Alaska)	6194	20 320
Copiapo or Azifre (Chile)	6080	19 947
Logan (Yukon, Canada)	6051	19 524
Cotopaxi (volcanic) (Ecuador)	5896	19 344
Kilimanjaro (volcanic) (Tanzania)	5895	19 340

Name (location)	*Height*	
	m	*ft*
Ollagüe (Chile-Bolivia)	5868	19 250
Cerro del Potro (Argentina-Chile)	5830	19 127
Misti (volcanic) (Peru)	5822	19 101
Cayambe (Ecuador)	5797	19 016
Huila (volcanic) (Colombia)	5750	18 865
Citlaltepi (Mexico)	5699	18 697
Demavend (Iran)	5664	18 582
Elbrus (volcanic) (Russian Fed.)	5642	18 510
St. Elias (volcanic) (Alaska, Canada)	5489	18 008
Popocatepetl (volcanic) (Mexico)	5453	17 887
Cerro Lejfa (Chile)	5360	17 585

Name (location)	*Height m*	*ft*
Foraker (Alaska)	5304	17 400
Maipo (volcanic) (Argentina-Chile)	5290	17 355
Ixtaccihuati (volcanic) (Mexico)	5286	17 342
Lucania (Yukon, Canada)	5228	17 150
Tomila (volcanic) (Colombia)	5215	17 109
Dykh Tau (Russian Fed.)	5203	17 070
Kenya (Kenya)	5200	17 058
Ararat (Turkey)	5165	16 945
Vinson Massif (Antarctica)	5140	16 863
Kazbek (volcanaic) (Georgia)	5047	16 558
Blackburn (Alaska)	5037	16 523

Name *(location)*	*Height* *m*	*ft*
Jaya (Irian Jaya, Indonesia)	5030	16 502
Sanford (Alaska)	4941	16 208
Klyucheveyskava (volcanic) (Russian Fed.)	4750	15 584
Mont Blanc (France-Italy)	4808	15 774
Domuyo (volcanic) (Argentina)	4800	15 748
Vancouver (Alaska-Yukon, Canada)	4786	15 700
Trikora (West Irian, Indonesia)	4750	15 584
Fairweather (Alaska-British Colombia, Canada)	4670	15 320
Monte Rosa (Switzerland-Italy)	4634	15 203
Ras Dashan (Ethiopia)	4620	15 158
Belukha (Kazakhstan)	4506	14 783

Name (location)	*Height* m	ft
Markham (Antarctica)	4350	14 271
Meru (volcanic) (Tanzania)	4566	14 979
Hubbard (Alaska-Yukon)	4557	14 950
Kirkpatrick (Antarctica)	4528	14 855
Karisimbi (volcanic) (Rwanda-Zaire)	4508	14 787
Weisshorn (Switzerland)	4505	14 780
Matterhorn/Mont Cervin (Switzerland-Italy)	4477	14 690
Whitney (California)	4418	14 495
Elbert (Colorado)	4399	14 431
Massive Mount (Colorado)	4397	14 424
Harvard (Colorado)	4396	14 420

Name (location)	*Height* *m*	*ft*
Rainier or **Tacoma** (Washington)	4392	14 410
Williamson (California)	4382	14 375
La Plata (Colorado)	4371	14 340
Blanca Peak (Colorado)	4364	14 317
Uncompahgre (Colorado)	4361	14 306
Crestone (Colorado)	4356	14 291
Lincoln (Colorado)	4354	14 284
Grays (Colorado)	4351	14 274
Evans (Colorado)	4347	14 260
Longs (Colorado)	4345	14 255
White (California)	4343	14 246

Name (location)	*Height m*	*ft*
Colima (volcanic) (Mexico)	4340	14 236
Shavano (Colorado)	4337	14 229
Princeton (Colorado)	4327	14 196
Yale (Colorado)	4327	14 196
Elgon (volcanic) (Uganda-Kenya)	4321	14 176
Shasta (volcanic) (California)	4317	14 162
Grand Combin (Switzerland)	4314	14 153
San Luis (Colorado)	4312	14 146
Batu (Ethiopia)	4307	14 130
Pikes Peak (Colorado)	4301	14 110
Snowmass (Colorado)	4291	14 077

Name (location)	*Height m*	*ft*
Culebra (Colorado)	4286	14 070
Sunlight (Colorado)	4284	14 053
Split (California)	4283	14 051
Redcloud (Colorado)	4278	14 034
Finsteraarhorn (Switzerland)	4274	14 022
Wrangell (Alaska)	4269	14 005
Mount of the Holy Cross (Colorado)	4266	13 996
Humphreys (California)	4259	13 972
Ouray (Colorado)	4254	13 955
Guna (Ethiopia)	4231	13 881
Mauna Kea (Hawaii)	4205	13 796

Name (location)	*Height* m	ft
Gannet (Wyoming)	4202	13 785
Hayes (Alaska)	4188	13 740
Fremont (Wyoming)	4185	13 730
Sidley (Antarctica)	4181	13 717
Mauna Loa (volcanic) (Hawaii)	4169	13 677
Jungfrau (Switzerland)	4158	13 642
Kings (Utah)	4124	13 528
Kinabalu (Sabah)	4102	13 455
Cameroon (volcanic) (Cameroon)	4095	13 435
Fridtjof Nansen (Antarctica)	4068	13 346
Tacaná (volcanic) (Mexico-Guatemala)	4064	13 333

Name (location)	*Height* *m*	*ft*
Bernina (Switzerland)	4049	13 284
Summit (Colorado)	4046	13 272
Waddington (British Colombia, Canada)	4042	13 262
Lister (Antarctica)	4025	13 205
Cloud Peak (Wyoming)	4016	13 176
Yu Shan (Taiwan)	3997	13 113
Truchas (New Mexico)	3994	13 102
Wheeler (Nevada)	3981	13 058
Robson (British Colmbia, Canada)	3954	12 972
Granite (Montana)	3902	12 799
Borah (Idaho)	3858	12 655

Name (location)	*Height* m	ft
Baldy (New Mexico)	3848	12 623
Monte Viso (Italy)	3847	12 621
Kerinci (volcanic) (Sumatra)	3805	12 483
Grossglockner (Austria)	3797	12 460
Erebus (volcanic) (Antarctica)	3794	12 447
Excelsior (California)	3790	12 434
Fujiyama (volcanic) (Japan)	3776	12 388
Cook (New Zealand)	3753	12 313
Adams (Washington)	3752	12 307
Lanín (volcanic) (Argentina-Chile)	3740	12 270
Teyde or **Tenerife** (volcanic) (Canary Islands)	3718	12 198

Name (location)	*Height m*	*ft*
Mahameru (volcanic) (Java)	3676	12 060
Assiniboine (British Colombia-Alberta, Canada)	3618	11 870
Hood (vocanic) (Oregon)	3428	11 245
Pico de Aneto (Spain)	3404	11 168
Rheinwaldhorn (Switzerland)	3402	11 161
Perdido (Spain)	3352	10 997
Etna (volcanic) (Sicily)	3323	10 902
Baker (Washington)	3286	10 778
Lassen (volcanic) (California)	3188	10 457
Dempo (volcanic) (Sumatra)	3159	10 364
Siple (Antarctica)	3100	10 170

Name (location)	*Height* *m*	*ft*
Montcalm (France)	3080	10 105
Haleakala (volcanic) (Hawaii)	3058	10 032
St. Helens (Washington)	2950	9677
Pulog (Philippines)	2934	9626
Tahat (Algeria)	2918	9573
Shishaldin (volcanic) (Aleutian Islands)	2862	9387
Roraima (Brazil-Venezuela-Guyana)	2810	9219
Ruapehu (volcanic) (New Zealand)	2797	9175
Katherine (Egypt)	2637	8651
Doi Inthanon (Thailand)	2594	8510
Galdhöpiggen (Norway)	2469	8100

Name (location)	*Height m*	*ft*
Parnassus (Greece)	2457	8061
Olympus (Washington)	2425	7954
Kosciusko (Australia)	2230	7316
Harney (South Dakota)	2208	7242
Mitchell (North Carolina)	2038	6684
Clingmans Dome (North Carolina-Tennessee)	2025	6642
Washington (New Hampshire)	1917	6288
Rogers (Virginia)	1807	5927
Marcy (New York)	1629	5344
Cirque (Labrador)	1573	5160
Pelée (volcanic) (Martinique)	1463	4800

Principal Rivers of the World

Name (location)	Length km	miles
Nile (Africa)	6695	4160
Amazon (South America)	6516	4050
Yangtze (Chang Jiang) (Asia)	6380	3965
(Mississippi-Missouri) (North America)	6019	3740
Ob'-Irtysh (Asia)	5570	3460
Yenisey-Angara (Asia)	5553	3450
Hwang Ho (Huang He) (Asia)	5464	3395
Zaïre (Africa)	4667	2900
Mekong (Asia)	4426	2750
Amur (Asia)	4416	2744

Name (location)	*Length* km	*Length* miles
Lena (Asia)	4400	2730
Mackenzie (North America)	4250	2640
Niger (Africa)	4032	2505
Paraná (South America)	4000	2485
Missouri (North America)	3969	2466
Mississippi (North America)	3779	2348
Murray-Darling (Australia)	3750	2330
Volga (Europe)	3686	2290
Madeira (South America)	3203	1990
St. Lawrence (North America)	3203	1990
Yukon (North America)	3,187	1,980

Name (location)	*Length km*	*miles*
Indus (Asia)	3180	1975
Syrdar'ya (Asia)	3079	1913
Salween (Asia)	3060	1901
Darling (Australia)	3057	1900
Rio Grande (North America)	3034	1885
São Francisco (South America)	2897	1800
Danube (Europe)	2850	1770
Brahmaputra (Asia)	2840	1765
Euphrates (Asia)	2815	1750
Pará-Tocantins (South America)	2752	1710
Zambezi (Africa)	2650	1650

Name (location)	*Length* km	miles
Amudar'ya (Asia)	2620	1630
Paraguay (South America)	2600	1615
Nelson-Saskatchewan (North America)	2570	1600
Ural (Asia)	2534	1575
Kolyma (Asia)	2513	1562
Ganges (Asia)	2510	1560
Orinoco (South America)	2500	1555
Arkansas (North America)	2350	1460
Colorado (North America)	2330	1450
Xi Jiang (Asia)	2300	1427
Dnepr (Europe)	2285	1420

Name (location)	*Length* km	miles
Negro (South America)	2254	1400
Aldan (Asia)	2242	1393
Irrawaddy (Asia)	2150	1335
Ohio (North America)	2102	1306
Orange (Africa)	2090	1299
Kama (Europe)	2028	1260
Xingú (South America)	2012	1250
Columbia (North America)	1950	1210
Juruá (South America)	1932	1200
Peace (North America)	1923	1195
Tigris (Asia)	1900	1180

Name (location)	*Length km*	*miles*
Don (Europe)	1870	1165
Pechora (Europe)	1814	1127
Araguaya (South America)	1771	1100
Snake (North America)	1670	1038
Red (North America)	1639	1018
Churchill (North America)	1610	1000
Marañón (South America)	1610	1000
Pilcomayo (South America)	1610	1000
Ucayali (South America)	1610	1000
Uruguay (South America)	1610	1000
Magdalena (South America)	1529	950

Name (location)	*Length* km	miles
Oka (Europe)	1481	920
Canadian (North America)	1459	906
Godavari (Asia)	1449	900
Parnaíba (South America)	1449	900
Dnestr (Europe)	1411	877
Brazos (North America)	1401	870
Fraser (North America)	1368	850
Salado (South America)	1368	850
Rhine (Europe)	1320	825
Narmada (Asia)	1288	800
Tobol (Asia)	1288	800

Name (location)	*Length* km	*Length* miles
Athabaska (North America)	1231	765
Pecos (North America)	1183	735
Green (North America)	1175	730
Elbe (Europe)	1160	720
Ottawa (North America)	1121	696
White (North America)	1111	690
Cumberland (North America)	1106	687
Yellowstone (North America)	1080	671
Donets (Europe)	1079	670
Tennessee (North America)	1050	652
Vistula (Europe)	1014	630

Name (location)	*Length km*	*miles*
Loire (Europe)	1012	629
Tagus (Europe)	1006	625
Tisza (Europe)	997	619
North Platte (North America)	995	618
Ouachita (North America)	974	605
Sava (Europe)	940	584
Neman (Europe)	937	582
Oder (Europe)	910	565
Cimarron (North America)	805	500
Gila (North America)	805	500
Gambia (Africa)	483	300